# The Evolution of Large Corporations in Korea

# The Evolution of Large Corporations in Korea

A New Institutional Economics Perspective of the *Chaebol*

Sung-Hee Jwa

*President, Korea Economic Research Institute, Seoul, South Korea*

**Edward Elgar**

Cheltenham, UK • Northampton, MA, USA

Published by
Edward Elgar Publishing Limited
Glensanda House
Montpellier Parade
Cheltenham
Glos GL50 1UA
UK

Edward Elgar Publishing, Inc.
136 West Street
Suite 202
Northampton
Massachusetts 01060
USA

Reprinted 2003

A catalogue record for this book
is available from the British Library

**Library of Congress Cataloguing in Publication Data**
Jwa, Sung-Hee
    The evolution of large corporations in Korea : a new institutional economics
perspective of the chaebol / Sung-Hee Jwa.
        p. cm.
    Includes index.
    1. Corporations—Korea (South)—History. 2. Conglomerate corporations—
Korea (South)—History. 3. Industrial concentration—Korea (South)—History.
4. Industrial organization—Korea (South)—History. 5. Big business—Korea
South—History. 6. Industrial policy—Korea (South)—History. I. Title.

HD2908.C485 2002
338.095195–dc21                                                      2002021390

ISBN 1 84064 883 X

Printed and bound in Great Britain by the MPG Books Group

# Contents

# Tables

# Figures

# Preface

This book tries to convey the essence of large corporations in Korea or what is referred to as the *chaebol* in terms of its past, its current status and its future prospects. Relatively speaking, the reason for the demise of any entity is usually easier to explain than putting forward an acceptable explanation of how that particular entity came into being. For example, an innocent boy can easily be held accountable for the death of a bug that he purposely stepped on, but he can hardly be expected to explain how and why that insect came to cross his path. This book faces this difficult challenge to present to its readers a concise picture of the unique circumstances that prompted the growth and behavioral characteristics of large corporations in Korea.

It is common to find that the *chaebol* have been looked upon as an 'evil monster'. Ever since the 1997 economic crisis, the *chaebol* have increasingly been brought to the spotlight internationally as well, and there is now a flood of discerning commentaries. Discussions surrounding the *chaebol* besides being highly controversial are usually preceded by unfavorable pre-judgements that quickly erase any hope of objective analyses, thereby resulting in nothing but confusion. Furthermore, although international concern is highly welcome in this day and age, the lack of proper understanding of *chaebol* issues is reflected by inconsistencies in policy recommendations, which should be promptly corrected. In fact, a strong motive for writing this book has been my frustration with widespread misunderstanding and misconceptions about the *chaebol*. This book serves to fill the void in objective research in economics as the reader will recognize immediately the application of positive economic analyses to *chaebol* issues, thereby providing a challenge to the widespread ethical and normative discussions common in the media and among professionals up until now.

Many of the ideas in this book began to crystallize at about the time when I wrote a Korean book of a similar title addressing *chaebol* issues. Also, I discuss various aspects of the recent corporate sector reform in my *A New Paradigm for Korea's Economic Development* (Palgrave, 2001). Needless to say, this book is not only an extension of the discussions touched upon in my previous works, but it is in many ways a much more comprehensive study containing many new ideas, analyses and insights. To produce a manageable and comprehensive volume, various important issues surrounding the evolution of large corporations have been selected, presented and thoroughly discussed, on the theoretical as well as the empirical levels. That notwithstanding, I have avoided being too technical or writing an encyclopedia and thus the book should appeal to all those interested in understanding the evolution of large corporations. A unique feature of this book is the application of new-institutional economics, which, as this book will demonstrate, is a highly applicable discipline to understanding the evolution of economic phenomena, including corporate formation, growth and behavior. I hope this book results in not only a better understanding of how large corporations, in particular the *chaebol*, have evolved, but also a clearer appreciation of why public policy as well as recent reform efforts directed at restructuring corporations in Korea have so far been rather ineffective. Development economists and policy-makers should find here a viable policy framework suitable to enhancing corporate efficiency, as well as national economic growth.

I am grateful to both the Korea Development Institute (KDI) and Korea Economic Research Institute (KERI) - leading think-tanks in the public and private domain, respectively, in Korea - for providing me with a pleasant environment in which I could carry out extensive research over so many years. I would like to extend my special appreciation to Yoon Yong for editing as well as being available for discussion throughout the writing of this present volume. Needless to say, I bear full responsibility for the judgements reflected in this book. This book is dedicated to my loving family: Soo, HoonJoon (Eddie) and JungWon (Annie).

# 1. The *chaebol* problem and the economic policy dilemma

## 1. WHAT IS THE *CHAEBOL*?

The *Chaebol*. Quickly browse through any magazine or newspaper article on the modernization of Korea's economy and it is highly probable that this word will appear not once but repeatedly. But what exactly is the *chaebol*? A reader may well consider the *chaebol* as synonymous with the modern conglomerate, often having in mind an image of a huge US or European or Japanese corporation such as IBM, BMW or Sony, of course, with some minor reservations. Many people, including academics, policy-makers and the layman, often have a very unclear understanding of the *chaebol*. This book is meant to de-mystify the *chaebol* by bringing together, in a concise and simple manner, important facts and analysis accessible to all those who may be interested.

One of the most remarkable features of Korea's modern history is the extremely rapid pace of economic development experienced during the four decades following the Korean War, as evidenced by a series of record-breaking growth rates. Much of this phenomenal feat was initiated by the government's active industrialization policy that focused on accelerating the growth of the heavy and chemical industries, which also led to the formation of the big businesses or the so-called *chaebol* in the 1970s. The government-initiated and managed growth strategy, however, was not free from problems. Various economic and socio-political problems appeared such as economic concentration, underdevelopment of markets, moral hazard, cronyism, and others. In this book, we focus our discussions around what is more broadly referred to as the *chaebol* problem, which has manifested itself in the many ubiquitous regulations, as well as in anti-*chaebol* sentiment. We discuss in detail such reaction to the *chaebol* as well as other structural bottlenecks that have become major obstacles to the implementation of more rational, market-oriented economic policies.

In this book, we define the '*chaebol*' as multi-product firms composed of smaller subsidiaries with the purpose of maximizing group benefits and which operate under a single (or closely connected) managerial center, mostly through cross-shareholding and managerial connections. Accordingly, we

*1*

consider a *chaebol* as a single multi-product firm in and of itself – a business organization functionally integrated rather than a simple grouping of firms. Here we note that although the *chaebol*s are not legal entities in themselves, they have important economic implications as economic entities, being comprised of many legally recognized corporations. We emphasize this point because, for our purposes, we need only to define the *chaebol* strictly from an economic point of view regardless of their legal status.

In other discussions of the *chaebol*, it is interesting to note that almost everyone – whether or not they are academically or policy oriented – chooses to treat the *chaebol*s as if they are legal entities, sometimes even suggesting that they be subject to legal action or that they be dismantled. This oddity can probably be explained by the fact that the Korea Fair Trade Commission has been identifying and closely monitoring the top 30 *chaebol*, disregarding the fact that none of the *chaebol*s has any legal status. Nevertheless and despite the fact that a holding company system has only very recently been reintroduced in Korea after having been banned for a long time, the *chaebol*s play the same economic function as a group of firms under the control of a holding company.[1] This is why we believe that our definition of the *chaebol* can be meaningfully applied in general economic analysis.

Commentaries often define the *chaebol*s as 'groups of large and diversified firms under the ownership and managerial control of a particular family'. However, from the point of view of economics, the definition of *chaebol* should contain in it the fact that they act and are treated as a *single* economic group that undertakes business activities consistently under the pursuance of a common interest regardless of the particular management structure. It is precisely this general pattern of concerted economic effort as a group that is more important in making the *chaebol* what they are as economically significant entities rather than the mere pattern of particular ownership and management connections among affiliated firms, that is, who owns or manages a *chaebol*.

Viewed from this standpoint, if we take an extreme case of a group of firms that operate as one entity, possibly through cross-shareholding and/or managerial connections, such a grouping will be classified as a *chaebol* even though they may not be under the central ownership of a single family. On the other hand, where firms are under central or family ownership, but are for some reason managed independently, then it is not economically meaningful to classify them as a *chaebol*.

Put differently, to analyze the *chaebol* from an economic perspective, it is not particularly helpful to place undue emphasis on family ownership and management. In fact, although the use of the phrase 'family manage-ment' usually contains an abnormal prejudice, such managerial patterns are often observed in the early stages of firm growth, when this form of management is inevitable to a certain degree. Here, ownership and management are not yet separated and, before the firm goes public, the owner-manager of the firm usually receives a helping hand from other family members. Thus, simply to conclude that family management is a vice is grossly inaccurate.[2]

It is common to find discussions about *chaebol*s in conjunction with their wide-ranging business diversification. Emphasizing diversification behavior in the definition of *chaebol* is, however, not particularly useful as far as economic analysis is concerned because most modern firms are generally diversified multi-product firms of varying degree. As in many real life situations, this is a distinct break from the treatment of firms in standard textbooks, which are usually restricted to the analysis of 'single product' firms. Although our study defines the *chaebol* as multi-product firms diversified into various economic activities, what is intended in this definition is not to emphasize the behavioral aspect of diversification, but simply to emphasize the fact that the *chaebol*s themselves are also 'firms'. Therefore, when deciding if a firm can be classified as a *chaebol*, the extent to which that firm is diversified should not be a critical feature.

Moreover, once we modify the concept of the firm in accordance with the realities of actual firm behavior by broadening this concept from the textbook single-product to the real life multi-product firm, the economic significance of distinguishing between *chaebol*s and other large firms disappears. This is because although the *chaebol*s may in a legal sense be somewhat inconsistently defined, they are nothing but large firms from the standpoint of their economic significance. Therefore, in what follows, there is no harm if we use '*chaebol*' and 'large corporation' interchangeably.

## 2. THE *CHAEBOL* PROBLEM: A PRELIMINARY

The term '*chaebol* problem' has traditionally been used to denote mainly economic concentration of the *chaebol*, but our treatise will broaden the term slightly by adding to it the anti-*chaebol* sentiment that stems from the general public's criticisms about the fairness of the *chaebol* formation process.

The *chaebol* problem in the context of economic concentration is actually a condensation of two rather complex elements. The first is the excessive ownership of economic resources by the *chaebol* (also known as general economic concentration), and the second element is the monopolistic market structure in which the *chaebol* are usually the dominant actors (also known as market concentration). Another element, often associated with the *chaebol* problem, is the managerial behavior of the *chaebol*, which is generally considered to be unsound. In many cases, the *chaebol* problem is meant to imply the complex interplay of the above elements.

In general, the *chaebol* problem will be viewed in this book strictly from the standpoint of economic analysis. However, we shall also look into some non-economic aspects of the problem, more specifically, the ethical aspects of the formative and growth processes of the *chaebol*. Misgivings have been expressed over the legitimacy of the *chaebols*' wealth accumulation process because the *chaebols* were formed and have subsequently flourished under government protection, which the general public deems to be both unfair and unethical. This historically rooted view of the formation and growth of the *chaebol* still exerts great influence on the general public's perception of them today.

In the meantime, the existence of the *chaebol* problem has presented a perennial policy dilemma for the government. As the *chaebols* have grown into leading players in many of Korea's major industries, one of the most pressing tasks facing the government has been to ensure that their economic performance is continuously enhanced for the benefit of the national economy. However, public sentiment against the *chaebol* has often impeded this policy goal. According to general perception, the *chaebols* have managed to grow monstrously large through unjust government favors to the extent that they are perceived to have caused actual economic harm as well as contributing to political problems by their influence over various national policies. An implication then is that the future of the Korean economy will hinge on efforts to keep the *chaebol* from growing any larger. Regardless of whether or not this view of the *chaebol* is in fact accurate or not, such anti-*chaebol* sentiments have greatly constrained the government's ability to design and implement economic policies effectively. As a result, the government has been forced to deal with the difficult task of harmonizing the two conflicting directions of economic policy toward the *chaebol*: that is, to provide support for them while at the same time finding an appropriate way to regulate them.

In order to achieve the macroeconomic goals of high economic growth and a current account surplus through export promotion and economic vitality, the government needs to provide support to the *chaebol* or at the very least, it must avoid getting in their way. Furthermore, following the prevalent though incorrect view that protecting the domestic market is necessary to secure Korea's economic vitality means that the government has been taking measures to protect the *chaebols*' domestic market. However, the effect of such measures will be to make it easier for the *chaebol* to expand their business operations or to strengthen their monopolistic position. Therefore, once the government decides on the macroeconomic targets of high growth, high exports and a current account surplus, it will have no other alternative but to adopt policies which strengthen the economic status of the *chaebol*.

Moreover, in many cases, it may be pointed out that such policies are not usually sector- or firm-specific and are not restricted to the support of an individual large firm or *chaebol*. Instead, they usually take the form of general economic policies that affect the entire economy and include the nation's monetary and fiscal policies. For example, financial policy instruments such as access to low interest rates and easy loan facilities, and various fiscal expenditure and tax incentives in general and specifically to provide support for exports, as well as to protect the domestic market, have been common. Furthermore, policy goals themselves are generally framed to achieve macroeconomic targets. Therefore, such policies do not usually provoke criticism for being pro-*chaebol* in nature. Until recently, as long as government policies emphasized macroeconomic goals such as growth and exports, they were implemented successfully without much resentment from the public – despite the fact that these policies, whether intended or not, provided opportunities for the *chaebol* to flourish. Thus, it is not surprising that the role of the *chaebol* has increasingly expanded and become more important to the Korean economy.

On the other hand, microeconomic policy measures that seek to constrain the economic concentration of the *chaebol*, such as the Fair Trade Act, have been enforced to stifle their operations by regulating their monopolistic behavior and economic influence. The government has often decided to regulate the *chaebol* for a number of reasons. Politically speaking, such regulatory action would pander to public anti-*chaebol* sentiment and would help suppress the political influence of the *chaebol*. Economically, regulations were meant to restrict the *chaebols*' ability to monopolize the domestic market as well as to reduce competitive market pressure. Policies to regulate the *chaebol* would include, for example, the control of bank loans to the *chaebol*, forced business specialization thereby restricting diversification, and regulation of cross shareholding and cross-debt guarantees among affiliate firms.

Such measures, however, amount to the implementation of *macroeconomic* policies that support the *chaebol* on one hand, while simultaneously implementing *microeconomic* policies suppressing their economic activities on the other. This policy conflict is exactly the policy dilemma of the Korean government.

As mentioned earlier, the *chaebol* problem is related to all aspects of economic policy. This implies that looking at and acting upon the *chaebol* problem from a single viewpoint is highly likely to lead to a worsening of the policy dilemma. Put differently, it will remain very difficult to resolve such an issue unless we approach the *chaebol* problem in a comprehensive way, that is, by interpreting it within the context of the overall economic policy strategy, as well as the Korea-specific economic and institutional environment.

## 3.   A NEW THEORETICAL FRAMEWORK TOWARD UNDERSTANDING THE *CHAEBOL* PROBLEM

A giant among modern economists, Alfred Marshall suggested over a century ago that 'in the more advanced stages in economics ordinary static concepts change their meaning and acquire a definite "biological" tone when economists focus their attention on the historical development of economic institutions'.[3] Institutions are constantly evolving, and they do so following different paths, and the results are discontinuities and disturbances of a most interesting sort, which are effectively studied through the evolutionary perspective and the new-institutional economics. These two distinct but related disciplines constitute the theoretical background upon which we build a clearer and better understanding of the *chaebol*.

### 3.1   The Evolutionary Perspective in Economics

The evolutionary perspective that looks at economic phenomena from an evolutionary point of view has had a long history. In fact, it has been argued that the roots of the theory of evolution originally came from economic science. After all, Adam Smith's *The Wealth of Nations* was the main inspiration for Charles Darwin's evolutionary theory outlined in his classic *The Origin of the Species*.[4] The canvas upon which the economics of Adam Smith is constructed is the market economy, in which individual agents attempt to outdo each other by engaging in competition. Economic progress comes about through the competition process under the principle of the 'survival of the fittest', where those who are best equipped to compete with others will survive into the next generation and enjoy greater economic prosperity. This competition process is guided by what Adam Smith termed the 'invisible hand'. To Adam Smith, economic development was directly linked to the division of labor. It is important to understand that working behind this economic process were the human mechanisms of rivalry and greed, which encourage the individual to continually find new ways of outdoing their competitors, under the auspices of the 'invisible hand'.

Therefore, the approach that interprets economic phenomena from an evolutionary perspective involves giving a new interpretation to the meaning and role of competition. For all economic phenomena, there are corresponding economic environmental features that constrain the nature of such economic phenomena that usually include not only material limitations but also institutional factors such as the legal system, customs, traditions, culture and so on. In this context, a specific economic phenomenon in a given economic environment can be viewed as the result of competition for economic survival that takes place within the specific environment. Thus, if we interpret the concept of competition as the dynamic competition for survival, this means that we come to interpret economic phenomena from an evolutionary perspective.

For Adam Smith, competition was not just a static concept. Rather, competition was viewed as essential for survival in a dynamic process. In modern economic theory, this dynamic concept has been replaced by the more static concept of perfect competition that culminates in the sophisticated 'formalization and mathematization' of economics by neoclassical economists. Recently, however, Hayek (1968, 1988) and other proponents of the Austrian School imbued the concept of competition with its original dynamic meaning. It is especially noteworthy that Hayek (1968) conceptualized competition as a dynamic discovery procedure for uncovering unknown opportunities and possibilities. Through the resurgence of the Austrian School, the approach initiated by Adam Smith, of looking at economic reality from an evolutionary perspective has now come to the forefront of economic discussions. Such economists as Armen Alchian (1950), Milton Friedman (1953), Jack Hirshleifer (1977) and Geoffrey Hodgson (1993) have also tried to turn economics back into a discipline with high applicability. They have not only attempted to restore the concept of competition to its original meaning and its role as a key notion, but they also contend that it is more convincing to explain economic phenomena from an evolutionary perspective.

Another recent approach, known as 'sociobiology', analyzes social phenomena from the perspective of biological evolution. The two pioneers in this field, one from each side of the Atlantic, are Edward O. Wilson of Harvard University and Richard Dawkins of the University of Oxford. Dawkins (1976) argues that even social culture spreads through the self-reproduction of the selfish cultural gene, which he terms the 'meme'. In a similar vein, Hayek (1988) explains the evolution of the market order from the perspective of cultural evolution. Hayek perceives the market order as a spontaneous order that is formed through the interaction of market participants; and for him, it is this evolution of the market order that amounts to economic development. From Hayek's evolutionary approach, only those societies that choose to adopt a market order having higher survival value (higher likelihood of success) will endure, and the market order itself will evolve through this selection process and finally, again through the evolution of the market order, economic progress will be achieved. To take an example, the fact that capitalism survived its competition with communism means that capitalism endured because capitalistic societies adopted the superior market order based on the voluntary efforts of individual economic agents, while communist societies adopted an inferior command economy order based on central economic planning.

In this book, the evolutionary perspective is taken as the main philosophical standpoint. On another dimension, the new-institutional economics perspective provides the rigorously analytical tools that will be applied when analyzing the *chaebol*. We now offer a brief introduction to new-institutional economics.

## 3.2   New-institutional Economics and the *Chaebol* Problem

In this book, new-institutional economics derived originally from works by Coase (1937) and Alchian and Demsetz (1972), and more recently Eggertsson (1990) and North (1990) is applied to the discussions and analysis of the *chaebol*. Williamson (1975) first coined the term 'new institutional economics'. Since then, it has enjoyed rapid growth largely based on Coase's (1937) analysis of the firm, and Hayek's (1937, 1945) writings on knowledge. Other major works include contributions by Simon (1947), Arrow (1963), Davis and North (1971), Williamson (1985), Macneil (1978) and Holmstrom (1979), to name but a few. Its most prominent representatives are Coase, Williamson, Alchian, Demsetz and North.[5]

New-institutional economics is distinct from traditional neoclassical economics in that the existence of non-zero transaction costs is emphasized in their understanding of the real world economy, in which economic institutions are the ultimate determinants of the size of transaction costs influencing the structure of economic organization and performance. Hence a key concept in this modern approach to economic analysis is the importance of economic institutions in determining economic behavior, organizational structure and business performance. That is, the type of economic institution built into the economy becomes a most crucial factor in determining not only the nature of economic organization, but the general performance of the economy as well.

To illustrate this aspect more clearly, it is useful to distinguish three different levels of an economic system (Eggertsson, 1990). On the most general level, an economic system can be described as consisting of individual economic agents, economic organizations which organize individual agents, and finally, economic institutions which regulate the agents and organizations (see Figure 1.1).

According to this classification, three different levels of economic analysis of an economic system may be distinguished. The first and most simple level would be to analyze the effects of the given structure of economic organization and the given types of economic institution on the economic behavior of individual agents. The second and intermediate level would be to analyze the effects of the given types of economic institution on the structure of economic organization. Lastly, the most comprehensive level of analysis would be to treat economic institutions as endogenously formed and to explain

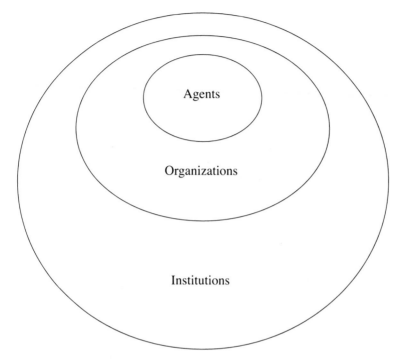

*Figure 1.1　Constitution of an economic system*

how the institution evolves through various political processes. At this level of analysis, economic agents and organizations are treated as the players who take the initiative in changing existing institutions for their own advantage.

This analytical framework provided by new-institutional economics will be applied to our discussion of the *chaebol*, basically in the sense that *chaebol* behavior is not independent of surrounding institutional constraints. The aim of this book, however, is not merely to exploit the relevance of new-institutional economics to our understanding of the various issues surrounding the *chaebol*, but also to show how policy should be framed in the future. This, of course, is then the realm of public policy, which also involves debates about the reform of institutions. In approaching the latter issue, we will reinterpret and define the distinct roles of the government and markets in disciplining the *chaebol*, and furthermore, develop a theory of corporate governance that will be useful in shaping the future policy paradigm.

As is commonly known, the Korean government has often directly intervened in the decision-making process of the private sector, thereby creating undesirable distortions in the economy's incentive structure. So how then should the role of government be defined so as to generate a viable business culture? Broadly speaking, we shall argue that the government should establish a regime of fair competition within the economic and social system so that the discovery function of the market order may become more effective. Specifically, the role of the government should be limited to defining the external economic and social environments, and should be confined to preserving the spontaneity and endogeneity of the market order. What is important here is the distinction between exogenous and endogenous economic variables, which is encountered in a beginner's economics class, but is unfortunately forgotten during discussions of real world economics and policies. We emphasize in this book that the government should create an economic environment with competitive markets buttressed by proper economic institutions (the rules of the game), which to the firm constitute the exogenous variables, while allowing all endogenous management decisions to be independently decided upon by private corporations. This, in essence, is one of the important implications derived from the new-institutional economics as outlined in Figure 1.1.

### 3.3   Implications of a New Policy Paradigm: Preliminaries

The analysis in this book examines the *chaebol* problem from an evolutionary perspective by applying the analytical tools of the new-institutional economics. The *chaebol* is appropriately viewed as a business organization that evolves according to the specific economic environment, which includes all aspects of the economic, political and socio-cultural institutions that are peculiar to Korea. The *chaebol* is a form of economic organization that seeks out the survival strategy best suited to the environment to which it belongs. Hence, it acts like a selfish organic entity, transforming itself according to the changes and challenges within that environment. The structural form and managerial pattern of the *chaebol*s have evolved under the Korea-specific economic environment through the process of the 'selection of the fittest' to its most viable form. While the existing form of the *chaebol* may have been considered the most appropriate in the context of the past and current economic environment, it is doubtful whether recent efforts by less developed countries to replicate the Korean *chaebol* can succeed. In fact, it is also unclear how long the current form of the *chaebol* can maintain its survival value in the rapidly changing internal and external economic environment. The *chaebol* are already undergoing rapid changes in response to the new economic environment prompted by the 1997 economic crisis. Many of these important issues will be studied in this book.

From the evolutionary perspective, we can draw the following important implications regarding *chaebol* policy and, more importantly, implications for national economic policy. First, the *chaebol* is a private enterprise, no more nor less so than any other economic organization seeking to maximize profits through the maximal utilization of resources within the given economic environment. Thus, regardless of their unpopularity, the *chaebol* are merely the product of the Korea-specific economic environment. Therefore, policies that aim to correct *chaebol* behavior, if they are to be at all successful, need to focus on reforming the economic environment. Without such changes, policies will not only be ineffective but may result in economic harm.

Second, the government clearly has the predominant influence in determining the economic environment. Indeed, in this sense, the *chaebol* can be said to be a product of government policy. If the government wishes to change the behavior of the *chaebol*, it should refrain from direct regulation, and rather focus on improving the economic environment through a change in its policy that has induced *chaebol* formation and growth. It is important that the government limit the scope of its policy to incorporate only exogenous factors affecting the organizations' economic behavior and performance, leaving endogenous management variables to be decided upon depending on the individual organization's goals and strategies.

Third, as the Korean economy becomes more liberalized and as the world economies become integrated into a single global market, direct intervention policies through protection and discrimination will increasingly become ineffective. The government will have no choice but to rely on the indirect management of the economy based on market principles. By indirect management of the economy, it is meant that the government should not intervene in the process of determining endogenous variables, but rather focus on facilitating the workings of the market order and indirectly influence endogenous variables through the management of the exogenous economic environment.

Fourth, the government cannot take effective measures to directly control the behavior of the *chaebol*, particularly in the era of rapid globalization, because the *chaebol* could exercise their option to emphasize international markets at the expense of the Korean market and become global firms. The government may reduce the *chaebol*'s market power and increase their competitiveness only by inducing greater competition among the *chaebol* and other firms regardless of their nationalities.

Fifth, the progress of a free private market order can only be secured through competition. Competition is a process through which dormant opportunities are discovered and explored, and hence, an economy with a stifled competitive environment cannot escape stagnation.

Sixth, the only solution to the policy dilemma resulting from the *chaebol* problem, specifically, the conflict between micro and macroeconomic goals, lies not in regulating or protecting the *chaebol*, but in introducing fierce competition into the industries in which they dominate. For this, it is urgent to liberalize market entry for all domestic and foreign firms into the business sectors. Only in this manner can both the competitiveness of the *chaebol* and the vitality of the national economy be achieved in harmony.

Approaching the *chaebol* problem from the evolutionary perspective and incorporating new-institutional economics, it becomes necessary to systematically analyze the economic environment that brought about the current form and behavior of the *chaebol*. In other words, if the whole evolutionary process of the *chaebol* – their genesis, development and current behavior – is ultimately the product of the economic environment, then successful policy formulation demands the inclusion of valuable knowledge of the economic environment and of the causal relationship between that environment and the evolutionary process of the *chaebol*. This book presents our efforts to meet this requirement.

The classic work that addresses the *chaebol* problem is undoubtedly Jones and Sakong (1980). Many other studies of the *chaebol* have concentrated on grasping the realities of the *chaebol* problem (Chung and Yang, 1993; Lee and Lee, 1990; Cho, 1991; Yoo, 1992). All in all, these studies were primarily designed to illuminate the seriousness of the *chaebol* problem, and usually trace the historical pattern of *chaebol* behavior through various indices of economic concentration and efficiency. However, they are for the most part commentaries and are relatively weak as far as the economic analysis of the *chaebol* problem and its possible solution is concerned. There are also recent efforts to analyze the causes of the *chaebol* problem. One such effort explains the process of economic concentration in the hands of a few people by regarding the phenomenon of resource concentration as the product of economic and political rent-seeking behavior (So, 1994). Another study analyzes the diversification behavior of the *chaebol* from an economic point of view, attempting to prove that the reason for *chaebol* diversification stems from the possibility of maintaining the stability of their consolidated profits through diversification (Yang, 1992). Recently, Hwang (2000) studied aggregate concentration, diversification and market structure in the 1980s and 1990s for Korea, and found that *chaebol* diversification may not be an important reason behind deepening aggregate concentration.

Be that as it may, the debate on the *chaebol* problem is far from being settled. From the evolutionary perspective adopted in this book, we shall address, by applying more systematic and rigorous economic analyses, many of the most important issues related to the *chaebol* problem. Jwa (1997) tried to analyze the diversification behavior of the *chaebol* as a process of endogenous (potentially optimal) response to changes in the economic environment, and to provide some prospects for change in their behavior in the era of globalization. This, perhaps, is the starting point for analyzing the *chaebol* from an evolutionary viewpoint, and this book is an extension to further this line of research.

## 4. STRATEGY OF STUDY

For analytical convenience, the strategy of this book is to break down the genesis of the *chaebol* problem into two separate stages. The first stage is the process by which the *chaebol* secure large amounts of economic resources and the second stage is the process through which the secured resources are put to use. An analogy from a famous Korean folktale should be illustrative. A farmer, named Heungbu, has suddenly become a millionaire because of the gourd seed brought to him by a swallow he cured.[6] He will probably face the problem of how to allocate this new wealth. In this case, the process through which Heungbu suddenly became wealthy can figuratively be compared to the process that enabled the *chaebol*'s initial concentration of ownership and resources. On the other hand, the decision-making process through which Heungbu allocated his wealth can be compared to the *chaebol*'s economic decision-making process for the maximization of their wealth through the appropriate choice of firm strategy.

This study re-examines the nature of the *chaebol* problem through this multi-stage decision-making system. It also sheds new light on the fundamental causes of the *chaebol*'s formation and managerial behavior, including its diversification behavior. Finally, it evaluates past and current *chaebol* policies and explores a new paradigm for *chaebol* policy based on an analytical framework developed by applying new-institutional economics to the understanding of the *chaebol*.

When approaching issues of *chaebol*-related policy, the factor that is most responsible for changes in the economic environment, and as a result deserves special consideration, is the increasing trend of globalization. We propose that *chaebol* policy should be consistently perceived within a broader framework of national economic policy consistent with the trend of globalization. Therefore this book not only attempts to conduct theoretical and empirical analyses of the formation and behavioral pattern of the *chaebol*, but also explores a new *chaebol* policy in light of the new national economic policy framework brought about by globalization.

## 5. STRUCTURE OF BOOK

The structure of this book is as follows. Chapter 2 provides an overview of the industrial policies in Korea during the past four decades, and explains how the *chaebol* have grown as an outcome of this development strategy. This chapter can be viewed as a general introduction to Korea's industrial policy as well as providing the background to the understanding of *chaebol* formation.

Chapter 3 attempts to clear the air with regard to the so-called '*chaebol* problem'. Here we distinguish between problems of general concentration, monopolistic market structure, and managerial behavior in the conventional manner, and proceed by critically re-examining these concepts to identify the real issues associated with the *chaebol*.

Chapter 4 views the *chaebol* problem by applying the concept of the two stage decision-making process, thereby providing a unique and what we think is a clearer way towards understanding *chaebol* formation and growth. Past and current government *chaebol* policies are then grouped in line with the analytical framework developed here and are comprehensively evaluated.

Chapter 5 analyzes the influence of institutions (rules of the game) and government policy on the evolution and behavior of the *chaebol*. This chapter explores the evolution of the *chaebol* through the new-institutional economics perspective. Specifically, we show that the lack of private property rights protection is of special importance in explaining the formation and the behavior of the *chaebol*. Hence we firmly establish that economic institutions and government policy have largely been responsible for creating an economic environment that led to the evolution of the *chaebol*.

Chapter 6 investigates the business diversification behavior of firms by providing theoretical as well as cross-country empirical analyses. Using cross-country data, the effects of economic institutions, market structure and characteristics of firms on diversification are empirically examined. This chapter also explores the prospects of *chaebol* diversification behavior in response to changes in market size and technology brought about by the arrival of the globalization age. It is argued that the government's arbitrary control will become less effective as we enter the era of globalization, a period accompanied by increased uncertainty that only markets may effectively manage. Furthermore, in the latter part of the chapter, the impact of economic institutions on national economic performance is also analyzed.

Chapter 7 presents our interpretation of the past economic development process, and also provides a new paradigm for Korea's economic future. Here we begin by evaluating Korea's industrial policy in terms of its effect on productivity during the period of the heavy and chemical industrialization drive. As an example of the deep-seated government intervention, we look at the case of the Samsung Motor Industry, which is a nice example illustrating how the government intervenes in the business decisions of private corporations. We also discuss the general impact the government-led industrial policies had on the financial crisis of 1997. In this chapter, we criticize past explanations of economic growth as somewhat insufficient at explaining Korea's 'miracle' growth. Rather, 'government-led discrimination' is singled out as one of the most critical factors contributing to Korea's development. However, by championing the firm as the most important engine for economic growth, a theory of corporate governance is presented which is later applied to provide a thorough understanding of the evolution of corporate governance systems across different countries. That is, we show how institutional factors such as culture, law, government policy, and the financial system affect corporate behavior, thereby suggesting how public policies toward the corporate sector should be approached.

Chapter 8 follows naturally from the previous chapter. Here, we spell out the details of the policy framework needed to encourage *chaebol* efficiency and competitiveness. Broadly speaking, emphasis is placed on improving market institutions when attempting to influence *chaebol* behavior, as this should strengthen the corporate monitoring roles of the various markets surrounding the *chaebol*, such as the product market and the financial market, and others. It is emphasized, however, that institutional reform cannot survive without appropriate enforcement, and we argue that only the government is equipped to take on this role. The government has the additional responsibility of setting up legal institutions that will minimize uncertainty in the property rights system, an issue thoroughly discussed in this chapter.

Chapter 9 concludes the book with a concise overview of both its theoretical contribution and empirical findings. The reader can find here a summary of the ideas developed throughout the book.

## Notes

1.  A Holding Company System was introduced in the Fair Trade Act (1998) but companies as groups have yet to satisfy some very restrictive conditions for eligibility. First, their debt-equity ratios must be lower than 100 per cent for the entire group of companies. Second, cross-debt guarantees must be eliminated. Third, the holding company must hold more than 50 per cent of stocks of subsidiary companies. Fourth, no grandson companies are allowed in related business areas. Finally, the joint holding of financial and non-financial firms is prohibited.
2.  This position is consistent with Demsetz (1983), who proposes that the structure of ownership of a firm or corporate does not matter to the firm's performance.
3.  *Principles of Economics* (1920, p. xv).
4.  See Hayek (1988, pp. 23-4, and its Appendix A).
5.  For overviews and commentaries see Eggertsson (1990), Furubotn and Richter (1997), Coase (1992), Werin and Wijkander (1992), Pejovich (1995), Drobak and Nye (1997). There is also an annual symposium issue of the *Journal of Institutional and Theoretical Economics (JITE)*.
6.  In case the reader is not familiar with this traditional folktale, a short summary of events is presented here. It is a story that involves two brothers: Nolbu the elder one who was greedy and ill-mannered, and the younger Heungbu who was good-natured but very poor. Nolbu always disliked Heungbu. One summer, a swallow that lived on Heungbu's roof broke its leg, Heungbu noticing this, quickly tied the broken leg with a scarf and the swallow was cured in time to make its journey south over the winter. The swallow was grateful. It returned the next summer with a gourd seed as a gift for Heungbu's kindness. Heungbu planted these seeds and when the grown gourds were open, countless gems of silver and gold were found in these gourds. This made Heungbu very rich. Nolbu, who was always lazy, came to hear of the news and became very jealous. He sent his wife to find out how Heungbu was able to acquire such

wealth. Upon hearing the story of the swallow, he devised a plan. What he did was to grab hold of a swallow and purposely broke its leg, only to bind it again with a scarf. The swallow did return with gourd seeds the following summer, but when the grown gourds were split, they did not yield gems and treasures. Rather, a very scary spirit appeared and scolded Nolbu for his misdeeds.

# 2.   Industrial policies and the growth of the *chaebol*

## 1.   INTRODUCTION

The *chaebol* is a corporate form emerging from the Korea-specific business environment that includes her political, social and economic institutions. In particular, Korea's industrial policy has loomed large in shaping the business environment. Thus without a proper understanding of the history and characteristics of her industrial policies, which have been greatly influenced by the dominance of government intervention, one cannot hope to fully understand the factors behind the establishment and growth of the *chaebol*. In this chapter, we review the pattern of Korea's industrial policies and show how the *chaebol* has evolved.

## 2.   INDUSTRIAL POLICIES IN KOREA

### 2.1   Overview of Korea's Industrial Policy

Schematically, the pattern of Korean industrial policies during the last 30 years may be depicted as a cycle of three phases as depicted in Figure 2.1. First, the government selects industries and corporations to be supported. In the second phase, it sets up trade policies as well as mobilizing tax and financial resources to support those selected industries. The third phase consists of government-led restructuring of industries and corporations that are found to be in distress. In essence, we find active government intervention in every phase of the cycle. Entry and exit barriers, and financial and tax supports acted as tools of industrial policy. Entry barriers basically allowed only selected large corporations to enter the targeted industries, and policies designed to support these corporations contributed to the rise of big diversified enterprises – the Korean *chaebol*s. Moreover, exit barriers, erected as a result of active governmental intervention in industrial and corporate restructuring, inhibited the natural flow of economic resources from non-viable firms to viable ones. Financial support included loans of scarce financial resources at preferential, subsidized rates, with long maturity periods, to corporations

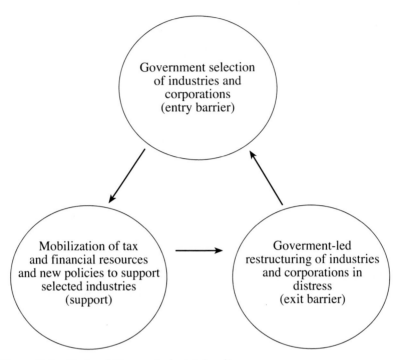

*Figure 2.1    Cycle of Korean industrial policy*

chosen to operate in selected industries. Consequently, it can be argued that
these practices may have resulted in resource misallocation.

Deliberate industrial policies in Korea were first implemented in the 1960s,
at which time the first Five-Year Economic Development Plan[1] was launched.
The early import substitution policies of the 1950s gave way to the export-led
development strategy. The government initially targeted the development of
key industries through import substitution selecting several strategic sectors,
including fertilizer and refined oil, to be supported extensively. Laws supporting these industries were quickly enacted. The government allocated most
investment resources, which were procured mainly through foreign loans, to
firms operating in these industries.

The period of the most extensive government intervention in Korea took
place in the 1970s with the heavy and chemical industrialization drive (HCI
drive). The government designated certain industries as key industries. These
included iron and steel, non-ferrous metals, shipbuilding, general machinery,
chemicals and electronics, and others, to which tax and financial resources as
well as trade policies were directed specifically to promote rapid and
uninterrupted development. As mentioned above, entry barriers were set up
thus contributing to the rise of the *chaebol*s. It is not surprising therefore to

find that during this period the size of heavy and chemical industries (HCIs) grew enormously.

Unfortunately, deficiencies and side effects of the HCI Drive eventually began to appear, and in the 1980s, the government had little choice but to initiate corrective measures. Over-investment in selected industries and high inflation caused by the expansionary monetary policy eventually led the government to refrain from its active industrial promotion policies. Priorities shifted and industrial policy was redrawn to support technology-intensive industries. The underlying motive for this shift was to correct the structural imbalances that started to appear in the manufacturing sector in the late 1970s. The massive inflow of funds into the HCIs was reduced drastically, leaving many of these industries with severe over-capacity. Nevertheless, despite the change in priorities, it is important to note that the government has continued its legacy of closely interfering in industrial and corporate restructuring even up to the present day.

In the 1990s, the government's economic policy experienced a turn toward emphasizing deregulation. The government rescinded many existing regulations, but sometimes revived ones it had repealed. Again, the government's interventionist 'habit' and the private sector's persistent expectations of government initiation and intervention in the market continued to impede the development of a market economy. Despite the numerous changes in government policies throughout the past four decades, government intervention remains a prominent feature, usually with consequences for the success or failure of individual corporations. Indeed, the *chaebols* can be thought of as the brainchild of the government itself. Whether the current form of the *chaebols* is what was intended or not is quite beside the point.

## 2.2  Selective Nurturing of Industries by Government

To induce rapid economic growth, the Korean government set up economic development plans and selected strategic industries. In the course of promoting these industries, the government often restricted entry through regulations, thereby contributing to the growth of a few selected large corporations.

In the early 1960s, fertilizer, refined oil, steel, synthetic chemical fibers and electric machinery were selected as the industries to be supported. The government also decided on the division of labor. For example, the government took responsibility for building the oil refineries while the private sector took the initiative in constructing other industries. During that period, 60 per cent of total investment was procured through foreign loans, 55 per cent of which was used for the fertilizer, refined oil, cement and textile industries. Moreover, 25 per cent of foreign loans was spent on social overhead capital (SOC) such as electricity, telecommunication and transportation.

In the second half of the 1960s, the government targeted the steel, petrochemical and general machinery industries. To gain a feel for the magnitude of the importance of these industries, these three industries absorbed 60 per cent of total investment in the manufacturing industry and 77 per cent of all foreign loans.

In the 1970s and early 1980s, with emphasis on export-oriented development and the HCI Drive, the government targeted various heavy and chemical strategic industries that included iron and steel, nonferrous metals, shipbuilding, general machinery, chemicals and electronics.[2] Once again, tax and financial resources as well as trade policy were designed and used to support these industries. Basically, the government allowed only existing large corporations to enter the targeted industries, with the obvious result that they enjoyed the benefits emanating from the government's support. Furthermore, the government allowed foreign loans for firms in the targeted industries on a preferential basis.

## 2.3   Entry and Exit Barriers

Once the strategic industries had been selected, the government decided on industries that it would take responsibility for and those it would delegate to the private sector. Fierce competition raged in the private sector as firms struggled to receive permission to enter the selected industries, since once entry permission was obtained, protection through entry restrictions and support through tax and financial policies were almost surely guaranteed.

The government later recycled corporations after the accumulation of industrial capital began. That is, firms that had been selected in the 1960s were selected again to participate in the HCI drive of the 1970s. For example, 'the Promotion Plan for Heavy and Chemical Industries', announced in June 1973, stated that those companies wishing to be considered as part of the promotion project must procure 30 per cent of total investment with their own capital. This can be interpreted as an indirect way to ensure that only those enterprises that had been selected in the 1960s would be selected again. This is easily seen to be the case as those companies already selected were precisely those able to put up such a large amount of capital.[3] Along with the promotion of HCIs, the government in the 1970s committed itself to export promotion and for that purpose sought economies of scale in export industries, which resulted in the establishment of the so-called 'General Trading Companies'. These were private enterprises having government backing that specialized in the export of Korean goods. Because the general trading companies were given permission to enter the HCIs, they therefore became deeply involved in the various priority industries.

Trade policy, or more specifically, access to international markets also became a preferential instrument geared toward the selected industries and corporations. For example, due to restrictions on imports to protect domestic markets, it was virtually impossible to import foreign products if similar goods were produced domestically. However, if the exporter needed to import inputs for the production of an export good, such items were exempted from this prohibition and, moreover, benefited from a tariff rebate system. As such, the general trading companies became highly active in the export and import businesses as well as in the HCI drive through their subsidiaries, and prospered greatly from this system. For example, HCI products accounted for 57 per cent of the general trading companies' total exports in 1980.[4]

In addition to entry selection, the government actively intervened in the corporate restructuring process, including the liquidation and merger and acquisition (M&A) of private firms, which can be interpreted as a way of determining the exit of firms. Table 2.1 shows principal features of the industrial and corporate restructuring that took place during the period of Korea's rapid economic development.

The country's export-oriented economic development strategy, financed by large investments allocated under government discretion eventually fostered many incompetent firms characterized by their lack of experience and managerial skills. The government worried that the emergence of many non-viable firms would lower the nation's credit status in international financial markets, thus impeding economic growth that, in turn, was greatly dependent on foreign loans. Despite criticism that it was itself partly responsible for the deterioration of firms as well as the widespread resource misallocation, the government nevertheless felt duty bound to activate and control the corporate restructuring process. Within the period 1969 to 1971, for example, over a hundred incompetent firms were either liquidated or acquired by other firms (see Table 2.1). We should bear in mind that the effect of the government's corporate restructuring strategy was essentially to transfer ownership at its discretion, thereby effectively deciding which companies would remain active and which would exit the market.

Despite this early action by the government, problems of excessive financial costs and capital structure vulnerability persisted in many firms. Moreover, in the early 1970s, the tight monetary policy recommended by the IMF in tandem with sharp currency devaluation aggravated financial problems. In reaction, the government enforced comprehensive measures and applied them uniformly to firms in order to alleviate their financial difficulties. Some of these measures included the transforming of short-term debt into long-term debt, lowering interest rates, and tax exemptions.

However, from the late 1970s, over-investment and persistent inflation caused by an expansionary monetary policy became the primary concerns.

*Table 2.1    Content of industrial and corporate restructuring prior to the 1997 economic crisis*

| Period | Content |
| --- | --- |
| 1969–1971 | 112 insolvent firms in the PVC, automobile, steel, chemical and textile industries were liquidated or acquired by other firms |
| 1972: Industrial rationalization | Due to a tight monetary policy recommended by the IMF and sharp devaluation, firms took out loans at high interest rates and with short maturity. Financial problems of these firms worsened.<br>Industrial rationalization:<br><br>• Covered 61 firms, including 30 in heavy industries, eight in chemical industries, and ten in light industries.<br>• Self-rationalization through specialization, M&As and R&D supported by the government through financial and tax support |
| Late 1970s– early 1980s restructuring of HCIs | The government decreased the flow of investment to HCIs to correct over-investment in those industries. The electricity-generating, heavy construction equipment, automobile, and diesel engine industries were covered. Main restructuring tools were M&As. The government supported restructuring with bail-out financing and interest rate subsidies |
| 1990s: Business specialization inducement | Induce the big 30 business groups to specialize. Regulations on the core business areas chosen by individual business groups will be eased |

Eventually the goal of economic policy was switched to economic stabilization and the scaling-down of investment in the HCIs. In 1979, for example, the government decided to slow down monetary growth[5] and also divert financial support toward the expansion of the consumer goods industries. This change in policy direction led to a reduction in investments in the HCIs. On the other hand, the government reorganized the HCIs throughout the 1980s in an attempt to raise their competitiveness through the creation of economies of scale and tried to reduce the social costs associated with massive corporate bankruptcies.[6] In addition, the government carried out a program of industrial rationalization and revised the tax reduction regulation law. The revision stated that (i) the government should set the industry rationalization criteria and (ii) firms going through rationalization according to these criteria would get tax reductions or exemptions. As of 1988, 70 firms were classified as firms necessitating rationalization. Among them, 67 were disposed of through government-led M&As, while two firms went through a reorganization process and one firm was liquidated. It is important to note that most firms were merged with or acquired by third parties based on criteria set primarily by the government. Yet again, we observe that the restructuring process, in effect, worked as an exit barrier that restricted the swift transfer of resources from non-viable to viable firms.

## 2.4   Financial and Tax Supports

The Korean government allocated financial resources and provided tax support to those corporations given permission to enter industries it deemed economically strategic. During the 1960s, the government put almost all of the domestic financial resources under its control. It revised the Korea Central Bank Law as well as the Commercial Bank Law, took over the stocks of commercial banks owned by private enterprises, and established special-purpose state banks such as the Kookmin Bank for the general public and the Industrial Bank of Korea for small and medium firms. In the early 1960s, the government allocated 55 per cent of foreign loans to the strategically selected industries. In the second half of the decade, 60 per cent of investments in the manufacturing sector were allocated to three strategic industries: petro-chemical, steel and machinery. In addition, the government applied low interest rates on loans to firms entering the selected industries.

Even after the industrial restructuring program of the late 1960s, many of the surviving firms (among those selected and helped by the government) experienced financial difficulties. The government rode to their rescue with comprehensive and uniformly applied measures. For example, it allowed short-term private-sector debt to be switched to long-term debt, lowered interest rates (from 19 to 15.5 per cent for the discount rate of commercial bills), issued special bonds (30 per cent of which were changed into long-term low interest rate loans), raised the depreciation rate of fixed facilities from 30 to 40 and then to 80 per cent, and raised the corporate tax exemption rate from 6 to 10 per cent.

In the 1970s, the government became increasingly involved in the allocation of investment funds not only to strategic industries but also to individual investment projects. To provide large investment resources in the heavy and chemical industries, the government established the National Investment Fund in 1974. Commercial banks, virtually controlled by the government at that time, were then directed to issue loans to targeted investment projects. In addition, the government gave priority to companies operating in the heavy, chemical and export-oriented industries to introduce foreign loans. The loans to these companies and other earmarked loans were called 'policy loans', which had interest rates kept deliberately low (see Table 2.3). Table 2.2 shows the share of policy loans compared to total domestic credit during the period 1975 to 1985. At the time, foreign trade loans were used to finance exports in general, while earmarked loans were reserved for the agricultural sector, small and medium firms, residential construction and so on. Hence the remainder of the loans became the likely source of investment funds for the heavy and chemical industries. More than half of total investment funds was placed under government control, with more than two-thirds allocated to HCI firms and exporters. In the late 1980s, more than 93 per cent of national investment funds and 42 per cent of the Korea Development Bank's loans were allocated to HCI industries.

*Table 2.2    Share of policy loans in domestic credit (%)*[a]

| Year | Not earmarked[b] | Foreign Trade[c] | Earmarked[d] | Total |
|---|---|---|---|---|
| 1975 | 27.67 | 8.86 | 18.52 | 55.04 |
| 1976 | 26.98 | 9.84 | 17.78 | 54.61 |
| 1977 | 29.52 | 10.20 | 18.03 | 57.76 |
| 1978 | 32.14 | 10.62 | 19.17 | 61.93 |
| 1979 | 33.05 | 10.49 | 16.34 | 59.88 |
| 1980 | 32.76 | 11.15 | 15.44 | 59.35 |
| 1981 | 31.52 | 12.56 | 16.24 | 60.31 |
| 1982 | 29.65 | 12.16 | 14.25 | 56.05 |
| 1983 | 27.70 | 12.56 | 15.98 | 56.24 |
| 1984 | 25.73 | 12.62 | 16.94 | 55.29 |
| 1985 | 25.03 | 12.75 | 16.98 | 54.76 |

*Notes*:
[a] Domestic credit includes all loans and discounts to the private sector by deposit money banks (commercial banks and special banks) and two development institutions, the Korea Development Bank and Korea Export Import Bank.
[b] 'Not earmarked' includes loans from the National Investment Fund, loans denominated in foreign currencies, all loans by the Korea Development Bank and other miscellaneous items.
[c] 'Foreign Trade' includes loans for foreign trade by deposit money banks and all loans from the Korea Export and Import Bank.
[d] 'Earmarked' includes loans for agriculture, small and medium firms, and residential construction.

*Source*:   Yoo (1989).

Table 2.3 shows the gap between the preferential interest rate and other interest rates. The difference between the earnings rate of commercial bills and the interest rate on loans for equipment grew from 3.0 per cent in 1965 to 12.6 per cent in 1970, and up to a further 15 per cent in 1980. The difference between commercial bills and loans for foreign trade was even greater. These differences started to shrink only after 1985. Furthermore, since the inflation rate ranged between 10 to 28.7 per cent during 1975 to 1985, real interest rates on policy loans were negative. Thus, it becomes clear that until the mid-1980s the export sector and the heavy and chemical industries enjoyed easy access to financial resources at low interest rates.

*Table 2.3   Various interest rates (annual rate, %)*

|  | 1965 | 1970 | 1975 | 1980 | 1985 | 1990 | 1992 | 1993 |
|---|---|---|---|---|---|---|---|---|
| Commercial bills | 14.0 | 24.6 | 20.1 | 30.1 | 14.2 | 16.5 | 16.2 | 12.6 |
| Loans for equipment | 11.0 | 12.0 | 12.0 | 20.0 | 12.0 | 12.0 | 12.0 | 9.5 |
| Loans for foreign trade | 6.5 | 6.0 | 9.6 | 15.0 | 10.0 | 10.0 | 10.0 | 8.5 |

*Source*:   Lee (1998).

In general, tax supports for corporations operating in selected industries included tax reductions on export sales, reductions of indirect and customs taxes on inputs for export goods, reductions of corporate tax, and a high rate of depreciation. Figure 2.2 shows the trend of corporate tax reduction. We observe that the reduction rate increased slowly until the early 1970s, but then surged to increase very sharply in the late 1970s and early 1980s.

Table 2.4 shows the effective marginal tax rate for selected industries. The favorable tax treatment for these industries lowers the tax rate to around three-quarters of what it would otherwise have been.

In addition, we note that the effective tax rate on HCIs during the 1970s was 20 per cent, while that of light industries was almost 50 per cent.[7]

## 3.   GROWTH OF THE *CHAEBOL* AND THE ORIGIN OF *CHAEBOL* REGULATION

The strategy of government-led economic development set the ground for the growth of the *chaebol*. As we have mentioned, in the early stages of economic

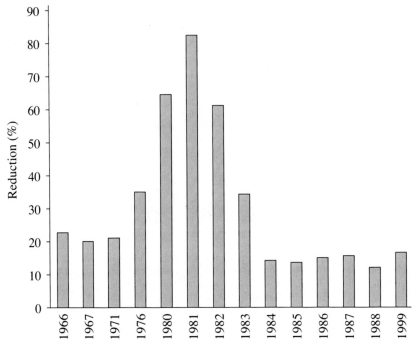

*Source*:   Lee (1998).

*Figure 2.2    Reduction of corporate tax (%)*

*Table 2.4    Effective marginal tax rates*

|  | Chemical products | | Basic metal and product | | Electrical and electronic machinery | |
|---|---|---|---|---|---|---|
|  | General | Special | General | Special | General | Special |
| 1973 | 48.90 | 46.30 | 49.00 | 46.90 | 49.30 | 47.10 |
| 1975 | 54.20 | 38.80 | 53.20 | 38.70 | 53.70 | 39.10 |
| 1978 | 41.10 | 29.50 | 41.20 | 31.00 | 42.00 | 30.90 |
| 1980 | 45.30 | 32.00 | 45.50 | 32.90 | 45.80 | 33.00 |
| 1981 | 55.80 | 42.40 | 55.00 | 42.60 | 55.60 | 43.00 |
| 1982 | 57.10 | 50.80 | 56.40 | 50.80 | 57.00 | 51.20 |
| 1983 | 37.60 | 34.80 | 38.10 | 35.80 | 38.40 | 36.00 |

*Notes*:   'General' rates are applicable to firms that are not qualified to get special tax treatment
and 'special' rates are for qualified firms.

*Source*:   Kwack (1984).

development, the government allowed a few corporations to enter the targeted industries. Since these industries usually belonged to the heavy and chemical industries, they were subject to strong economies of scale, and therefore the size of the corporations involved could not but grow increasingly larger. Afterwards, the government continued to make use of and rely on their experience and managerial skills in the course of economic development. The government gave the *chaebol*s preferential entry into targeted industries, offering financial and tax inducements to chosen firms, and this hindered the introduction of the spirit of rivalry in markets and cushioned the firms from losing ground to outside competition. Moreover, these large corporations had every incentive to diversify their operations according to the government's industry targeting policy. Consequently, they became larger and larger. Furthermore, in disposing of insolvent firms, the government reorganized the industrial structure by transferring their ownership to the big business groups, thereby reinforcing the growth of the *chaebol*. In addition, the government, to minimize the huge potential social cost of *chaebol* bankruptcies, resuscitated insolvent *chaebol*s or their subsidiaries through preferential measures. An important implication is that these big business groups, as a result, had little chance to restructure themselves according to market discipline. Basically, the formation and growth of the *chaebol* was a result of the interaction between the government's industrial policies and the *chaebol*'s responses to them.

The *chaebol* have a distinguishable management system. The controlling shareholder, usually referred to as the chairman, controls the management of all affiliates. The chairman of a *chaebol* maintains tight control over its subsidiaries mainly by owning shares in other firms (cross-shareholding). Consequently, the boards of directors and supervisors of other subsidiary firms do not function as they should in a contemporary sense (that is, monitoring management), and in fact, it is common for board members not to oppose the chairman in fear of being expelled.

Since the *chaebol*s are accountable for a large share of the Korean economy's assets, sales and debts, most industrial policy measures are inevitably connected with them. The growth of the *chaebol*s has become a burden to economic policy. The *chaebol*s, as leading companies in major export-oriented industries such as petrochemicals, automobiles and semiconductors, had initiated large-scale projects and were exposed to increasingly harsh international competition with domestic competition somewhat reduced. Moreover, strategic concerns in oligopolistic markets have forced them to expand their capacity. They have become larger and larger with little experience of how to restructure. The need to restructure, moreover, was diminished with the growth of the notorious 'too-big-to-fail' legacy of the *chaebol*. In addition, Korea's financial system has been heavily skewed toward indirect financing through banks in comparison to direct financing through the stock market. Furthermore, the government controlled the banking system, usually determining the allocation of financial resources to support big businesses and at times to resuscitate them. As a result, the *chaebol*s ended up with high debt–equity ratios as can be seen in Figure 2.3.

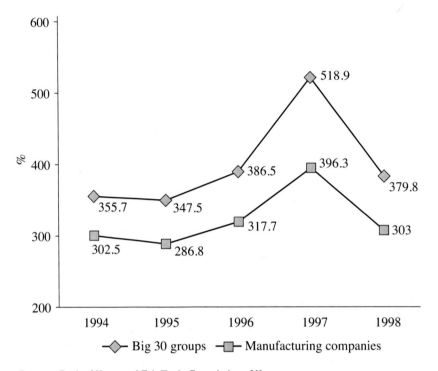

*Source*:   Bank of Korea and Fair Trade Commission of Korea.

*Figure 2.3   Debt–equity ratio of top 30* chaebol

From the early 1980s, Korea's anti-monopolist policy began to focus its attention on regulating economic concentration. The 'Regulation on Monopoly and Fair Trade Act' ('The Fair Trade Act' hereafter) was enacted in 1980 and the regulations on M&A and big business groups were introduced in 1986. The regulations on market concentration and cross-debt guarantees among *chaebol* affiliate firms were introduced in 1990 and 1992, respectively. Table 2.5 presents the main regulations regarding economic concentration as of 1990.

In Korea, the Fair Trade Commission selects on an annual basis the top 30 *chaebol*s, based on the size of their assets, as its main target for regulation. The government then puts up various regulations such as restrictions on loans to

*Table 2.5   Regulations on economic concentration as of 1990*

|  |  | Content |
|---|---|---|
| Market structure | Suppression of economic concentration | Holding companies are prohibited<br>Restrictions on total investment in subsidiaries<br>Restrictions on cross-debt guarantees<br>Restrictions on voting rights of financial and insurance companies having shares of affiliates |
|  | Restrictions on M&As | Anti-competitive M&As are prohibited<br>Unfair M&A is prohibited |
| Corporate behavior | Restrictions on exercising market power | Restrictions on unjust price determination and change<br>Restrictions on entry barriers<br>Restrictions on hindering other firms' operations |
|  | Restrictions on collusion | Restrictions on collusive determination of prices and sale conditions<br>Restrictions on regional demarcation and exclusive dealing |
|  | Restrictions on unfair transactions | Maintaining resale prices is prohibited<br>Restrictions on unfair international contracts |

the *chaebol* to prevent lending concentration. Also, during the 1990s, a business specialization policy was introduced that requires the *chaebol*s to limit diversification to two to three specialized business lines.

Nevertheless, these regulations were not as effective as expected. Both the net assets and cross-holdings of the *chaebol* have approximately doubled during 1993 to 1997. Market concentration is still high – the top 30 *chaebol*s accounted for 46.9 and 46.6 per cent of total sales in 1988 and 1997, respectively.[8] The top 30 *chaebol* accounted for 24.2 and 21.5 per cent of total financial loans in 1990 and 1995, respectively.

There are several reasons for the failure of regulations to contain economic concentration in Korea. First, restrictions on competition including entry barriers and price regulations were still effective. Second, the government could not commit the fate of incompetent *chaebol*s to the care of market mechanisms because of the potential social cost of their financial problems and bankruptcies. As a result, the government sustained incompetent *chaebol* subsidiaries with public money or merged them with other *chaebol* subsidiaries. Furthermore, the M&A market remained inactive and bankruptcy laws, including reorganization processes, were inadequate and usually ignored. Third, the financial industry was too immature to exercise its role as a check on the *chaebol*'s over-expansion. Korean banks did not perform their duty of loan screening thoroughly because they were used only as tools to support the government's industrial policies in the so-called 'government-controlled financial system' or *kwanchi kumyung* in the Korean expression. Local banks are therefore reduced to nothing more than an instrument of excessive government intervention in the banking sector. As banks and other financial institutions became accustomed to governmental guidance and coordination, they hardly needed and so lacked the requisite ability to conduct credit and project analyses. Since their ability to function as banks deteriorated, for every loan they provided, even for credit loans, they tended to prefer debt guarantees by a third party or collateral to reduce risks. So the *chaebol*s satisfied the banks with cross-debt guarantees among subsidiaries, with which they could obtain money needed for their expansion.

All these factors not only made regulating the *chaebol*s ineffective but also created inconsistencies in government policies toward the *chaebol* and possibly even led to the erosion of their competitiveness. In the next chapter, we turn to understanding the traditional perception of the *chaebol* problem.

## Notes

1. Five-Year Economic Development Plans were implemented every five years starting in 1961 during the 1960s and 1970s. However, from the 1980s on, the plans have merely been a broad profile of government economic objectives.
2. The main reason for the implementation of this policy appears to be security concerns raised by the reduction of US troops stationed in Korea. The Korean government at the time felt that this was the best response to the need to build up certain industries for national defense (see Yoo, 1989).
3. One more reason was that the heavy and chemical industries required a large production scale and therefore large amounts of money, and this gave a relative advantage to the big enterprises that had financial and managerial experience and ability.
4. In the same year, heavy and chemical industrial production accounted for 42 per cent of the nation's total exports.
5. The M2 growth rate was set at 25 per cent, 10 per cent lower than the rate in 1978.
6. For example, the restructuring process encompassed amongst others, the electricity generation, heavy construction equipment, automobile, and diesel engine industries.
7. Lee (1988), Lee (1998), Yoo (1991).
8. Hwang (1999).

# 3. Critical review of the traditional perception of the *chaebol* problem

## 1. INTRODUCTION

This chapter provides a critical review of the traditional perception of the *chaebol* problem. According to the prevailing view, economic concentration is cited as one of the most notorious features of the *chaebol*. Specifically, economic concentration has been conceptualized as consisting of aggregate concentration, market concentration, and conglomeration stemming from various business practices such as excess diversification and ownership concentration.[1] This traditional perception of the *chaebol* problem has become the basis for current regulatory policies that identify both economic and social problems as arising from economic concentration and aims to remove them comprehensively. In this chapter, we will first examine what is referred to as the *chaebol* problem as defined by the traditional perception, and then shed new light on the problems presented by the traditional perception itself.

## 2. MONOPOLIZATION OF ECONOMIC RESOURCES AND AGGREGATE ECONOMIC CONCENTRATION

In Korea, a particular controversial *chaebol* issue is the alleged 'excessive' influential position of a few powerful decision-makers (specifically, the chairmen of the *chaebols*) over major economic resources. We argue that care must be observed so as not to be overwhelmed nor misguided by the prevailing and, at times, groundless anti-*chaebol* sentiment among the public. Rather we should try to be objective about the *chaebol* in a scientific and objective manner. We begin by discussing the general trend of economic concentration in Korea and compare this to other countries. This should provide us with some objective conclusions about the legitimacy of the so-called *chaebol* problem in Korea.

### 2.1 Aggregate Concentration Trend in Korea

Let us look into the trend of economic concentration of the top 30 *chaebols* for the period 1985 to 1995. Table 3.1 shows statistics about the *chaebols* that are commonly used to show economic concentration: namely, the share of value-added in GNP, the share of the value of sales and assets held relative to the whole industry, and the ratio of national employment. During this period, two stable trends can be observed: first, the share of the 30 largest *chaebols* in terms of their creation of value-added is seen to have increased steadily, while their share of employment has remained stable. This reflects the increase in capital intensity of *chaebol* firms during this period, of which more later.

Second, the degree of assets and sales concentration has fluctuated during this period. Both indices increased during the period of Korea's rapid economic growth until the late 1980s. These indices show a decline in the early 1990s reflecting the recession experienced in Korea at the time. A moderate increase from the mid-1990s is observed due largely to the prosperity in the semiconductor industry, as well as the petroleum and chemical industries and the shipbuilding industry – all of which are major business areas of the *chaebol*. It is worth noting that during this period the *chaebol* also adopted a policy of foreign asset acquisition in response to the worldwide globalization trend.

Our brief review shows that the general public's belief that the economic power of the 30 largest *chaebols* has constantly been increasing is inconsistent with the facts just described. Furthermore, every year the Korea Fair Trade Commission, in an attempt to reveal the *chaebols'* grip on the economy, publishes the 30 largest *chaebols'* share of value-added together with the number of affiliated firms belonging to each group. However, relying simply on value-added indices is questionable, as it is not obvious which index (for example, among those mentioned above – value added, employment, sales, or assets) should be used as a reliable indicator of economic concentration. Moreover, looking again at Table 3.1, we find that the indices used to describe economic concentration have not all moved in the same direction, thereby suggesting that it may be premature to draw any definite conclusions about the movement of economic power based only on a few indices. More specifically, we cannot conclude that economic power has, in fact, become more concentrated within a few *chaebols*.

As mentioned, the Korea Fair Trade Commission categorizes the 30 largest *chaebol* as a separate special group. However, by mistakenly treating the *chaebols* as a homogeneous entity, many of the current regulation policies advocated by the Commission fail to take into account various individual characteristics across different *chaebols*. Furthermore, the grouping of *chaebols* lacks serious theoretical underpinning with such an arbitrary grouping being adopted mainly for administrative convenience. Table 3.1 shows that the five largest *chaebol* account for over 60 per cent of economic

*Table 3.1 Trend of chaebol economic concentration: selected indices[a] (unit: %)*

| | Value-added[b] | | | Sales[c] | | | Asset[d] | | | Employment[e] | | |
|---|---|---|---|---|---|---|---|---|---|---|---|---|
| | Top 5 | Top 10 | Top 30 | Top 5 | Top 10 | Top 30 | Top 5 | Top 10 | Top 30 | Top 5 | Top 10 | Top 30 |
| 1985 | 6.6 | 8.8 | 12.3 | 30.8 | 38.6 | 48.8 | 23.5 | 31.3 | 42.9 | 2.54 | 3.06 | 4.34 |
| 1986 | 6.2 | 8.3 | 11.3 | 31.4 | 38.7 | 49.2 | 23.7 | 31.4 | 43.2 | 2.52 | 3.10 | 4.26 |
| 1987 | 6.1 | 7.9 | 11.0 | 31.5 | 38.7 | 48.7 | 25.1 | 33.8 | 45.0 | 2.53 | 3.09 | 4.29 |
| 1988 | 6.4 | 8.9 | 11.9 | 29.6 | 36.2 | 45.8 | 24.3 | 32.5 | 44.3 | 2.63 | 3.35 | 4.54 |
| 1989 | 7.4 | 9.8 | 12.9 | 30.5 | 37.5 | 47.3 | 25.5 | 33.7 | 45.9 | 2.61 | 3.29 | 4.52 |
| 1990 | 7.2 | 9.6 | 12.7 | 27.0 | 33.2 | 41.5 | 23.4 | 29.9 | 40.3 | 2.53 | 3.17 | 4.22 |
| 1991 | 7.2 | 9.6 | 13.0 | 27.2 | 32.8 | 41.3 | 24.0 | 32.5 | 43.5 | 2.55 | 3.30 | 4.29 |
| 1992 | 7.6 | 10.1 | 13.5 | 28.6 | 35.4 | 43.8 | 24.5 | 33.3 | 44.4 | 2.42 | 3.20 | 4.16 |
| 1993 | 7.8 | 10.2 | 13.6 | 27.6 | 34.1 | 41.7 | 24.0 | 32.6 | 43.2 | 2.40 | 3.20 | 4.14 |
| 1994 | 8.3 | 10.9 | 14.2 | 28.2 | 34.8 | 42.4 | 23.5 | 31.6 | 41.7 | 2.49 | 3.31 | 4.21 |
| 1995 | 10.1 | 12.8 | 16.2 | 30.7 | 37.8 | 45.8 | 25.4 | 33.8 | 44.6 | 2.62 | 3.48 | 4.41 |

*Notes:*
[a] All industries except for the finance and insurance industries.
[b] Weight of the largest 30 *chaebols* in GNP.
[c] Weight of the largest 30 *chaebols* in whole industry.
[d] Weight of the largest 30 *chaebols* in total employment.

concentration within the 30 largest firms regardless of the index used. This illustrates the stark difference in economic power, for example, between the top five *chaebol* and the rest of the top 30, thereby stressing the artificiality of such a categorization and its potential danger to policy formation. Although we have argued above that the economic concentration by the top five *chaebols* has been very high and that the uniform regulations under which all of the 30 largest *chaebols* are required to operate, regardless of their individual sizes, are somewhat irrational, it would be wrong to conclude that we must therefore regulate the top five differently from the rest of the top 30 *chaebols*.

But why shouldn't we select the top five, or top four, or top three *chaebols* to be placed under special regulation? To begin with, we need to realize that an important reason why economists are concerned about economic concentration is because firms with high market shares tend to exercise monopoly power, thereby eliminating benefits originating from competitive markets. However, we must bear in mind that this potential danger in exercising economic power should not be judged merely by the size of the firm, but must be more accurately evaluated by looking into the market environment of incentives structure that influences the willingness to exercise potential economic power. It follows, therefore, that the potential for the exercise of monopoly power should be judged not simply by static market structures but also by degrees of effective dynamic competition over time. The indices frequently used for measuring economic concentration, as shown in Table 3.1, only reveal the distribution of economic power at particular points in time. Consequently, they fail to provide a good indication of dynamic competition that may exist among the different economic units.

To analyze more accurately the extent or degree of actual competition in the market, that is, the dynamic aspect of competition, it is more appropriate to use 'mobility statistics', which reflect the changes with respect to the size, ranking and composition of *chaebols*. These indices, in fact, better reflect the essence and degree of effective competition, taking into account market entry and exit, as well as the rise and fall of individual firms and the changes in market share resulting from competition. It is inadequate to describe a particular market as being under monopoly influence merely by looking at the market structure at a particular point in time. In essence, mobility statistics measuring effective competition do more than merely resort to a static description of a particular market's monopoly structure and hence are more relevant to our study. The Appendix at the end of the chapter shows how we devised mobility statistics to measure the degree of dynamic competition among the *chaebols*. Basically, we find that despite criticisms about economic concentration among the *chaebol*, there has in fact been a significant degree of dynamic competition even among the top five *chaebol*.

## 2.2   International Comparison of Aggregate Concentration

Another frequently cited public criticism against the economic behavior of the *chaebols* is that economic concentration in Korea is said to be relatively much higher than in other countries. The Fair Trade Act of Korea ostensibly supports this perception. In contrast to other countries in which fair trade acts are used to promote competition, in Korea, the first Article declares that its purpose is 'to prohibit the excessive concentration of economic power'. Needless to say, economic concentration by large firms is frequently observed in advanced industrialized countries as well as Korea, and, moreover, we shall show that economic concentration in Korea is relatively moderate by comparison, contrary to popular belief. At this point, an important question may be raised: 'Are there any particular aspects of the Korean case of economic concentration that are so different from advanced countries as to require any special regulation?' To provide an adequate answer to this question, it will be useful to compare indices of economic concentration in Korea to those of advanced countries. Yet it must again be stressed that simple numerical comparisons of these indices should be interpreted with care because they also tend to reflect the unique economic environment peculiar to each country.

Table 3.2 shows the aggregate concentration figures of eight selected countries in 1993. Compared to other OECD countries, Korea has relatively lower concentration ratios for employment and sales, whereas it has higher concentration ratios for aggregate assets. This essentially reflects not only the relatively higher weights of land, buildings and cross-shareholding in the asset

*Table 3.2   International comparison of aggregate concentration in the manufacturing sector (1993)[a] (unit: %)*

|  | Korea | USA | Japan | Germany | UK | France | Sweden | Switzerland |
|---|---|---|---|---|---|---|---|---|
| Asset | 32.2 (46.5) | 22.4 | 22.7 | 22.7 | 29.5 | 28.6 | 37.3 | 56.0 |
| Employment | 11.3 (18.5) | 22.9 | 15.0 | 31.7 | 32.6 | 36.9 | 58.6 | 93.1 |
| Sales | 31.3 (42.5) | 34.6 | 25.8 | 38.8 | 48.6 | 46.2 | 65.5 | 51.6 |

*Notes:*
[a] Relative to the whole manufacturing sector. The largest 30 companies for Korea, USA, Japan, Germany, UK. The largest 20 for France, ten for Sweden, and nine for Switzerland.
In parentheses: Degree of concentration of largest 30 *chaebols* in Korea.

composition of Korean firms, but the bubble in prices of land and buildings in Korea, as well. Table 3.2 shows that results of international comparisons differ according to the indices of economic concentration, and consequently any conclusions should be drawn with care.

Employment indices, Scherer and Ross (1990) point out, have distinctive merits relative to the indices of sales or total assets particularly in studies of international comparisons of economic concentration. For example, sales indices cannot account for differences in the accounting system of each country, and total asset indices are sensitive to the rate of asset price changes, which varies from country to country. Employment indices, however, are immune from these differences across countries because employment is a real variable.[2] Viewed from this point of view, economic concentration in Korea can be said to be the lowest when compared to major advanced countries. This is true no matter how we compare the share of employment taken by the 30 largest firms of other OECD countries to that taken by either the 30 largest firms or the 30 largest *chaebols* in Korea.

Some critics argue that the employment index for Korea suggests that the *chaebols* do not contribute much to the creation of new jobs. In reality, what this implies is that the *chaebols* tend to specialize in industries having high capital/labor ratios, reflecting the fact that the Korean government encouraged large firms to enter capital-intensive industries through its policy of fostering heavy and chemical industries.[3] Furthermore, the *chaebols* opted for factory automization and other labor-saving technologies in response to the upward pressure on wage rates. It is beyond positive economics to discuss whether it is 'right' or 'wrong' for the *chaebols* to adapt to changes in the economic environment created by governmental policies and rapid wage increases. In fact, from the evolutionary perspective, it is imperative that the *chaebol* adapt to changes in the environment if it is to continue its existence.

Furthermore, despite the popular reproach often heard about the *chaebols'* tendency to put too much emphasis on their sales volume, even to the extent of including internal transactions among affiliated firms,[4] an international comparison shows that even this 'exaggerated' sales concentration ratio of the 30 largest *chaebols* in Korea is in the lower to middle range. This clearly refutes the mistaken view held by foreigners as well as Koreans that sales concentration (or concentration of general economic power) is a uniquely 'Korean' phenomenon not found elsewhere.

From the viewpoint of effective competition, a quick glimpse at the mobility statistics, found in the Appendix to this chapter (see Table A3.2), shows that Korea is no less competitive than other advanced countries such as the US or Japan. When we take the largest 100 firms in the manufacturing sectors of Korea, the US and Japan, and compare such dynamic indices as entry-exit, market instability and changes in the ranking of firm size, we find, surprisingly, that the Korean economy has exhibited an environment of more dynamic competition than either its American or Japanese counterparts.

## 2.3 Evaluation

Our discussions above show clearly that the general perception about the economic concentration of the *chaebols* has many aspects that differ significantly from reality. The data suggest that we should refrain from relying on general perceptions as we try to answer the many pressing questions of interest such as: (a) Has economic concentration in Korea been worsening? (b) Is the degree of economic concentration in Korea relatively much higher than in other countries? And (c) has the degree of effective competition among large firms or *chaebols* in Korea been so weak as to attract our special attention? The facts examined show that answers to the questions above are in the negative and therefore suggest that the problem of economic concentration may, in fact, not be the core of the *chaebol* problem in Korea.

Accordingly, we are led to the following question: why has the *chaebol* problem been perceived mostly as a problem of economic concentration despite the fact that all the indices in this regard show no significantly higher values for Korea than for other OECD countries? We believe that the confusion may have originated in part from the lack of serious studies comparing Korea with other countries in this regard. However, this is far from being the whole story.

The issue of economic concentration can be approached essentially from three different perspectives – efficiency, equality, and commercial empire building. These three approaches each provide a different angle on the causes and perils of economic concentration. So far, we have discussed the problem from an efficiency angle by focusing on the degree of effective competition among the *chaebols*. However, a large part of the animosity toward the *chaebols* in Korea stems neither from their high concentration ratio of economic power nor from the low effective competition among them. Rather, animosity seems to stem from the fact that the *chaebols* were formed and grew in a privileged environment, rather than from fierce free competition. Put differently, accumulated wealth is often perceived as resulting, not from market competition, but from various support schemes of the government. This may be termed the 'unfair rules of competition'. Hence the notion of unfairness with respect to the competition process undermines the legitimacy of the *chaebols'* wealth, which seems to be the principal underlying source of the animosity toward the *chaebols* in Korea. We will expand on this theme in Chapter 4.

According to the theory of empire building, once a very popular theme of the 'Old Institutionalist' school of thought in Europe and the US, conglomerates try to influence policy-making directly, bypassing the democratic political process of elections, in order to protect and enlarge their vested interests. In the socio-cultural realm, conglomerates try to spread their influence and to imprint it on the culture.

Many people, adopting this popular view, worry that the *chaebol* may exert their hegemonic power not only in the economic sphere but also in the political and socio-cultural arenas. Many Koreans today perceive the *chaebol* as monstrous industrial organizations, with all the usual connotations such as big, frightening, threatening, uncompromising, dangerous and so on. Accordingly, they feel that power is distributed unevenly among interest groups, allowing the *chaebol* to exert excessive influence on all aspects of the economic, social and political realms.

## 3.　MONOPOLISTIC MARKET STRUCTURE: THE PROBLEM OF MARKET CONCENTRATION

All forms of economic concentration can be a source of concern. However, in Korea, aggregate economic concentration has received more attention than market concentration, as is evidenced by the government's policy to suppress the economic power of the top 30 *chaebols*. In its efforts to curb aggregate concentration, the Fair Trade Commission in Korea has implemented various measures to monitor and regulate monopolistic firms and products, anti-competitive mergers and acquisitions, and other anti-competitive firm behavior. However, such regulations are not far from being purely cosmetic measures compared to the emphasis given to the regulation of market concentration. In advanced countries, however, the issue of aggregate economic concentration has been treated – at the theoretical as well as policy-making levels – as a problem of market power concentration.

As we have already seen, advanced industrialized countries do not always have lower degrees of aggregate economic concentration than Korea. Yet they are more preoccupied with market concentration. The reason for this is two-fold. First, the most important problem resulting from economic concentration is the distortion of economic resource allocation as a result of monopolization. However, it has been noted as in Bain and Qualls (1987) that an increase in aggregate concentration does not necessarily imply an increase in market monopolization. Second, various indices of economic concentration do not necessarily move in the same direction, and some may actually move in the opposite direction. Furthermore, changes in these indices may have different ramifications on the economy. It is therefore not only impossible but also inappropriate for the government to seek regulation of all types of economic concentration.

In sum, whether from the standpoint of economic efficiency or the effectiveness of economic policy, it is our contention that the *chaebol* problem in Korea be treated as a problem of market concentration.

## 3.1 *Chaebol* and Market Concentration

Various market concentration indices have been used to measure the degree of distortion in economic resource allocation caused by the monopolization of a particular market. The Herfindahl index incorporates the relative weights of all firms in a particular industry and therefore differs from $CR_4$, which only takes into account the sum of the top four firms. Among these measures, the market concentration ratio of the top $k$ firms ($CR_k$) and the Herfindahl index (HI) have been widely used for both academic studies and governmental regulation purposes. For either the monopolization test of a particular market or an anti-competitiveness test of mergers, the market share of the top three firms ($CR_3$) has been more frequently used in Korea, whereas the Herfindahl index has been more commonly used in the US.[5] The Appendix at the end of the chapter contains calculations of market concentration ratios for manufacturing industry in Korea for the period 1991 to 1995 (see Table A3.3). A quick glance provides two observations: market concentration ratios increased for some industries and decreased for others, and on average, the market concentration ratio increased only slightly.[6]

However, except for a few industries, in Korea, the Herfindahl and $CR_4$ indices generally move in the same direction, as is shown by almost perfect correlation[7] for the period 1991 to 1995. A possible explanation for this phenomenon is that the growth of large Korean firms affiliated to a *chaebol* group may constitute the major factor in the increased degree of market concentration. Here one may suggest the hypothesis that a close relationship exists between market concentration and *chaebol* industry concentration.[8]

In order to verify this hypothesis, the market concentration ratio in manufacturing industry by firm type for the period 1991 to 1995 is shown in Appendix Table B3.1. This can be compared to Table B3.2 which shows the industry concentration of the *chaebol* in the manufacturing sector for 1991 and 1995. We find three characteristics: first, in the 1990s, almost all industries have shown an increase in the weight of the 30 largest *chaebol*. Except for a few industries such as textile manufacturing, publication, printing, copying and recording media, and metal product assembly, where the weight of the 30 largest *chaebol* declined, their weighted average concentration ratio in all 21 industries is seen to have increased from about 46 per cent in 1991 to 51 per cent in 1995.

Second, the varying sizes of *chaebols* show a manifest difference in industry concentration and this gap has widened further during the period

1991 to 1995.[9] It is worth noting that despite the fact that the number of firms affiliated to the top five *chaebol* in the manufacturing industry declined significantly between 1991 and 1995 from 91 to 75, the weight of these firms increased quite starkly from 29.0 to 34.2 per cent. This implies that more economic resources have been gravitating toward the top five *chaebol*.

Lastly, statistics confirm that the market concentration ratio as represented by $CR_4$ or the Herfindahl index displays a very high positive correlation with the concentration of *chaebols* in the industries.

Figure 3.1 summarizes the correlation coefficients between the concentration of *chaebol* groups and market concentration ratios as represented by $CR_4$ and the Herfindahl index respectively.[10] In 1995, depending on the size classes of *chaebol* groups, the correlation coefficients of the weights of *chaebol* by industry with the Herfindahl index and $CR_4$ ranged between 0.81 to 0.84 and 0.77 to 0.80, respectively.[11] Such findings imply that the *chaebol* have made a significant contribution to the increase in the market concentration ratio. Such a high correlation between market concentration and *chaebol* industry concentration seems to support the assertion that the *chaebol* may be a major

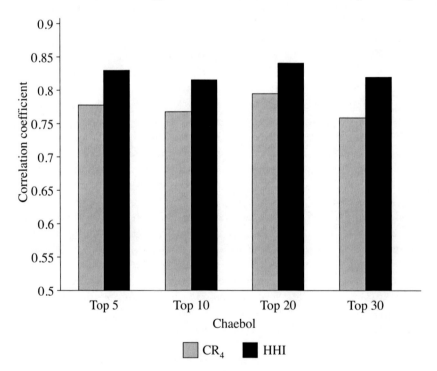

*Figure 3.1   Correlation coefficient between market concentration and industry concentration ratio by* chaebol *(1995)*

obstacle to the development of competitive market structures. On the other hand, one may look beyond mere correlation figures and observe that heavy government regulations with artificial entry barriers and price controls across many products in the manufacturing sector as well as across the economy as a whole, could be a major obstacle constraining competition.

Having stated the foregoing, it should be added that an examination of the correlation coefficient alone does not necessarily reveal which perspective is correct. Thus, a final judgment as to whether the *chaebols* or various government regulations are responsible for limiting competition cannot be established at present. The issue of 'what limits competition' is a totally different question.

Of course, there are structuralists who believe in the strong causality between structure, conduct and performance. As such, a strong correlation between the industry concentration by the *chaebol* and market concentration ratios constitutes 'evidence' for the assertion that market dominance by the *chaebols* is responsible for the low market efficiency experienced in Korea.[12] We hasten to add that many different alternative explanations to this traditional analysis of structure–conduct–performance now exist. For example, the contestable market theory denies a simple causal relationship between concentration ratio, market dominance and economic efficiency. A high concentration ratio does not necessarily lead to increased market dominance and monopolistic pricing unless potential entry into the market is blocked. Especially when the emergence of market dominance is the result of the growth of an efficient firm, a monopolistic market structure does not bring about economic inefficiency.[13] It is therefore an empirical question, which requires empirical corroboration, whether large firms can, in reality, exercise market dominance and furthermore, if they can, to what degree would social loss be incurred?

## 3.2   Market Concentration and Inefficienct Resource Allocation

What about the empirical relationship between market concentration and inefficiencies in resource allocation? We measure the degree of market inefficiency as the value of social costs (arising from imperfect competition in an industry) divided by the total value-added created by that industry. We proceed to ask whether there is a close positive correlation between the market concentration ratio and economic inefficiency. Structuralists have asserted the existence of a positive correlation. However, one study reports that although both indices show a statistically significant positive relationship, the strength of the relationship is much weaker than is surmised by structuralists.[14]

When confined to the manufacturing sector in Korea, irrespective of the type of market concentration measure ratio employed, as it increases, the degree of market inefficiency also tends to increase. It is noticeable that compared to both $CR_3$ and the Herfindahl index, which are commonly used as concentration ratios, the concentration ratio of the *chaebol* in the relevant industries shows a closer relationship[15] to the degree of market inefficiency as is seen in Figure 3.2. This interesting result reflects a particular aspect of the market structure in Korea. Theoretically, the degree of market inefficiency and the Herfindahl index should have the closest relationship. However, the Korean case shows a different result implying that the *chaebols*, a characteristically Korean organizational form, exert a strong influence on the formation of market power and resource allocation.

On the other hand, the somewhat weak correlation suggests that the market concentration ratio cannot be safely argued to be a reliable proxy of market power. Some structuralists have traditionally conceived a very strict one-to-

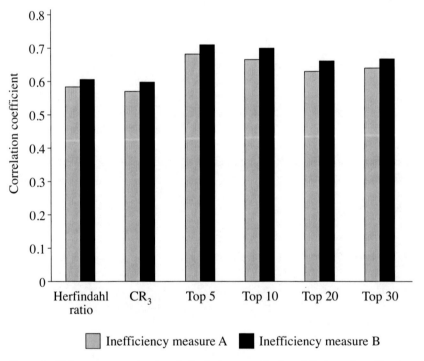

*Note*: Inefficiency measure A value obtained after normalization of Harberger's welfare loss triangle by relevant industry's value-added. Inefficiency measure B includes costs of advertising and other services in welfare loss calculation. All the coefficients are statistically significant at the 1 per cent level.

*Figure 3.2    Correlation coefficient between market concentration ratio and degree of market inefficiency in the manufacturing sector (1995)*

one positive relationship between the market concentration ratio and market inefficiency. This structuralist viewpoint has influenced the government's competition policy, which has adopted the market concentration ratio as an appropriate proxy variable for measuring market power. However, as we have seen, empirical evidence does not support this as a correct conception of reality. Rather, we suggest that there could be limits to the market concentration ratio as a reliable measure of market power and it is dangerous to interpret the degree of market power and the resulting resource misallocation simply by using the concentration ratio. To more accurately judge the degree of market inefficiency, it is necessary therefore to consider other statistical indicators such as the dynamic mobility indices, examples of which were discussed in the previous section, as these will better reflect the real aspects of market competition.

### 3.3   Evaluation

The industry concentration ratios of the *chaebols* show a high correlation with the $CR_4$ and the Herfindahl index. These concentration indices also show a statistically significant positive relationship with the index for economic inefficiency. These two results imply that to some degree the *chaebols* have exercised some influence on the monopolization of markets, and may imply that the government needed to take steps to make market structures more competitive in order to reduce the perils of monopolization (and consequently to reduce economic inefficiency). However, this does not mean that simply suppressing the *chaebols'* economic power through various regulations is desirable. Such regulations could be not only ineffective but also inappropriate. As will be argued throughout this book, it would be more appropriate to expedite market opening, liberalize markets further by removing various entry regulations imposed by the government, and strengthen competition policy by monitoring and penalizing non-competitive market behavior if necessary. All these measures will contribute to the promotion of competition.

   In fact, in order to reduce market concentration and to promote competition, it is most important to shift policy paradigms away from focusing on aggregate economic concentration as at present to emphasizing market monopolization. We have seen that concerns over economic concentration have been biased toward the suppression of aggregate concentration rather than the reduction of market concentration. The old policy of regulating and suppressing aggregate economic concentration needs to be changed into a new policy of promoting competition and thereby reducing market concentration. Viewed from the standpoint of economic efficiency rather than from an equity or hegemony-struggle perspective, market concentration is of more importance than aggregate concentration. Furthermore, regulations on large firms for the suppression of aggregate concentration are currently applied only to Korean firms. This raises the issue of reverse discrimination against domestic firms *vis-à-vis* large foreign firms. Therefore the existing policy runs counter to the global trend of the increasing openness of domestic markets. If current policy is aimed at increasing social welfare, the nationality, size and organizational form of a firm should not matter. It is necessary to provide and implement open norms of competition, which can be applied to any firm, either domestic or foreign, doing business in Korea.

In fact, the *chaebols'* industry concentration turns out to be highly correlated not only with market concentration but also with market inefficiency. Therefore any traditional anti-market concentration policies will be effective at reducing the *chaebols'* industry concentration and aggregate concentration as well as reducing market concentration itself. In this sense, regulatory policies specifically geared to suppressing the phenomenon of aggregate and industrial concentration of the *chaebols* can effectively be replaced by more orthodox competition promotion policies, without incurring any loss of substance of antitrust policies in general.

## 4.  CONGLOMERATION OF THE *CHAEBOL*: PROBLEMS OF *CHAEBOL* BEHAVIOR

The *chaebol* problem often carries the connotation of characteristic managerial behavior that seeks to expand through conglomeration. The *chaebols* have often been criticized among other things for their excessive diversification behavior, concentration of ownership as well as management and the practice of cross-debt guarantees.

### 4.1  *Chaebol* Diversification

Among the problems created by the *chaebols'* behavior, diversification into various industries has been identified as the most notorious. *Chaebol* diversification strategy has been widely mentioned as the main culprit for weakened competitiveness in the Korean economy. This is supposed to be so because the *chaebol* have not concentrated their energy on core competencies by specializing and creating scale economies, but instead have excessively 'penetrated' large numbers of business areas only very remotely related to their core businesses or considered best suited to medium and small firms. In the process, it has been argued that they have misused and squandered scarce resources.

Table 3.3 shows the average number of business areas and subsidiaries per *chaebol* for the top 30. Despite enforcement of the Fair Trade Act and

*Table 3.3    Change in the number of businesses and subsidiaries of the top 30 chaebol*

| Year | 87.4 | 88.4 | 89.4 | 90.4 | 91.4 | 92.4 | 93.4 | 94.4 | 95.4 | 96.4 | 97.4 | 98.4 | 99.4 |
|---|---|---|---|---|---|---|---|---|---|---|---|---|---|
| Average number of businesses[a] | - | - | - | - | - | 17.9 | 18.3 | 19.1 | 18.5 | 18.8 | 19.9 | - | - |
| Number of subsidiaries | 501 | 516 | 531 | 573 | 593 | 608 | 604 | 616 | 623 | 669 | 821 | 804 | 686 |
| Average number of subsidiaries | 16.7 | 17.2 | 17.7 | 19.1 | 19.8 | 20.3 | 20.1 | 20.5 | 20.8 | 22.3 | 27.4 | 26.8 | 22.9 |

*Note*:    [a] Year end.

inducement policies encouraging the *chaebol* to concentrate on their core competencies, the data show little change in their diversification behavior.

Table 3.4 summarizes international comparisons with respect to diversification behavior as reported in Yang (1992).[16] As compared to other

*Table 3.4    International comparison of diversification based on the Rumelt method (unit: %)*

| Forms of diversification | Country | | | | | | |
|---|---|---|---|---|---|---|---|
| | Korea (1989) | Japan (1973) | US (1969) | UK (1970) | Germany (1970) | France (1970) | Italy (1970) |
| Specialization | 36.8 | 53.3 | 35.4 | 40.0 | 44.0 | 48.0 | 43.0 |
| Total (SR>0.95) | 8.2 | 16.9 | 6.2 | 6.0 | 22.0 | 16.0 | 10.0 |
| Partial (0.95>SR>0.7) | 28.6 | 36.4 | 29.2 | 34.0 | 22.0 | 32.0 | 33.0 |
| Diversification | 63.2 | 46.7 | 64.6 | 60.0 | 56.0 | 52.0 | 57.2 |
| Related (SR>0.7, RR>0.7) | 6.1 | 39.9 | 45.2 | 54.0 | 38.0 | 42.0 | 52.0 |
| Unrelated (RR<0.7) | 57.1 | 6.8 | 19.4 | 6.0 | 18.0 | 10.0 | 5.0 |

*Notes*:
SR: sales of the largest subsidiary/total sales of the *chaebol*.
RR: sales of the largest related subsidiary/ total sales of the *chaebol*.
Forty-nine *chaebol*s for Korea, 118 business groups for Japan, 100 business groups for other countries. The values are obtained through the Rumelt method for Korea, and Yoshihara (1981) for other countries.

*Source*:    Yang (1992).

advanced countries, this table shows that *chaebol* diversification into unrelated business areas in Korea is, in fact, high.

Another empirical finding about *chaebol* diversification behavior is that the bigger *chaebol*s tend to diversify more widely (Yang, 1992; Lee, 1996). This implies that diversification has been a major means of expansion for Korean *chaebol*s. Scherer and Ravenscraft (1984) report a similar pattern for large American firms between 1950 and 1975. They found that American firms during that period had expanded and diversified through mergers and acquisitions rather than through internal growth. In this regard, the behavior of large firms in Korea has not been much different from those in advanced countries such as the US. Chapter 6 will address corporate diversification behavior in greater detail, particularly in the context of Korea's *chaebol* behavior as well as cross-country firm behavior.

## 4.2   Concentration of Ownership and *Chaebol* Management

With respect to the management of the *chaebol*, the concentration of ownership and management in the hands of a few shareholders through cross-shareholding among affiliated firms has been pointed out as another serious problem. The above-mentioned business diversification strategy of the *chaebol*s is closely related to this management issue. It has been argued that business diversification has been not only a cause for, but also a reflection of, the concentration of managerial power in the hands of a few individuals.

Table 3.5 analyzes time series data for the ownership distribution of *chaebol* shares. Although not clearly obvious, we find a decrease in the ratio of cross-shareholding among affiliated firms to the total net worth of individual *chaebol*s and a continued decline in the ratio of internal shareholding within the *chaebol*. In relation to the internal shareholding ratio among the *chaebol*, the ratio of the founding family shares to total shares has continually declined, while the ratio for affiliated firms has remained quite steady at around 33 per cent in the 1990s. It should be noted here that the declining weight of internal shareholding does not mean a decline in its absolute level. The decline in the relative weight of internal holdings – especially by a specific family – can be explained by the expansion of external funding due to the rapid growth of the Korean stock market. On the other hand, the stabilization of the weight of affiliated firms' shareholdings can be explained by the fact that diversification (as a way to expand their businesses) has stabilized in recent years.

Some people believe that not only the concentration of ownership but also the concentration of managerial power contributes significantly to the *chaebol* problem. This view holds that the anti-*chaebol* sentiment in Korea has its origin in the fact that a particular family, despite possessing only a meager 10

*Table 3.5   Cross-shareholding   among   affiliated   firms   and   internal
          shareholding of top 30* chaebol *(unit: %)*

| | Year | | | | | | | | | |
|---|---|---|---|---|---|---|---|---|---|---|
| | 1987 | 1989 | 1990 | 1991 | 1992 | 1993 | 1994 | 1995 | 1996 | 1997 |
| Cross-shareholding | 43.6 | – | 32.1 | 31.8 | 38.8 | 28.0 | 26.8 | 26.3 | 24.8 | 27.5 |
| Internal shareholding | | | | | | | | | | |
| Family | | 15.1 | 14.7 | 13.7 | 13.9 | 12.6 | 10.3 | 9.7 | 10.5 | 10.3 | 8.5 |
| Affiliated firms | | 41.1 | 32.5 | 31.7 | 33.0 | 33.5 | 33.1 | 33.1 | 32.8 | 33.3 | 33.7 |
| Total | | 56.2 | 47.2 | 45.4 | 46.9 | 46.1 | 43.4 | 42.8 | 43.3 | 43.6 | 41.2 |

*Source*:   Korea Fair Trade Commission.

per cent of the total shares, not only controls over 40 per cent of total ownership of a *chaebol*, but through affiliates' cross-shareholdings controls most of the managerial power as well. Put more dramatically, in the case of the 30 largest *chaebol*, an 'owner' (or his family) typically invests, on average, only 2 per cent of the total assets of the *chaebol* while exercising almost unchallenged overall managerial discretion. Yet, because of the concentration of managerial power, external stakeholders who invest in the remaining 98 per cent of total assets – external individual shareholders, institutional investors, banks or individual depositors whose deposits in banks are ultimately used for loans to *chaebol* – are excluded from exercising influence on the management of a *chaebol*. In fact, those outside stakeholders inherently do not tend to have any strong incentive to protect their assets by monitoring the *chaebols*. In addition, institutional foundations to enhance their incentives to monitor *chaebol* management more closely are lacking. These factors are alleged to have allowed *chaebol* 'owners' to gain wide-ranging discretionary power, recognized as being the source of the various problems associated with the *chaebol*.

It may be beyond the ability of economics to answer whether this situation is desirable or not. This is because the behavior of various stakeholders – *chaebol* owners, those who monitor them and other shareholders – is the result of survival adaptations made under the harsh conditions created by the economic environment, which include government policies as well. Hence, value judgments about these kinds of behavior do not provide clues for the formulation of better economic policies.

It is true that the government, while dealing with the anti-*chaebol* sentiment, may have reason to consider the current behavior of *chaebol* owners as a serious political problem. Even so, one needs to understand how state policies and the lack of a proper institutional framework have induced this kind of behavior. If, in fact, those factors turn out to be contributory causes of the *chaebols'* undesirable behavior, then perhaps there is need to eliminate such policies and introduce an appropriate institutional framework. For example, it is more appropriate to leave the right to make decisions regarding the degree of ownership concentration and hence the internal governance structure of firms to individual actors in the marketplace as such areas are better determined endogenously. More specifically, individual actors should be given the right to make decisions regarding a variety of factors. Autonomy is necessary in areas that include the percentage of ownership that will maximize management effectiveness, and the appropriateness of invest-ments in other affiliate firms of the same *chaebol* group that will increase the performance of a particular firm in a particular industry given a particular institutional environment. Those choices are inherently endogenous and, therefore, it is not constructive for outsiders to pass judgment on the appropriateness of those decisions made by the *chaebols* in the marketplace and to regulate them. Even when their behavior is judged inappropriate for non-economic reasons, the government needs to investigate what type of economic environment is responsible for instigating certain behavior. Simply put, the government should concentrate on establishing a proper institutional framework to correct the distorted incentive structure behind the observed behavior of the *chaebol*.

### 4.3   The Practice of Cross-Debt Guarantees

Cross-debt guarantees between affiliates of the same *chaebol* are yet another highly controversial practice typical of Korean conglomerates. The practice of cross-debt guarantees is the act by which a firm, or a few firms, in a *chaebol* will guarantee loans made from the bank on behalf of another firm of the same *chaebol*. This practice is criticized for encouraging excess diversification and for increasing the potential for the contagious failure of a cluster of firms under cross-debt guarantee relations. There is, therefore, potential for the simultaneous failure of a series of big firms triggered by the failure of another firm of the same *chaebol*. This tends to limit the degree of freedom that the government can exercise in forcing any big firm to be declared bankrupt, and so, in general, tends to create exit barriers. Within this context, the Korean government first imposed an upper limit on the size of cross-debt guarantees in its revision of the Fair Trade Act. Through its 1997 revision, the Act forces each firm to reduce the size of its debt guarantees written for other firms affiliated to the same *chaebol* to within 100 per cent of its own assets by the end of March 1998 – effective from 1 April 1997. The Act's 1998 revision prohibits banks from requesting any new cross-debt guarantees from affiliates.

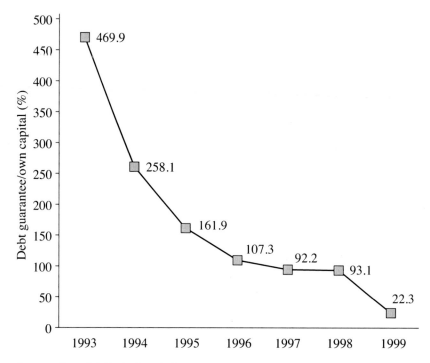

Source:    Korea Fair Trade Commission.

*Figure 3.3    Trend of cross-debt guarantees of top 30* chaebol

As of the end of March 2000, further aims to eliminate any remaining cross-debt guarantees were established.

Recently, the size of cross-debt guarantees among firms of the 30 largest *chaebol* has decreased at a precipitous rate as illustrated in Figure 3.3. On the other hand, Table 3.6 indicates that the smaller *chaebol*s tend to rely more on cross-debt guarantees in their business activities than the bigger ones.

*Table 3.6    Cross-debt guarantees of top 30* chaebol *(1999) (Unit: debt guarantee/own capital: %)*

| Top 5 *Chaebol* | Top 6–30 *Chaebol* |
| --- | --- |
| 6.5 | 69.9 |

*Source*:    Korea Fair Trade Commission.

It is revealing to note that the practice of cross-debt guarantees is a derived business practice that originated in the banking industry – requesting cross-guarantees for debts was widespread despite the fact that the guarantors, in fact, belonged to the same *chaebol*. The banking industry used to require two or three firms in the same *chaebol* to write debt guarantees, usually one-and-a-half times the amount of the original debt. We have already pointed out that firms in the smaller *chaebols* usually have a higher ratio of cross-debt guarantees with respect to their own asset values. This implies that for a loan of a similar amount, relative to the larger *chaebol*, banks demand a greater amount of guarantees from the smaller *chaebol*.

The key problem with the cross-guarantee practice is that the *de facto chaebol* business group is not legally recognized. Due to interconnected ownership as well as its business relationships, it is more appropriate to view firms belonging to a *chaebol* group as a single economic unit. However, individual firms belonging to a *chaebol* are in fact legally regarded as independent entities, completely separate from other firms. Cross-debt guarantees among firms belonging to the same *chaebol* group subsequently have become a common practice. A legal practice widely accepted by Korean banks, cross-debt guarantees make little sense in terms of economics, because they cannot function as a safety device against potential default, particularly among economically integrated *chaebol* affiliates.

Therefore if cross-debt guarantees are deemed problematic by the government, this can be resolved naturally through improving banks' loan practices. For example, the Financial Supervisory Commission may more strictly enforce the existing regulation limiting lending concentration to a single borrower by correctly identifying affiliates of the same *chaebol* collectively as one single economic entity. Beyond any doubt, this strict enforcement of banking regulations will greatly reduce the practice of demanding cross-debt guarantees. However, it is important to stress that the government should not require banks to be bureaucratic in interpreting the concept of a *chaebol* as a single economic entity. Degrees of integration among affiliates either within the same *chaebol* or across different *chaebol* will of course be different. Therefore it is natural to allow banks to decide how far they should apply the concept of a single economic entity based on the bank's own judgment of the degree of integration within a given *chaebol*, and to treat that *chaebol* accordingly.

## 4.4 Evaluation

So far, in this section we have examined (a) the diversification behavior of the *chaebol*, (b) the concentration of ownership and managerial power, and (c) the practice of cross-debt guarantees. Trends, at least, of all three behavioral indicators show no alarming sign of 'worsening' although the degree at each point in time remains high. Even so (or for that matter, even if it is becoming more severe through time), we should recall that the managerial behavior of the *chaebol* cannot be evaluated merely by examining the trend of their behavioral patterns without considering the 'managerial environment' which has caused such behavior. Furthermore, it is not desirable or even possible for outsiders to unilaterally pass judgment on a firm's optimal behavior from their own standpoint, or any other standpoint, other than that of the firm itself.

Management is simply a means for survival in a given environment. Whether a particular type of 'management' is desirable depends on the economic environment a firm finds itself in. Those firms that fail to adapt to the environment will soon be selected out, while those firms that are successful in adapting will continue to survive. Different environments will determine the probability of success of different types of management. Changes in the environment will put pressure on managers to change their managerial style in order to increase the probability of the firm's survival. This point of view supports an important contention of this book that the managerial style is not an exogenous variable but an endogenous one. Furthermore, it is almost absurd to judge a particular behavioral pattern as either 'right' or 'wrong' without examining the context and nature of the social and political environment, as well as the economic environment. Hence some outsiders may view certain kinds of firm behavior as undesirable from their own subjective standpoint. However, from the standpoint of the firms, such behavior, if it survives the test of time, will be considered a wise choice.

Value judgment on a particular type of firm behavior is usually beyond positive economics. Furthermore, government policy-making based on this kind of judgment is even more dangerous for it is more likely to distort resource allocation. Such policies tend to regulate the outcome of firms' behavior without a fundamental cure for the original causes. In particular, such policies may force individual agents to follow a path dictated by the government that may be against the underlying incentive structure, thereby possibly resulting in a corner solution.

Thus far we have seen that many of the factors or reasons that led to the so-called *chaebol* problem derive from various social and political perceptions formed over the past few decades. These are rather complex and at times difficult to judge given that we must understand these sentiments within their social and historical context. In the following chapter, we propose the analytical framework that is used in this book in developing a clear and precise understanding of the issues and problems surrounding the *chaebol*s.

# APPENDIX

## A1   Mobility Statistics to Measure Effective Competition within the *Chaebol*

Table A3.1 summarizes the trends in mobility indices that reflect the degree of effective competition among the *chaebols* for each year for the period 1985 to 1995. First, we observe that, for the top 30 *chaebols*, the changes in the index of entry and exit as well as the index of internal mobility were not insignificant in the long run.

More specifically, we find that the sum of changes in market share, the market instability index, among the 30 largest *chaebol* between 1985 and 1995 can be explained mostly by the changes in the shares of the top five *chaebols*. Of course, it is difficult to establish which aspects of the market instability index should be attributed to effective competition and which parts can be attributed to the inherent unpredictability of business prospects. Yet it is reasonable to assume that a higher degree of market instability is related to a higher degree of effective competition. If we look more closely at the market instability index which is obtained by adding the absolute values of the changes in the *chaebol*'s relative market shares within the top 30 *chaebol*, we find that this index for the top five *chaebol* stands at about 10.7 per cent for the period between 1985 and 1995. This reflects changes that may occur in two ways: first, changes in the relative weight of the top five as a group as a percentage of the top 30 *chaebols*; and second, changes in market shares within the top five while their weight as a percentage of the top 30 *chaebol* remains unchanged. We calculate that the relative weight of the top five *chaebols* (the change in $CR_5$) increased by only 4.0 per cent. The difference of 6.7 per cent, produced by subtracting 4.0 from 10.7 per cent, represents the transfer of market share among the top five *chaebols* that does not lead to any changes in their relative weight among the top 30. This difference is the result of a struggle among the top five to extend their market share, showing that there has in fact been significant dynamic competition among the top five *chaebols*.

Table A3.2 shows comparative statistics as in Table A3.1 for Korea, the US and Japan. Two sets of warnings need be mentioned here. First, it should be noted that the dynamic indices used in this section are not completely problem-free themselves. For example, they have limits of accuracy in measuring degrees of potential competition and efficiency because the mobility indices have been calculated using data on the value of shipments of a sample of incumbent *chaebol* only. Due to lack of relevant data, those indices cannot take into full account the diverse aspects of potential market competition, and therefore cannot accurately gauge the degree of market

Table A3.1  *The mobility statistics and effective competition among the top 30 chaebol*

| | Top 30 | | Internal mobility among remaining *chaebol* | | | | |
| | Entry and exit index | | Market instability index (%)[b] | | | Correlation of *chaebol* ranking[c] | Change in $CR_5$[d] (%) |
| | Number of entry and exit | Index (%) | Top 5 | Top 10 | Total | | |
|---|---|---|---|---|---|---|---|
| 1985–86 | 2 | 1.22 | 3.91 | 5.55 | 8.73 | 0.9414 | 0.8 |
| 1986–87 | 1 | 0.64 | 2.38 | 2.66 | 5.53 | 0.9571 | 0.8 |
| 1987–88 | 2 | 1.35 | 5.69 | 7.67 | 9.77 | 0.9781 | 0.0 |
| 1988–89 | 2 | 1.22 | 4.37 | 4.94 | 6.03 | 0.9940 | -0.2 |
| 1989–90 | 3 | 2.22 | 3.02 | 3.86 | 5.67 | 0.9890 | 0.5 |
| 1990–91 | 4 | 2.39 | 2.39 | 5.45 | 6.68 | 0.9822 | 1.0 |
| 1991–92 | 3 | 1.63 | 1.25 | 4.20 | 5.69 | 1.0000 | -0.8 |
| 1992–93 | 1 | 0.48 | 1.83 | 2.70 | 3.96 | 0.9961 | 1.0 |
| 1993–94 | 0 | 0 | 2.50 | 3.54 | 4.85 | 0.9867 | 0.2 |
| 1994–95 | 2 | 0.96 | 3.89 | 5.08 | 7.02 | 0.9869 | 0.5 |
| 1985–95 | 9 | 6.03 | 10.7 | 13.8 | 19.6 | 0.8922 | 4.0 |

*Notes:*

[a] Entry and Exit Index $= 1/2 \times \Sigma_i \Sigma_j (X_{it} + E_{jt})$, where $X_{it}$ is the weight of exited *chaebol* $i$ in year $t$, $E_{jt}$ is the weight of entered *chaebol* $j$ in year $t$. The higher this index, the more frequent entry and exit.

[b] Market Instability Index $= \Sigma_j | S_{t,\tau} - S_{t,t} |$, where $S_{t,\tau}$ and $S_{t,\tau}$ denote the weight of *chaebol* $i$ in year $t$ and $\tau$, respectively. The higher the index the more variability in each *chaebol*'s weight and so the higher the degree of competition among them.

[c] Rank correlation among the *chaebol* that remained in the top 30 during the relevant period. A high value of this index represents little changes in the ranking.

[d] The variability of the market share of the five largest *chaebols*.

*Table A3.2  International comparison of mobility indices of top 100 firms, measured by the value of shipments*

| Years | Change of composition | | | | | | Change of ranking | | | | | |
|---|---|---|---|---|---|---|---|---|---|---|---|---|
| | Number of entry and exit | | | Entry and exit index | | | Market instability index (%) | | | Correlation of *chaebol* rankings | | |
| | Korea | USA | Japan | Korea | USA | Japan | Korea | USA | Japan | Korea | USA | Japan |
| 1986–87 | 9 | 7 | 8 | 4.16 | 3.10 | 4.25 | 4.35 | 3.39 | 4.12 | 0.968 | 0.927 | 0.973 |
| 1987–88 | 14 | 7 | 10 | 6.75 | 4.50 | 6.09 | 3.72 | 4.12 | 1.87 | 0.927 | 0.984 | 0.985 |
| 1988–89 | 9 | 10 | 4 | 3.55 | 4.30 | 2.07 | 3.67 | 2.81 | 5.70 | 0.935 | 0.976 | 0.981 |
| 1989–90 | 5 | 7 | 5 | 1.82 | 3.18 | 1.77 | 3.93 | 4.87 | 2.07 | 0.950 | 0.980 | 0.988 |
| 1990–91 | 10 | 9 | 7 | 3.75 | 3.71 | 2.67 | 3.15 | 3.47 | 1.64 | 0.978 | 0.981 | 0.990 |
| 1991–92 | 11 | 4 | 7 | 3.90 | 1.44 | 2.82 | 2.96 | 2.78 | 3.57 | 0.964 | 0.984 | 0.973 |
| 1992–93 | 9 | 6 | 6 | 2.99 | 2.88 | 3.37 | 3.88 | 4.63 | 1.54 | 0.982 | 0.971 | 0.990 |
| Yr Avg. | 9.6 | 7.1 | 6.7 | 3.84 | 3.30 | 3.29 | 3.67 | 3.72 | 2.93 | 0.958 | 0.979 | 0.983 |

*Note:*  See notes to Table A3.1 for details of each index.

competition. Another point is that these indices do not include data on the level of competition and mobility indices of potential foreign entrants, as this could not be estimated, and thus do not adequately reflect the degree of competitive pressure that exists in the entire Korean economy.

A second warning is that we should not lose sight of the fact that in pursuing the industrial policy of 'picking winners,' the Korean government has been instrumental in determining which *chaebol* should be allowed to enter or exit particular industries. In this situation, a particular *chaebol*'s success or failure and its rank to a certain extent may reflect its lobbying power rather than economic efficiency alone. If this is indeed the case, although the mobility index may be relatively high, particular individual *chaebols* tend to behave as monopolistic entities. As mentioned in the chapter, it is important therefore to examine whether each *chaebol* is, in fact, characterized by monopolistic behavior, despite high mobility indices being found in such markets.

# A2 Market Concentration and Industry Concentration (1991–95)

*Table A3.3 Market concentration ratio in the manufacturing industry by firm type (1991–95)*

| | Herfindahl concentration ratio | | | | | $CR_4$ | | | | |
|---|---|---|---|---|---|---|---|---|---|---|
| | 1991 | 1992 | 1993 | 1994 | 1995 | 1991 | 1992 | 1993 | 1994 | 1995 |
| 15 Food products and beverage | 0.0183 | 0.0178 | 0.0183 | 0.0175 | 0.0170 | 0.1738 | 0.1700 | 0.1728 | 0.1687 | 0.1605 |
| 17 Manufacture of textile | 0.0220 | 0.0208 | 0.0202 | 0.0203 | 0.0228 | 0.2060 | 0.1952 | 0.1933 | 0.1863 | 0.2054 |
| 18 Wearing apparel and fur articles | 0.0145 | 0.0158 | 0.0191 | 0.0223 | 0.0253 | 0.1393 | 0.1503 | 0.1707 | 0.1953 | 0.2342 |
| 19 Tanning and dressing of leather | 0.0218 | 0.0261 | 0.0305 | 0.0322 | 0.0329 | 0.1944 | 0.2248 | 0.2488 | 0.2572 | 0.2558 |
| 20 Wood and products of wood and cork | 0.0067 | 0.0713 | 0.0871 | 0.1136 | 0.1166 | 0.4251 | 0.4532 | 0.5162 | 0.6137 | 0.6234 |
| 21 Pulp, paper and paper products | 0.0264 | 0.0288 | 0.0316 | 0.0344 | 0.0328 | 0.2324 | 0.2494 | 0.2704 | 0.2729 | 0.2587 |
| 22 Publishing, printing and recording | 0.0360 | 0.0317 | 0.0340 | 0.0394 | 0.0347 | 0.2908 | 0.2667 | 0.2743 | 0.3221 | 0.3054 |
| 23 Coke, refined petroleum products | 0.2633 | 0.2518 | 0.2584 | 0.2579 | 0.2477 | 0.9036 | 0.9037 | 0.9136 | 0.9066 | 0.9121 |
| 24 Chemicals and chemical products | 0.0273 | 0.0239 | 0.0247 | 0.0262 | 0.0246 | 0.2419 | 0.2331 | 0.2296 | 0.2349 | 0.2350 |
| 25 Manufacture of rubber and plastic products | 0.0649 | 0.0714 | 0.0844 | 0.0702 | 0.0751 | 0.3697 | 0.4183 | 0.4568 | 0.4194 | 0.4366 |

| | Industry | | | | | | | | | | |
|---|---|---|---|---|---|---|---|---|---|---|---|
| 26 | Non-metallic mineral products | 0.0322 | 0.0310 | 0.0330 | 0.0318 | 0.0321 | 0.2797 | 0.2831 | 0.2840 | 0.2806 | 0.2799 |
| 27 | Manufacture of basic metals | 0.1377 | 0.1336 | 0.1400 | 0.1256 | 0.1109 | 0.4891 | 0.4816 | 0.4929 | 0.4763 | 0.4555 |
| 28 | Assembling metal products and outfits | 0.0421 | 0.0095 | 0.0111 | 0.0110 | 0.0111 | 0.2738 | 0.1064 | 0.1098 | 0.1214 | 0.1224 |
| 29 | Manufacture of outfits, n.e.c. | 0.0555 | 0.0498 | 0.0305 | 0.0458 | 0.0872 | 0.3863 | 0.3630 | 0.2708 | 0.3593 | 0.4361 |
| 30 | For office, calculating, accounting | 0.0826 | 0.0726 | 0.0725 | 0.0785 | 0.0874 | 0.4693 | 0.4461 | 0.4286 | 0.4731 | 0.5199 |
| 31 | Electrical machinery and converters, n.e.c. | 0.0688 | 0.0745 | 0.0868 | 0.0302 | 0.0609 | 0.4508 | 0.4613 | 0.4940 | 0.3865 | 0.4597 |
| 32 | Television and communication equipment | 0.1174 | 0.1082 | 0.1178 | 0.1292 | 0.1457 | 0.5724 | 0.5439 | 0.5525 | 0.5726 | 0.6118 |
| 33 | For medical, precision and optical | 0.0466 | 0.0380 | 0.0427 | 0.0376 | 0.376 | 0.3388 | 0.2918 | 0.3146 | 0.2752 | 0.2898 |
| 34 | Motor cars and trailers | 0.1665 | 0.1336 | 0.1357 | 0.1286 | 0.1218 | 0.6770 | 0.6118 | 0.6190 | 0.5959 | 0.5890 |
| 35 | Other transport equipment | 0.2456 | 0.2514 | 0.2465 | 0.2882 | 0.2693 | 0.7849 | 0.8130 | 0.8782 | 0.8488 | 0.8844 |
| 36 | Manufacture of furniture and n.e.c. | 0.0376 | 0.0375 | 0.0489 | 0.0354 | 0.0395 | 0.3224 | 0.3159 | 0.3708 | 0.2965 | 0.3184 |
| | Weighted concentration ratio | 0.0889 | 0.0854 | 0.0924 | 0.0911 | 0.0949 | 0.4284 | 0.4180 | 0.4370 | 0.4326 | 0.4522 |

*Sources:* Korea Credit Evaluation Co. and Annual Report of Korean Companies.

Table A3.4  Industry concentration by chaebol in the manufacturing industry (1991 and 1995) (unit: %)

| | Share of top 5 | | Share of top 6–10 | | Share of top 11–20 | | Share of top 21–30 | | Total share | |
|---|---|---|---|---|---|---|---|---|---|---|
| | 1991 | 1995 | 1991 | 1995 | 1991 | 1995 | 1991 | 1995 | 1991 | 1995 |
| 15 Food products and beverage | 7.53 | 7.46 | 11.56 | 10.18 | 7.25 | 8.91 | 10.33 | 7.07 | 36.67 | 33.62 |
| 17 Manufacture of textile | 7.77 | 8.87 | 3.39 | 0.04 | 10.47 | 10.17 | 10.40 | 7.12 | 32.03 | 26.20 |
| 18 Wearing apparel and fur articles | 0.58 | | 0.00 | | 0.00 | | 0.00 | | 0.58 | |
| 19 Tanning and dressing of leather | 0.00 | 0.00 | 0.01 | 0.00 | 8.59 | 0.00 | 0.00 | 10.00 | 8.60 | 10.00 |
| 20 Wood and products of wood and cork | 0.00 | 0.00 | 0.00 | 0.00 | 5.07 | 11.19 | 0.00 | 0.00 | 5.07 | 11.19 |
| 21 Pulp, paper and paper products | 13.94 | 0.00 | 0.98 | 4.21 | 0.00 | 0.00 | 0.00 | 15.54 | 14.92 | 19.75 |
| 22 Publishing, printing and recording | 8.02 | 1.27 | 2.21 | 3.06 | 5.63 | 3.36 | 0.00 | 0.00 | 15.86 | 7.69 |
| 23 Coke, refined petroleum products | 43.90 | 67.71 | 46.46 | 29.88 | 0.00 | 0.00 | 0.00 | 0.00 | 90.36 | 97.59 |
| 24 Chemicals and chemical products | 16.30 | 24.20 | 13.22 | 11.83 | 1.72 | 7.08 | 5.57 | 3.94 | 36.81 | 47.05 |
| 25 Manufacture of rubber and plastics products | 1.03 | 1.58 | 0.37 | 0.00 | 0.68 | 22.51 | 21.54 | 0.67 | 23.62 | 24.76 |

| | | | | | | | | | | |
|---|---|---|---|---|---|---|---|---|---|---|
| 26 | Non-metallic mineral products | 20.68 | 7.13 | 1.22 | 11.87 | 2.24 | 7.08 | 1.03 | 7.85 | 25.17 | 33.93 |
| 27 | Manufacture of basic metals | 11.38 | 12.57 | 1.03 | 2.25 | 13.62 | 11.02 | 6.64 | 7.37 | 32.67 | 33.21 |
| 28 | Assembling metal products and outfits | 18.99 | 3.65 | 0.00 | 0.00 | 4.59 | 3.97 | 1.80 | 1.02 | 25.38 | 8.64 |
| 29 | Machinery and outfits, n.e.c. | 44.23 | 27.68 | 2.78 | 6.04 | 4.82 | 3.61 | 1.39 | 2.50 | 53.22 | 39.83 |
| 30 | For office, calculating, accounting | 0.00 | 18.86 | 6.09 | 2.98 | 0.93 | 0.31 | 0.00 | 0.00 | 7.02 | 22.15 |
| 31 | Electric-machinery and converters, n.e.c | 26.57 | 29.48 | 0.00 | 0.00 | 6.03 | 8.55 | 0.85 | 0.00 | 33.45 | 38.03 |
| 32 | Television and communication equipment | 72.10 | 77.07 | 0.81 | 0.51 | 0.43 | 0.46 | 0.59 | 1.06 | 73.93 | 79.10 |
| 33 | For medical, precision and optical | 19.34 | 17.25 | 0.00 | 0.00 | 0.00 | 0.00 | 0.00 | 0.00 | 19.34 | 17.25 |
| 34 | Motor cars and trailer | 48.88 | 45.66 | 0.06 | 24.67 | 25.95 | 4.67 | 4.16 | 0.28 | 79.05 | 75.28 |
| 35 | Other transport equipment | 78.15 | 84.35 | 8.68 | 0.72 | 0.01 | 8.97 | 4.62 | 0.03 | 91.46 | 94.07 |
| 36 | Manufacture of furniture | 14.11 | 13.75 | 0.00 | 0.00 | 0.00 | 0.00 | 0.00 | 0.00 | 14.11 | 13.75 |
| | Weighted Average | 29.00 | 34.24 | 6.35 | 8.29 | 6.94 | 5.43 | 4.33 | 3.31 | 46.62 | 51.26 |

*Sources*: Korea Credit Evaluation Co. and Annual Report of Korean Companies.

# NOTES

1. The popularity of the traditional perception is evident in the following statement from the Korea Fair Trade Commission: 'In general, "concentration of economic power" has been conceived in various ways, that is, general concentration, ... too high market share, ... ownership concentration, ... too much diversification. In our country, the concept of concentration of economic power entails the above conceptions and in addition has the Korea-specific characteristic that "a few persons" and their relatives have *de facto* ownership and control of many large firms ranging across a wide field of industries such that each firm belonging to the same *chaebol* has a monopolistic position in the industry and very weak managerial independence from "a few persons"' (Korea Fair Trade Committee, 1996, p. 115).

2. Of course, even employment indices are not completely free from the effects of firm-specific idiosyncratic factors such as differences in labor productivity, because these indices can be affected not only by the size of the firm but also by labor productivity. Low labor productivity will tend to make the employment index upwardly biased. However, if the index is lower for a country with relatively low labor productivity, then it can be safely argued that that country has a relatively lower degree of economic concentration in spite of a possible upward bias inherent in the index.

3. This can be seen from Table 3.1 where the employment concentration of the *chaebol* is seen to remain more or less constant while the value-added increases.

4. The volume of sales has been the most important criterion on the basis of which the 30 largest *chaebol* are selected and the sheer size of the volume itself has been regarded as the most important determinant of their credit-worthiness. Being one of the 30 largest *chaebols* brings not only additional regulations under the Fair Trade Act but also governmental favors such as easy credit and bankruptcy protection. Therefore, under such a scenario, the *chaebol* have tended to emphasize their sales volume excessively.

5. The market concentration ratio of the top $k$ firms is the sum of the market shares of the first $k$ firms among the total $n$ firms in an industry. The Herfindahl index (HI) is the sum of the squared shares of each individual firm in an industry. Formal definitions are as follows.

$$\text{Market concentration ratio of the top } k \text{ firms (CR}_k) = \sum_{i=1}^{k} S_i$$

$$\text{Herfindahl Index} = \sum_{i=1}^{k} S_i^2$$

6. The weighted average of $CR_4$ for all industries increased from 42.8 per cent in 1991 to 45.2 per cent in 1995. The weighted average of the Herfindahl index for the same period also increased from 0.0889 to 0.0949.

7. The correlation coefficient was calculated at 0.97 for this period.

8. Market concentration refers to the sum of the market shares of the $k$ leading firms. Firms that belong to the same group are counted as separate entities, which can lead to an underestimation of *chaebol* concentration. Industry concentration, on the other hand, is the sum of the market shares of the $k$ leading business groups, which may include several firms in the same industry, and is thus a better measure of the *chaebol*'s industrial dominance.

9. The weighted average of industry concentration of the top ten *chaebol* increased from 35.4 to 42.5 per cent. Also, during the same period, the corresponding figures for the top ten to 30 *chaebol* decreased from 11.3 to 8.7 per cent.

10. According to the *Annual Report of Korean Companies* (Korea Investors Service inc., 1995), the number of *chaebol*-affiliated firms in the manufacturing industry has decreased from 19 to 16 in the case of Hyundai, from 23 to 19 in the case of Samsung, and from 29 to 18 in the case of LG, from 1991 to 1995, while Daewoo has shown no changes in this regard, remaining at 12. The fifth rank in the top five *chaebol* that was held by the SsangYong group in 1991 (with eight affiliated firms) was overtaken by SunKyung (having seven affiliated firms) in 1995.

11. Similar results are found for 1991 data.
12. Analysis of structure-conduct-performance, one of the traditional theories of industrial organizations, shows that a more monopolistic market structure implies a monopolistic price above the competitive one, which in turn implies monopoly profits. For a typical structure-conduct-performance analysis, see Bain (1959) and Scherer (1980).
13. For this perspective, see Demsetz (1974) and Chapter 8, Section 4.2 in this book.
14. See Hwang (1998).
15. Correlation coefficient lies between 60 and 70.
16. The data may be a little out-dated but nevertheless serve as a good illustration.

# 4. A new interpretation of the *chaebol* problem and evaluation of *chaebol* policy

## 1. INTRODUCTION

This chapter presents and applies a new analytical framework to study the *chaebol* problem. Basically, the new framework utilizes the two-stage budgeting system based on a multi-stage decision-making model commonly employed in economic analysis. This chapter will pinpoint and distinguish between those aspects of the *chaebol* problem that can be addressed through economic analysis and those that need to be understood as being part of the political decision-making process. A second task of this chapter is to critically evaluate past and current *chaebol* policy in line with the categorization made in the first part of the chapter. Essentially, this chapter presents the first steps toward a new paradigm of *chaebol* policy, which is developed in the later chapters of this book.

## 2. REINTERPRETATION OF THE *CHAEBOL* PROBLEM

### 2.1 Application of the Two Stage Decision-Making Process to the *Chaebol* Problem

We make use of the multi-stage decision-making system usually applied to the analysis of consumer behavior patterns. Simply put, it is assumed that in the first stage, consumers will allocate their income to a wide range of categories such as food, clothes and leisure, while, in the second stage, they allocate their budget to specific goods and services within each category, for example, rice and meat, jackets and suits, and foreign and domestic travel.[1] In this manner, the consumer will optimize his consumption.

In the same vein, in the context of the *chaebol* problem, it may be assumed that the government pursues industrial policy intended to achieve an optimal allocation of resources to various industries. Thus, in the first stage the government allocates resources to entrepreneurs rather than to specific industries, while in the second stage, those entrepreneurs who have secured resources will allocate resources to specific industries according to their investment plans. This process may also be conceptualized in the form of a utility tree (see Figure 4.1), a tool that is often employed to analyze behavioral patterns of consumption. For analytical purposes, it is convenient to separate economic processes from political processes, both of which are an intricate part of the formation of the *chaebol* in Korea. More precisely, the first stage can be seen as primarily a political process by which a *chaebol* secures economic resources (including funds procured from banks) through various non-market means, particularly through the use of its business and political relations. The second stage is essentially a market process, where the resources allocated in the first stage are efficiently put to use.

The first stage involves political choices decided upon by the government through non-market means, particularly the assignment of rights over economic resources to entrepreneurs. Naturally, another aspect of this process is the competition among entrepreneurs to secure vested interests through various means such as political lobbying. The second stage involves purely economic decisions on the part of the entrepreneurs, that is, the allocation of the resources obtained to a multitude of activities according to the dictates of

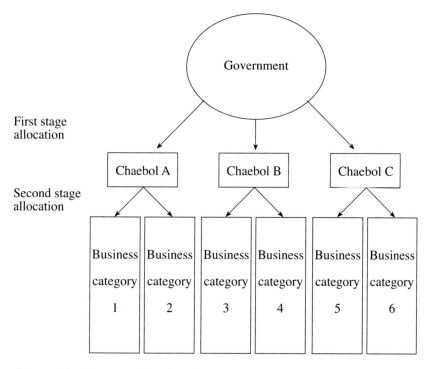

*Figure 4.1   Resource allocation tree*

the market mechanisms. Put this way, the choices made in the first stage are political while those made in the second stage are economic.

The use of the term 'political decision-making' is meant to denote behavior that influences the distribution of income by transferring property rights from one group (or any number of individuals) to another through non-market processes. Economic decision-making, on the other hand, denotes behavior that results in the allocation of resources through the market mechanism. Here it should be noted that political decision-making, which in Korea favors large firms over small ones for example, does not automatically result in the inefficient allocation of resources because it remains possible that the favored groups may in fact be the most efficient groups. 'Political decision-making' simply means the redistribution of property rights through means other than the market. Whether or not it happens to be efficient is another matter entirely.

## 2.2   Reinterpretation of the *Chaebol* Problem in Korea

Now let us re-examine the *chaebol* problem in Korea by employing the analytical framework developed above. To begin with, problems associated with economic concentration in the hands of a few *chaebol* originate mostly from the first stage decision-making process. As has already been pointed out, this first stage process involves two aspects. First, in pursuing its industrial policy of encouraging the growth of export-oriented and heavy and chemical industries, the government decided that certain entrepreneurs would enjoy the advantages of special loans and artificial entry barriers to protect their markets. At the same time, entrepreneurs worked to secure government support through non-market processes such as lobbying. The more successful these entrepreneurs became at mustering government support, the longer they were able to purchase resources for less than the market value and as a result, a growing trend of economic concentration emerged with these government-backed firms growing even larger.

The decision to promote the growth of the export-oriented and heavy and chemical industries is an important economic choice for a national economy. However, implementing government's industrial policy usually involves decisions as to which firms are to receive special loans and which will be protected from further competition through artificial entry barriers. This is ultimately a political activity, characterized by the limiting or transferring of property rights through non-market means. In the same way, the government's decisions regarding the qualifications required for the management of large firms or access to resources necessary for running large firms are basically political in nature.

In capitalist economies, when power to control economic resources becomes concentrated as a result of voluntary transfers of property rights through fair market competition, disputes over the political and ethical problems of economic concentration become meaningless. In the case of Korea, however, the rapid growth of the *chaebol* is generally considered to be the result of political decisions by the government – the result of governmental favoritism through interlocking relations between politicians or government policy-makers and entrepreneurs. Because of this and in addition to the potential economic side effects of economic concentration, moral and ethical problems related to the *chaebol* issue are commonly raised.

On the other hand, non-competitive market structures and the potential for monopolistic behavior on the part of the *chaebol* – associated with high market shares – can be linked to the results of entrepreneurial decision-making in the second stage. In the case of a small domestic market, such as Korea's, efforts by a few entrepreneurs to maximize the advantages of special loans and industry protection tend to expand their market share through a process of monopolization.

Generally, we can think of monopolization in market economies developing under two different economic scenarios. One is under free competition with free entry that exhibits subsequent increases in the market share of the surviving, most efficient firm. The other is monopolization through artificial measures such as government regulations, protection and restriction of market entry. It is widely accepted among scholars that under the first scenario monopolization does not tend to cause distortions in resource allocation, while in the second case monopolization usually causes economic inefficiencies and therefore requires some initiative by the government to improve market structures. In particular, the government should itself assume responsibility to remove barriers to competition in order to promote market competition when monopolistic structures emerge not from firms' initiative under conditions of free entry and exit, but from government regulations. Problems caused by the monopolization of most markets by the *chaebol* correspond to the latter case.

Now we turn to the issue of conglomeration and in particular what is referred to as the unsound managerial behavior of the *chaebol*, which is often associated with diversification. We note that this is the result of entrepreneurial decision-making geared toward maximizing the use of resources in the second stage. *Chaebol* diversification into unrelated business areas is a natural result of their taking the best options available given the easy access to financial resources resulting from the allocation decisions in the first stage and the narrow domestic markets for their products that do not favor specialization.[2] In general, one of the most important factors that influence decisions of whether to diversify into other areas of business is the existence of technological economies of scope. In the Korean case, the concentration of economic resources within a few firms and the small size of the domestic market have encouraged business diversification among the *chaebol*. Because regulations and barriers are components of the industrial policy under which explicit or implicit permission by the government is required for entry, it is interesting to point out that government-established entry regulations and exit barriers have also encouraged the *chaebol* to pursue a diversification strategy. Indeed, once the government has allowed entry, the selected firms are kept in business for as long as possible, even by the use of various measures to restrain incumbent firms from exiting (file for bankruptcy) when they become non-viable. It is not surprising, therefore, to find that given this pattern of industrial policy, the *chaebol* have exhibited a tendency to make pre-emptive strategic moves into unrelated business areas. However, given the many factors influencing a *chaebol*'s diversification behavior, including the government's industrial policy over the years, it is hardly a simple matter for external observers to judge whether or not the right degree of diversification has been achieved.

In a similar fashion, conglomeration and concentration of ownership, and managerial power, secured by the *chaebol* through other forms of managerial behavior such as cross-debt guarantees among affiliated firms, are all results of the optimizing behavior, or survival strategy, of the *chaebol* in the second stage. These behavioral patterns are the result of managerial decisions aimed at maximizing their survival probability by optimally allocating resources obtained during the political decision-making process in the first stage. Therefore, because no external observer is able to consider fully all aspects of the managerial strategy, it is just as difficult for an economist to judge whether or not behavioral patterns have been excessive.

Reflecting on the above discussion, we may divide the *chaebol* problem into three sub-problems: (a) economic resource concentration in the hands of only a few *chaebol* as a result of the political decision-making process in the first stage; (b) monopolization or oligopolization of individual markets by the *chaebol*; and (c) managerial behavior toward conglomeration such as the concentration of ownership and managerial power or diversification into related and unrelated businesses. The last two sub-problems, monopolization and managerial behavior (conglomeration) of the *chaebol*, are the by-products of both the first stage decision-making process, in this case the first sub-problem, and the Korea-specific economic environment, such as Korea's industrial policies and the limited extent of the Korean domestic market.[3]

In sum, the problem of economic resource concentration in the first stage of political decision-making is important, not just in terms of whether it has been fair but also because it constitutes the basis for the *chaebol*'s business behavior in the second stage. However, the problems related to both monopolization and managerial behavior in the second stage are the result of endogenous responses by the *chaebol* to the exogenously given economic environment, as well as the political decision-making at the first stage.

## 3.   EVALUATION OF THE *CHAEBOL* POLICY

### 3.1   Classification of Past and Current *Chaebol* Policy into Two Stage Decision-Making Process

The government has made numerous efforts to regulate *chaebol* behavior over the past 30 years or so. Hence it is only natural that past and current *chaebol* policies are somewhat difficult to classify strictly according to the two stage decision-making model. Nevertheless, it is useful to do so and we will classify them into the two groups of policies as distinguished in the first part of this chapter – that is, (a) policies related to the first stage problem, aimed at limiting the *chaebol*'s capacity to mobilize economic resources; and (b) policies related to the second stage problems, aimed at constraining *chaebols*' economic behavior. Table 4.1 summarizes the major regulatory measures adopted by the government in terms of their influence on first stage and second stage decision-making process.[4]

Broadly speaking, *chaebol* policy has evolved under three broad specifications: the loan management system, the antitrust laws and the recent reforms initiated by the Kim Dae-jung administration, known widely as DJ Reforms, that followed the 1997 economic crisis. As discussed in Chapter 2, easy loans with preferential treatment by the government's arbitrary determination of interest rates constitute a major reason for resource concentration among the *chaebol*. Hence efforts were made to remove some of the various support programs that had been included by the government in several industrial and financial policies. Accordingly, the volume of low-interest loans for targeted industries shrank, interest rates were liberalized and various protective measures blocking the entry of foreign goods were removed. All these greatly contributed to a reduction in the scope for political decision-making power over the distribution of resources as described by the two stage decision-making model. However, serious doubts continue to be raised on the legitimacy and ethical justification of the *chaebols*' formation process as well as on its identity.

As such, the first stage policies usually took the form of putting direct restrictions on the *chaebols*' ability to raise funds for investment. These include: (a) various measures under what is known as 'the Loan Management System,' which is aimed at reducing the size of loans from financial institutions to the *chaebol*, (b) regulation on lending among affiliates and temporary payments to dominant stockholders, (c) the prohibition of cross-debt guarantees among affiliates, and (d) measures aimed at improving the *chaebols*' financial and capital structure, such as reducing the debt-to-equity ratio, imposing self-financing requirements, and forcing them to first seek means other than bank borrowing to finance projects.[5]

*Table 4.1  Government regulation affecting first and second stage decision-making process of chaebol*

| Regulation by government | Affecting | |
| --- | --- | --- |
| | First stage | Second stage |
| (1) The 'Loan Management System' – regulation on corporate borrowing, improvement of *chaebol*'s financial structure, restrictions on real estate acquisition and size of capital investment. | x | x |
| (2) Specialization of business lines – initially core firm system established, that switched to focus on core business areas. Later relaxed to induce autonomous business specialization. Currently aims at streamlining business activities by improvements in M&A procedure, adoption of corporate-split system, improving bankruptcy procedure and the 'big deals'. | | x |
| (3) Regulation on lending among affiliates and temporary payments to dominant stockholders. | x | x |
| (4) Regulation on unfair trade practices of big conglomerates – regulation on intra-conglomerate trade. | | x |
| (5) Regulation on cross-ownership between affiliated firms. | | x |
| (6) Regulation on holding company system. | | x |
| (7) Regulation on cross-debt guarantees. | x | x |
| (8) Enhancing transparency – appointment of outside directors, strengthening voting rights of shareholders, and adoption of international accounting standards. | | x |
| (9) Strengthening accountability – strengthening legal liability of controlling owner, introducing voting rights of institutional investors and the cumulative voting system. | | x |
| (10) Regulation on financial structure – improvement of bank's capital structure, introduction of asset-backed securities, requirement of a 200 per cent debt-equity ratio and the 'workout program'. | x | x |

In order to maintain the soundness of the banking industry, most countries have regulations preventing the concentration of bank loans to one particular economic entity. As we have described in the previous section, Korea is not an exception and in fact there have been additional features regulating bank lending to large *chaebol*-affiliated firms under the name of 'Loan-Limit Management Policy'. Since August 1997, however, the Korean government strengthened the regulation of bank loans by throwing away the existing Loan-Limit Management Policy and introducing in its place a new institution that shifts the focus from loans to individual affiliates to total loans to a *chaebol*, including all its affiliates. Integrating various existing regulations that limit loans to large firms into a bigger framework applicable to the *chaebol* group by expanding the concept of 'a single economic entity' to encompass all firms belonging to the same group is a step in the right direction. However, for its proper operation, it is necessary to define both the economic and legal concepts of the term 'same group' clearly and meaningfully. The holding company system being historically prohibited by the Monopoly Regulation and Fair Trade Law was a primary cause of much confusion as regards the economic role of the *chaebol*. Although this system has recently been reintroduced, it is too restrictive and rather impractical and ineffective; there is therefore an urgent need to activate the holding company system in order to put into perspective the economic functions of the *chaebol*.[6]

On the other hand, policies related to the second stage, which are aimed at regulating the *chaebol*s' market and management behavior, include those (a) affecting equity investment and ownership of affiliated firms, (b) prohibiting cross-debt guarantees among affiliates, (c) prohibiting unfair trade practices, such as intra-conglomerate trade, (d) enhancing managerial, accounting and corporate transparency, and (e) streamlining business activity and discouraging diversification behavior.

During the latter 1980s and much of the 1990s, the government increasingly resorted to antitrust laws in its attempts to regulate the *chaebol*s' management behavior. Essentially, antitrust laws were put in place as a means to regulate what were considered unfair trade practices of big business conglomerates. These included regulation on cross-investment and ownership of affiliates, intra-conglomerate trade, as well as the ban on cross-debt guarantees. In general, all these policies were aimed at affecting the second stage decision-making process.

The government also regulated the competitive entry of *chaebol* firms into key industries as it considered competitive entry wasteful. As mentioned earlier, *chaebol* diversification has always been highly controversial and until recently, the government has pursued policies encouraging the *chaebol* to specialize in a few business lines or 'core competencies' by exempting from several regulations only those *chaebol*s that conform to its guidelines.

A somewhat different approach to *chaebol* regulation emerged following the 1997 economic crisis. A flood of new policy measures was introduced not only to limit economic concentration, but also directly to improve management transparency as well as the efficiency and competitiveness of *chaebols*, emphasizing issues of corporate governance and financial prudence. 'Old style' regulation seems to be giving way to 'new style' reform efforts that tend to address economic environmental factors, thus moving away from the direct control of managerial decision variables. In line with this shift, there is also a change in the terms commonly used from 'regulation' to 'reform'. This, in a sense, is a big improvement in the right direction.

Broadly speaking, the post-crisis *chaebol* reform policies have emphasized three broad areas. First, reforms seek to improve the corporate governance structure and managerial transparency and this can be viewed broadly as addressing second stage problems. The commercial code now requires the establishment and appointment of outside directors. Limits on the voting rights of institutional investors have been lifted, and the rights of minority shareholders strengthened. On the other hand, the legal liability of controlling owners has also been strengthened in order to enhance accountability, in addition to the adoption of consolidated financial statements and international accounting principles. These reforms should help increase the accountability of the owner-managers, or the group chairmen in the case of the *chaebol*, and decrease the hold on power that they currently have. One of the problems in the *chaebol* has been the absolute dominance of the chairman over all affiliated firms. For example, the chairman of a *chaebol* has the power to fire members of the board of directors, who should be the ones keeping the chairman in check. It is hoped that further reforms will help reverse this situation and create a more independent and effective board.

A second area of emphasis in the post-crisis reform seeks to improve financial conditions and the capital structure of firms, which can be viewed as directed to addressing first stage *chaebol* problems as well as second stage problems. This includes the elimination of cross-debt guarantees among group affiliates and also the reduction in the debt–equity ratio to 200 per cent by the end of 1999. For example, the debt–equity ratios of the top 30 *chaebol* have decreased from about 480 per cent in 1997 to a level lower than 200 per cent by the end of 1999.[7] Most of the top five *chaebols*' cross-debt guarantees have been dissolved as of January 2000. Also in place agreements to improve the financial structure of the business sector have been signed between creditor banks and their corporate clients under government guidance with the process of financial restructuring being closely monitored by the government. Furthermore, the 'workout program', a kind of private corporate reorganization process between debtor firms and creditor banks was recently introduced. This aims to restructure debtor-firms before they become non-viable so that firms and banks can avoid the agony of corporate bankruptcy.[8]

A third area of reform, which can be viewed as addressing the second stage problems, aims at improving business competitiveness primarily by stream-lining business activity. To facilitate the exit or reorganization of insolvent firms, the bankruptcy and corporate reorganization laws have been revised. In the early phase of the crisis, 55 non-viable firms belonging to the 30 largest *chaebol*s were forced to close down. In particular, as part of the efforts to streamline business activity, the top five *chaebol*s agreed to reduce the number of their affiliates and to concentrate on three to five core businesses in order to solve the problems of over-diversification and over-investment.[9] These firms would reduce the number of affiliates by up to 70 per cent by the year 2000 in return for comprehensive tax breaks and other benefits, including debt–equity swaps by creditors. Also, as part of the efforts to streamline business activity, the top five *chaebol*s had agreed to decrease the number of affiliates and to concentrate on three to five core businesses in order to solve the problems of over-diversification and over-investment. Moreover, the government continues strongly to encourage 'big deals', essentially a form of business swaps among various firms with the aim of restricting the number of business lines of each *chaebol*.[10]

## 3.2   Problems with Policies of the First Stage *Chaebol* Formation

We find that problems regarding the first stage resource concentration cannot be resolved simply by eliminating preferential loans to the *chaebol*s or by limiting their ability to access funds. This is because both the current existence of special favors to them and the past practices during their formative years are all part of the problem. It seems that we cannot find an appropriate solution to this problem without rigorously evaluating the *chaebol*'s contributions and harm to the Korean economy, and more importantly, understanding whether it will be desirable fundamentally to change the current industrial structure in which the *chaebol* dominate.

First, regarding the merits and faults of the *chaebol*, two interrelated issues are relevant to our discussion: the fairness of resource allocation, and the degree to which the *chaebol* have contributed to the development of the Korean economy. The issue of fairness of resource allocation will involve judgment on whether governmental support has been conducted under fair rules. As such, answers to this question cannot avoid eventually becoming a matter of political or value judgment, as has been clearly established in the earlier part of this chapter, and is thus beyond the scope of this book.

The question of whether the *chaebol* have made any positive contribution to the development of the Korean economy also does not lend itself to an easy and definite answer. It is evident that the development of the Korean economy and the *chaebol*'s growth will show a positive correlation. Hence, one may easily be led to conclude that the *chaebols*' growth has made a positive contribution to the development of the Korean economy. One must, however, be careful, as a positive correlation is not sufficient to allow us to conclude that the Korean economy would not have been able to achieve its past level of economic growth if it had not been for the *chaebol*. It is stretching logic to draw such a conclusion from the simple existence of a positive correlation. In fact, the market system may have operated well in an economy with an industrial structure devoid of *chaebol* dominance, and to a greater extent might have evolved even in the absence of governmental initiatives and industrial policies that have encouraged the formation of large firms.

There is also another question concerning the most desirable industrial structure for the Korean economy in the future. In this regard, for example, one may argue (by either political judgment or economic evaluation) that the *chaebols*' influence has been negative and that, therefore, it is desirable to change completely the current industrial structure in which they dominate. It is important to note, however, that the possible negative role of the *chaebol* in the past does not automatically lead to the conclusion that the destruction of the current industrial structure is desirable. The question regarding the optimal industrial structure in the future is far more complicated and cannot be addressed simply by looking at the role of the *chaebol* in the past. In fact, an evaluation of the *chaebols*' positive or negative contribution in the past might not have a decisive influence on the choice of our future industrial structure because the type of industrial structure in the future will depend on choices that are basically of a forward-looking nature. Even if it is the case that the current *chaebol*-dominated industrial structure should be replaced by some other structure, it does not necessarily follow that the existing structure should be destroyed. The policies for introducing a new structure could be revolutionary, through the destruction of the existing structure, or evolutionary, by allowing the next structure to evolve gradually out of the existing one in response to the newly emerging market environment. Thus, if it is indeed the case that it is economically unwise to destroy the current industrial structure considering the prospects for the evolution of a future structure and consequent costs and benefits of alternative policies, the arguments over the merits and demerits of the *chaebols*' past practices will in fact be meaningless. Therefore, in my judgment, it will be difficult to resolve the problems originating from the first stage decisions during the *chaebol* formation process without answering such fundamental questions as the ones about the optimal industrial structure of the future and how to bring it forth.

## 3.3   Problems with Policies of the Second Stage *Chaebol* Behavior

Having discussed the problems with policies addressing the first stage *chaebol* formation, we will now turn to address problems with policies designed to influence *chaebol*s' management behavior. In many respects, the pre-crisis *chaebol* policies, in particular, toward the correction of *chaebol* behavior, have largely been symptom-regulating rather than addressing fundamental causes. On the other hand, post-crisis reform efforts, especially as relates to issues of corporate governance such as transparency, accountability, strengthening of shareholder rights and so on, by addressing the external environment rather than being directed to a certain feature of *chaebol* behavior are a huge improvement in the right direction. Nevertheless, old habits do not die out fast. Without having to go into too much detail, let it suffice at this stage to discuss three controversial measures that continue to exhibit elements of the 'old style' regulation legacy – namely, the ban on cross-debt guarantees, the uniform application of 200 per cent debt–equity ratios, and the ban of the Planning and Coordination office. Other issues of corporate governance will be discussed fully in Chapter 8, when we are able to benefit from important insights developed in Chapter 7 that are necessary to put into better perspective issues related to corporate governance behavior.

As mentioned in Chapter 3, the regulation on cross-debt guarantees[11] between *chaebol* affiliates has recently been strengthened on the grounds that through lending concentration they might become a major cause of economic concentration, thereby acting as obstacles to the exit of failing businesses. However, a more fundamental problem is that bank supervisory authorities have not strictly enforced the regulation. Nor have commercial banks abided fully by the prudential regulations on the single borrower lending limit system. Since cross-debt guarantees must involve a third party, once affiliate firms are understood as belonging to a single *chaebol*, the term 'cross-debt guarantee' then becomes a misnomer. Thus, the single borrower lending limit system on the *chaebol* should be reinforced strictly in recognition that a *chaebol* is an economically single identity, thereby acting as an effective way to restrain *chaebol* affiliates from cross-debt guarantee practices among each other. That notwithstanding, banks have maintained the practice of accepting cross-debt guarantees between affiliate firms that belong to the same *chaebol*. Therefore, without due improvements in the banks' lending practices, outright regulations prohibiting all cross-debt guarantees would bring about inefficient financial resource allocation. It is important to recognize that cross-debt guarantees should be acted upon at the discretion of corporate management, while the banking regulation authority should monitor banks so as to ensure that the loan limit system is abided by, as well as maintaining a sound banking system.

The uniform application of a predetermined 200 per cent debt–equity ratio is also unjustifiable. Essentially the debt–equity ratio shows how much leverage, or debt, a company is carrying compared to its shareholders' equity, and in general, in the real world, the lower the figure the stronger the firm's financial position in cushioning any adverse effects of the business cycle. Nevertheless, an acceptable debt load must vary from industry to industry.[12] The government, however, has called for the reduction of the debt–equity ratio to be uniformly applied to each of the big five *chaebol*s without taking into account the diversity of each of the corporations. Considering that each of these *chaebol*s has different managerial objectives and business strategies, their debt management plans and capability cannot but be different. The government, nevertheless, has stated that the *chaebol* stick to the 200 per cent debt–equity ratio as from the year 2000. This, in our opinion, is bound to restrict the freedom of the corporate sector in managing financial options.

Another controversial area of the post-crisis reform, which is reminiscent of pre-crisis regulations, is the outright banning of the planning and coordination office. This had been set up in lieu of the banned holding company system so as to manage diversified business interests in the manner of a holding company but was largely informal, that is, without legal authorization. It has been argued that a more transparent corporate governance system be institutionalized through the removal of the planning and coordination office. Nevertheless, we must appreciate that functions of an organization that emerge due to economic necessity cannot be easily discarded by legal regulations. Moreover, many regulatory measures may induce firms to try and avoid such regulations, thereby increasing transaction costs and eventually adding to the burdens of corporate management, as well as the economy as a whole. As mentioned earlier, interestingly enough, the *chaebol* instituted a restructuring committee in lieu of the banned planning and coordination office, where this new committee performs essentially the same functions as the planning and coordination office.

The introduction of a non-executive director system, which is meant to correct unsound management behavior such as management abuse by dominant shareholders and managers through the operation of the planning and coordination office, has also been suggested. It is true that the current governance structure of the *chaebol* even with the restructuring committee has drawbacks, and therefore serious reform efforts are needed. In reaction to a variety of legal transparency problems raised concerning the corporate governance structure that utilized either the planning and coordination office or the restructuring committee, the government eventually re-established the holding company system in 1998.[13] If, for example, the holding company system had been introduced earlier, then quite naturally, the endogenously formed planning and coordination offices would have evolved as the main administrative center of the *chaebol*, that is, the holding company itself. In any case, with the *chaebol* recognized as a legal entity through the holding company system, many of the legal transparency problems may be avoidable. However, a better understanding and application of the holding company system is needed, as current requirements have been too restrictive to be of much use.

Broadly speaking, as can be seen from the various measures directed at regulating *chaebol* behavior, as well as from the above three cases, problems with policies addressing second stage *chaebol* behavior can be attributed to a lack of effort to find a fundamental cure to the causes of *chaebol* managerial behavior in the case of second stage policies. While the post-crisis restructuring policy has improved in many respects compared to past policy measures as mentioned earlier, the existing policies, as can be seen, still continue to lay too much emphasis on directly regulating business management. Unfortunately, such direct regulation of management behavior without addressing fundamental causes will eventually result in distortions in the process of resource allocation by restricting firm activity. That is, policies that attempt directly to regulate management behavior and ownership and business structures are very likely to lead to industrial inefficiency.

Thus, in order to improve the effectiveness of these policies, an evolutionary perspective is needed to address the *chaebols'* management behavior. An economic entity, whether a single firm or corporation, should be viewed as adopting a set of optimal management behavior encouraged by its efforts to maximize profits, where this self-selected behavior is an economically determined endogenous variable.[14] That is, it must be understood that the *chaebols* are themselves the product of economic circumstances and consequently their managerial behavior is also a response to the demands of the economic environment to maximize the probability of their own survival in the competitive world. Therefore, if one looks at the *chaebols'* behavior from this viewpoint, their managerial behavior, which may be considered as undesirable from the political-social or moral viewpoints, should also be interpreted as a result of efforts to maximize profits or its survival probability.

## 4. CONCLUDING REMARKS

In this chapter we have separated *chaebol* problems using the two stage decision-making process model commonly used in economics. We have also reviewed past and present *chaebol* policies and distinguished and criticized those that address first stage problems and those that address second stage problems. Our discussions lead us to suggest that it is better to address first stage problems by looking forward rather than trying to justify or negate, one way or another, political decisions that led to the formation of the *chaebol*. Also, it is better not to try determine the type of industrial structure *ex ante*. In the same vein, we argue that problems with second stage *chaebol* behavior are better tackled by adopting an evolutionary perspective of the growth of the *chaebol*, where a firm's strategic choice variables should be left to be decided upon by the firm and not determined by government.

It could be argued that Korea should adopt policies to correct the *chaebols'* behavior precisely because the *chaebols* have become an issue owing to their growth by non-economic means. Whatever the case may be, the evolutionary perspective on the *chaebol* implies that, even for non-economic reasons, the government should change or improve the economic environment in order to induce behavioral changes on their part. Behavioral changes forced upon the *chaebol* without the necessary creation of an appropriate economic environment would result in the removal of their survival capability and will be accompanied by resource misallocation. Thus, irrespective of problems related to the *chaebols'* formation and behavior (that is, whether first or second stage problems), our analysis here suggest that it is highly likely that direct regulation which does not address the fundamental causes will amount to nothing but unnecessary constraints adversely affecting the firm. 'Corner solutions' become increasingly likely if policies are 'excessive' or too strictly binding and more often than not will result in policy ineffectiveness as firms try to evade these regulations. Needless to say, firms will then have an incentive to increase their lobbying efforts against such policies, thereby adding to policy ineffectiveness as well as transaction costs. Hence, we suggest that the government lift or at least soften all direct regulations, whether they be on decisions to diversify, the extent of business specialization, ownership concentration, degree of separation between ownership and management, cross-debt guarantees and cross ownership between affiliates, and so on. The government should restrain itself from trying to affect decision variables best left to the *chaebol* to act upon. Broadly speaking, the government should rather focus on establishing a regime of fair competition in the economic and social system by providing proper economic institutions, that is to say, the rules of the game, so that the discovery function of the market order may become effecive.

In Chapter 7, we consolidate our arguments here by introducing a novel approach to understanding *chaebol* behavior, and in particular corporate governance systems, by refining and applying analytical tools of the new-institutional economics. Before that, we first take a closer look at further issues related to the *chaebol* problem in the next two chapters – the effect of property rights on the alleged abnormal behavior of the *chaebol* in general, and then more specifically, the *chaebols'* diversification behavior.

# APPENDIX

## A1. Summary of Regulation on *Chaebol*

We summarize in this part of the Appendix in some detail the most important regulation policies that have been implemented in the government's attempt to lower economic concentration over the past 30 years or so.

Table A4.1 contains details of the government's loan management system that was the first significant attempt at curbing the *chaebols'* economic power mainly by limiting bank borrowing and inducing financial structure improvements. Bank borrowing was restricted through major creditor banks on the basis of proportion guidelines for equity capital, while financial restructuring was encouraged through the imposition of a self-financing requirement in the case of capital investment and in the acquisition of real estate. In order to ease the problem of skewed loans and to inhibit management practices from being heavily dependent on bank loans, the loan-limit manage-ment or basket management system was introduced in 1987. Following the guidelines at the time, the largest groups were classified according to their rank and were not allowed to borrow more than a fixed proportion of the total available bank loans.

Furthermore, firms were obliged to get *ex ante* approval from the main banks for the acquisition of real estate and capital investment. Also, the stipulation prohibited certain activities along with the anti-real estate speculation measures of 8 May 1990 that was intended to inhibit the enlargement of firm size arising from excessive investment and speculation on real estate.

The loan limit system for a single economic entity (borrower) established by the Banking Law currently sets the limit for loans to a single entity at 15 per cent of the bank's equity capital, and the limit for payment guarantees at 30 per cent of the equity capital. Furthermore, the approval limit by the Banking Supervision Authority for bank loans is set at 20 per cent of bank's equity capital and for payment guarantees at 35 per cent of the equity capital of each bank. Also, a total amount limit system for large loans that became effective as from June 1995 placed limits on the total amount of loans at five times the bank's equity capital. Here, 'large loans' are defined as the total credit (loans plus payment guarantees) to a single entity or affiliated firm exceeding 15 per cent of the equity capital of each bank. Finally, the loan limit system for a group of affiliates replaced the loan management system in August 1997, and is supposed to strengthen loan-related regulations by turning the loan limit system for a single entity into a loan limit system for a group of affiliates.

Based on the loan management system outlined above, the government also

*Table A4.1  Major contents of regulation policies to lower economic concentration*

| Policy (related laws and enforcement) | Enactment date | Major contents |
|---|---|---|
| Loan management system, with loan operation regulations for financial institutions in 1982 and detailed regulations of loan management for affiliated firms in 1984. | Established 1972 with many revisions thereafter. | (1) Loan-limit management – basket management system for loans to the five largest and 30 largest *chaebol* (introduced in 1984), whereby restrictions on corporate borrowing to a fixed proportion of total available bank loans was established. |
| | | (2) Induce improvement of *chaebol*'s financial structure by major creditor banks on the basis of proportion guidelines for equity capital and imposition of self-financing requirement in the case of capital investment and acquisition of real estate. |
| | | (3) *Ex-ante* approval or prohibition measures for the acquisition of real estate and capital investment to restrict the enlargement of firm size. Banking law reinforced a loan limit system for a single borrower. |
| | | (4) Limit on total amount for large loans to a single borrower or *chaebol* to five times the equity capital of each bank. |
| | | (5) |
| | | (6) Loan limit system for a group of affiliates rather than an individual affiliate established in August 1997, which replaces the loan-limit management system. |
| Specialization of business lines (based on the loan management system). | June 1991 | (1) Establishment of core firm system. |
| | | (2) Firms with widely diffused ownership structure excluded from the application of the loan management system. |

| Regulation category | Date | | Description |
|---|---|---|---|
| | October 1993 | • | Extension of core firm system to core business areas. |
| | June 1998 | • | Removal of business specialization policy to induce autonomous business specialization. |
| Regulation on lending and temporary payments (based on the loan management system). | Reinforced after February 1992 | (1) | Prohibition of temporary payments to dominant stockholders and individuals specially linked to a certain group. |
| | | (2) | Partial regulation on lending among affiliated firms. |
| Regulation on unfair trade practices of big business conglomerates (Antitrust Law). | July 1992 | (1) | Regulation on intra-conglomerate trade restraining competition through the abuse of one's dominant position. |
| | | (2) | Specification of six types of unfair trade practices and investigation of actual cases of intra-conglomerate trade covering 23 firms affiliated to eight *chaebols*. |
| Regulation on cross-ownership between affiliated firms (Antitrust Law) | September 1998 | (1) | Prevention of cross-ownership between affiliated firms and dissolution of excessive cross ownership. |
| | | (2) | Prohibiting holding company systems thereby preventing a holding company from governing affiliate firms. The holding company is introduced under rather restrictive conditions in 1998. |
| | | (3) | Regulation on equity investment in affiliated firms for the 30 largest *chaebol* to 25 per cent of net assets of investing firm. |
| | February 1998 | • | Abolition of regulation on equity investment in affiliated firms. |
| | April 2000 | • | Equity investment permitted to 25 per cent of net assets of investing firm to be effective as from 1 April 2001, a grace period of one year. |

| Policy (related laws and enforcement) | Enactment date | Major contents |
|---|---|---|
| Regulation on cross-debt guarantees (Antitrust Law and Post-crisis Reform). | December 1992 | • Reducing cross-debt guarantees of the 30 largest *chaebol* to 100 per cent of equity capital by the end of March 1998. |
|  | February 1998 | (1) Prohibition of new cross-debt guarantees between affiliated firms. (2) Full dissolution of all outstanding cross-debt guarantees by the end of March 2000. |
| Enhancing transparency (Post-crisis Reform). | February 1998 | • Compulsory establishment and appointment of outside directors. |
|  | May 1998 | • Strengthening the voting rights of minority shareholders. |
|  | October 1998 | • Adoption of international accounting principles and standards and, as from 1999, the adoption of combined financial statements. |
| Strengthening accountability (Post-crisis Reform). | June 1998 | • Strengthening the legal liability of controlling owners. |
|  | September 1998 | • Allowing voting rights of institutional investors. |
|  | December 1998 | • Introduction of cumulative voting system. |
| Improvement of financial structure (Post-crisis Reform). | February 1998 | • Removal of restriction on capital infusion to affiliates. |
|  | April 1998 | • Agreement with banks to improve their capital structure. |
|  | September 1998 | • Introduction of asset-backed securities. |

| Streamlining business activities (Post-crisis Reform) | December 1999 (deadline) | • Requirement by firms to reach a 200% debt/equity ratio. |
| | June 1998 | • Introduction of the 'workout programs'. |
| | February 1998 | • Streamlining bankruptcy procedures. |
| | May 1998 | • Full liberalization of M&As. |
| | June 1998 | (1) Adoption of corporate-split system. |
| | | (2) Continued improvement in M&A procedures. |
| | | (3) Liberalization of foreign ownership of real estates. |
| | September 1998 | • Introduction of the 'big deals'. |

81

directly intervened in the specialization of business lines and the diffusion of the ownership structure. In June 1991, to induce more specialization, a core firm system was set up that excluded 76 core affiliates of the 30 largest *chaebols* from the application of the loan limit system. This also excluded firms with widely diffused ownership structure from the application of the loan management system. In October 1993, the core firm system was extended to a core business area system whereby affiliates in core business areas were exempted from the application of loan management and stock investment regulations. However, in January 1997, the business specialization policy was removed, with the abandonment of government-driven business specialization policy, thereby encouraging autonomous business specialization.

From February 1992, and also based on the loan management system, a policy regulating lending and temporary payment among affiliates was re-enforced, in particular, temporary payments to dominant stockholders and individuals specially linked to a *chaebol* was prohibited. Partial regulation on lending among affiliated firms, for example, cutting off outward leakage of capital not related to normal business activity, and blocking the misappropriation of borrowed money was also implemented.

During the later 1980s and the 1990s, the government increasingly resorted to antitrust laws in its attempts to regulate the *chaebols'* management behavior. Antitrust laws have also been used as a means to regulate unfair trade practices of big business conglomerates. In July 1992, regulations were introduced that addressed intra-conglomerate trade that restrained competition through the abuse of one's dominant position. In fact, six types of unfair trade practices were specified and investigations on actual cases of intra-conglomerate trade, covering 23 firms affiliated to eight *chaebols*, were conducted. However, the implementation of regulations on 'unfair trade practices' has often been exercised in a haphazard manner, and largely remains the prerogative of the government.

In April 1987, attempts were made to regulate the cross-ownership between affiliate firms within certain limits and the dissolution of any excessive cross-ownership was pursued. Furthermore, the prohibition of the holding company system prevented a holding company from governing affiliated firms, a measure which was reintroduced in 1998.[15] Regulation on equity investment in affiliated firms was also made that limited the total amount of equity investment in affiliated firms for the 30 largest *chaebol* to 25 per cent of the net assets of the investing firm. In February 1998, regulation on equity investment in affiliated firms was abolished but has been reintroduced as from April 2000.

Under the antitrust law, the government also established regulation on cross-debt guarantees among affiliate firms. In December 1992, it was announced that cross-debt guarantees of the 30 largest *chaebol* would be reduced to 100 per cent of equity capital by the end of March 1998. Consequently, following the financial crisis and recommendations by the IMF, there was a nation-wide prohibition on new cross-debt guarantees between affiliated firms and the full dissolution of all outstanding cross-debt guarantees was made effective at the end of March 2000.

Following the 1997 economic crisis, a new set of policy measures has been introduced not only to limit economic concentration but also directly to improve the efficiency and competitiveness of *chaebols*. In particular, to enhance transparency of *chaebol* management, in February 1998 the compulsory establishment and appointment of outside directors became effective, and in May 1998, the voting rights of minority shareholders were strengthened. Furthermore, in October 1998, firms were to adopt international accounting principles and standards and, as from 1999, consolidated financial statements are being produced. Around the same time, in order to strengthen accountability, firms have been asked to strengthen the legal liability of controlling owners by designating them as outside directors (June 1998) and to allow voting rights to institutional investors (September 1998).

Policies adopted to improve the financial structure include, as mentioned earlier, in February 1998, the removal of restrictions on capital infusion to affiliates with consideration to defend against hostile takeovers, which however was reinforced in Arpil 2000; in April 1998, the agreement with banks to improve the capital structure; in September 1998, the introduction of asset-backed securities, and; in December 1999, the requirement for the debt–equity ratio to be set at 200 per cent. 'Workout programs' have been introduced to help relieve the financial burden of almost insolvent firms.

In order to streamline business activities, the bankruptcy procedures were revised in February 1998. Also in May 1998, there was full liberalization of M&As and as from June 1998, laws were made to allow for the adoption of a corporate-split system, the improvement in the M&A procedures, and the liberalization of foreign ownership of real estates. 'Big deals' have also been encouraged.

## A2.   Notes on the 'Big Deals' and the 'Workout Program'

In this part, we will take a brief look at two aspects of corporate reforms which have been very much reminiscent of past industrial policies: namely, the 'big deals' that aim at improving business competitiveness by streamlining business activity, and the 'workout program' that aims at restructuring debtor firms before they become insolvent.

As part of the measures to revitalize the domestic M&A market, the government has strongly encouraged big deals among the large corporations. The big deals, or more precisely business swap deals, have been taking place in eight major industries including the semiconductor and automobile industries (see Table A4.2). The big deals, however, are controversial and run counter to the liberalization trend in that these represent government intervention, despite claims by the government that the deals stem from the *chaebols'* own initiative.[16] At the same time they do nothing to improve the property rights situation in Korea as these involve the forced merger and acquisition of companies.[17]

For the top six to 64 *chaebols* and other mid-sized corporations, an out-of-court workout program was introduced by an association of financial institutions. The workout program is a kind of private corporate reorganization process between debtor firms and creditor banks. It aims to restructure debtor firms before they become non-viable so that firms and banks can avoid the agony of corporate bankruptcy. In this workout program, the creditor banks allow a grace of payment and enforce debt–equity swaps as shown in Table A4.3.

The most important thing to note is that the process of these restructuring policies remains reminiscent of the past interventionist industrial restructuring attempts of the 1970s and 1980s.[18] In the big deals, the government forced M&As upon firms and provided deadlines by which they must be completed, and even determined the acquiring and acquired firms in advance. By doing so, the government underestimated the transaction costs of M&As as well as the differences in production technologies and the technological levels of the merged firms or the acquired and acquiring firms, leading to a time-consuming negotiation process. In addition, the government is in fact infringing on the property rights of the companies participating in the restructuring programs. With pre-set deadlines and strong governmental pressure, the participating companies had to go ahead with the forced M&As without having enough time to consider their viability. Consequently, the big deals may raise doubts as to the consistency of government policy: first, they may lead to a significant increase in market concentration, which could be in conflict with governmental regulations on economic concentration. Second, after the deals are complete, the question of whether the government should prohibit new entry in the industries affected by the big deals remains. What if the potential entrants are foreign investors?

The workout program, on the other hand, was initially put in place by the government with the intention of assisting weak corporations to recover from debt burdens which if left alone would have led to bankruptcy. Through this measure, a firm engaged in the workout program usually came to some agreement with their creditors so as to relieve their financial obligations, for example, through the provision of a grace period for debt repayment, or through debt-to-equity swaps, and so on. This was meant to allow the firm an opportunity to transform itself into a viable well-functioning firm. The result

Table A4.2  Progress in big deals

| Industry | Before big deals | Progress |
|---|---|---|
| Semiconductor | Samsung Electronic Co.<br>Hyundai Electronic Ind.<br>LG Semicon Co. | Samsung Electronic Co.<br>Hyundai and LG merged into one company (Equity share-out to be discussed later) |
| Petrochemicals | Samsung General Chemical Co.<br>Hyundai Petrochemical Co.<br>Hanwha Petrochemical Co.<br>Daelim Petrochemical Co. | Samsung and Hyundai merged into one company (foreign investment is under negotiation)<br>Hanwha and Daelim merged into one company |
| Aircraft parts | Samsung Aerospace Industries Co.<br>Daewoo Heavy Industries Co.<br>Hyundai Space & Aircraft Co. | Form a new, joint company and introduce foreign capital |
| Rolling stock | Hyundai Precision & Ind. Co.<br>Daewoo Heavy Ind. Co.<br>Hanjin Heavy Ind. Co. | Unified into one company |
| Power generation equipment | Korea Heavy Industries & Construction Co. (Hanjung)<br>Samsung Heavy Ind. Co.<br>Hyundai Heavy Ind. Co. | Unified into one company<br>Hanjung takes over Samsung's Business |
| Ship engine | Samsung Heavy Ind. Co.<br>Hyundai Heavy Ind. Co.<br>Hanjung | Hanjung takes over Samsung's Business |
| Oil refining | Hanwha Energy Co. | Acquired by Hyundai Oil Co. |
| Auto | Hyundai Motor Co.<br>Kia Motors | Samsung Motors was acquired by Renault<br>Various companies including Ford are negotiating to take over Daewoo motors |
| | Daewoo Motors<br>Samsung Motors | Hyundai Motor Co. took over Kia Motor Co. |

*Table A4.3  Debt restructuring plan and accomplishment of the workout program (100 million won, %)*

| | Grace of payment | | Debt–equity swaps (value) | Others | Total | New loans |
| --- | --- | --- | --- | --- | --- | --- |
| | Reduced interest rate | Normal interest rate | | | | |
| **Top 6-64 chaebols** | | | | | | |
| Plan | 204 228 | 33 119 | 40 495 | 18 995 | 296 897 | 14,744 |
| Accomplished | 194 914 | 30 533 | 31 696 | 19 602 | 276 745 | 13,795 |
| **Mid-sized firms** | | | | | | |
| Plan | 28 773 | 15 452 | 2 798 | 5 126 | 52 109 | 5,505 |
| Accomplished | 28 508 | 14 611 | 1 985 | 5 613 | 50 717 | 3,745 |
| **Total** | | | | | | |
| Plan (composition ratio) | 233 021 (66.8%) | 48 571 (13.9%) | 43 293 (12.4%) | 24 121 (6.9%) | 349 006 (100%) | 20,249 |
| Accomplished (% of the plan) | 223 442 (95.9%) | 45 144 (92.9%) | 33 681 (77.8%) | 25 215 (104.5%) | 327 462 (93.8%) | 17,450 (86.6%) |

*Source*: Financial Supervisory Service, November 1999.

of the program, however, is far from satisfactory as the arrangement in fact encouraged moral hazard to prevail. Moreover, the weak firms continued to participate in the market through dumping practices and this led to all sorts of distortions in the markets. Again, we observe the inefficiencies brought about by the direct intervention of the government.

As a last point, we warn that such instruments of the restructuring process pay too much attention to changing outward symptoms rather than addressing the causes of the problems by establishing correct institutional and incentive structures. Government-led restructuring which does not provide an appropriate institutional foundation will not have a lasting effect.

## NOTES

1. For a more detailed discussion of the application of a multi-stage decision-making process to the analysis of consumer behavior patterns, see Deaton and Muellbauer (1980), Part Two.
2. For a detailed theoretical and empirical examination regarding diversification-or-specialization behavior, see Chapters 5 and 6, and Jwa (1997).
3. Here the optimization of resource utilization by the *chaebol* in the second stage will, of course, contribute to the overall relative economic power of each *chaebol*. Therefore there is a mutually enhancing feedback relationship between the first and the second stages of the decision-making process. However, as far as the optimal allocation of resources in the national economy is concerned, the feedback process from the second to the first stage, even if it also ends up with greater concentration of economic power, does not cause more serious problems than the opposite case. This is because this process of concentration of economic power would not raise such concerns over the legitimacy of wealth accumulation by the *chaebol* although their possible monopolization of individual markets may still become an important issue for debate.
4. For further details and discussion, see the Appendix to this chapter.
5. See Appendix at the end of this chapter for further details.
6. See Chapter 1 note 1.
7. Some economists, however, point out that debt has simply been transformed into bonds and that although formal debts have decreased, the actual amount of money owed may have in fact increased. Along these lines, it is also argued that the achievement of 200 per cent debt-equity ratio is simply nothing more than a kind of accounting gimmick.
8. For details and evaluation of the 'workout program', see the Appendix at the end of the chapter.
9. In the turmoil of corporate restructuring, the Daewoo group, which at the time was the fourth largest *chaebol* in Korea, collapsed in 1999 and has entered the workout program.
10. For details and evaluation of the 'big deals', see the Appendix at the end of the chapter.
11. Strictly speaking, although we discuss cross-debt guarantees here, they are actually also part of the first stage decision-making process, as well as the second stage decision-making process. That is, cross-debt guarantees affect both the source of funds to the *chaebol*, and also affect behavioral decisions, for example, such as whether to diversify or expand current businesses.
12. The Modigliani–Miller (M–M) theorem states that 'the market value of any firm is independent of its capital structure', and 'the average cost of capital to any firm is completely independent of its capital structure'. Essentially, the M–M theorem argues that in an efficient capital market with no tax distortions the relative proportion of debt and equity in a corporate capitalization does not affect the total market value of the firm. However, this theorem should not be expected to hold in the real world characterized by information asymmetry, tax distortions and so on.

13. There has been some concern that legalizing the holding company system may deepen the concentration of economic power. Even though it may appear so if a holding company system is adopted, like any other organizational form such as the subsidiary and multidivisional system, it does nothing more than attempt to function efficiently. That is, it is a way to manage diversified economic activities, and as such is endogenously formed though the process of minimizing transaction costs. A rational discussion on the approval or disapproval of the establishment of the holding company system would require a systematic analysis of the relationship between economic concentration and corporate organization. However, theoretical or empirical studies in this field are still very scant. In my opinion, even such studies may not lead to a meaningful resolution of this issue because such economic organizations are in essence an endogenous variable. It is my judgment that curing the underlying causes determining firm behavior (diversification) and performance (economic concentration) is more rational and effective than directly regulating the management behavior of firms, that is, the choice of the holding company system.
14. See Chapter 7.
15. The holding company system has been recently reintroduced. See Chapter 1 note 1.
16. In fact, there was always strong government pressure for the *chaebols* to participate in these deals.
17. See chapter 5 for detailed discussion and analysis on the private property rights situation in Korea.
18. We shall argue later in the chapter that corporate governance systems can only be improved by adopting wider measures that essentially encourage the functioning of market disciplinary systems effectively to monitor and check corporate behavior.

# 5. The role of institutions and government in the evolution of *chaebols*

## 1. INTRODUCTION

This chapter analyzes the economic and political environment under which the *chaebols* emerged, as well as their effect on the behavioral and business pattern of the *chaebol*. Here, we also provide a glimpse of the future prospects for their structural change. Discussions in this chapter should shed more light on the nature of the first stage decision-making process of *chaebol* formation as well as the second stage decision-making process of *chaebol* behavior described in the previous chapter.

Throughout the chapter, it is important to bear in mind that a capitalist free market economy is, simply, an economic system where the spontaneous market order guides resource allocation under the given institutional framework in place. Hence the efficiency of market determination will depend largely on the characteristics of such institutions that constrain the way the market order evolves endogenously.

Economic institutions in a broad sense include rules and conventions that regulate the behavior and decision-making processes of economic agents. It is a recognized fact among economists that one of the most important institutions in the market economies is the property rights system. Market efficiency greatly hinges on the nature of the property rights system in place because it constrains the workings of the market system.

Recently, new-institutionalism[1] has emerged as an important new perspective in the field of economics. This new and exciting economic school of thought re-examines the importance of economic institutions and emphasizes institutional problems as fundamental and deserving of economists' urgent attention and analyses. Coase (1937, 1960, 1984), Alchian (1950), Alchian and Demsetz (1972), North (1990, 1992), and Eggertsson (1990) have brought, *inter alia*, important contributions to the field by emphasizing the existence of non-zero transaction costs in the real world economy and the importance of economic institutions, especially the property rights system, in determining economic behavior and performance in the economy. These pioneer authors have shaped the new-institutional approach and have returned economic institutions, considered only as a 'pale' background in the traditional neoclassical world, back to the forefront of 'vivid' economic analysis.

This chapter surveys Korea's property rights system. The relationship between the property rights system in place, and the formation and characteristics of Korean industrial organizations will then be discussed in some detail. This will clarify issues about the origins of the *chaebols*' business behavior. More specifically, the following two questions are asked: (1) could large firms, or *chaebols*, as they exist now be formed in the absence of the government's active industrial policy promoting large businesses for rapid economic growth? (2) What is the primary cause and reason for the rise of the managerial behavior of the *chaebols* as it is observed today?

In Section 2, the analytical framework linking new-institutional economics to property rights systems is discussed. In Section 3, a brief historical overview is presented using anecdotal evidence of the Korean property rights system from the second half of the Chosun dynasty to modern times. We observe that the feeble and insecure property rights system in Korea has probably contributed to the high transaction costs in the economy. In Section 4, we look into some further empirical (quantitative) evidence of the impact of property rights systems on economic organizations. In Section 5, we discuss the economic behavior of the *chaebols* and argue that their evolution can be traced partly to the nature of property rights protection. We conclude this chapter in Section 6 by suggesting briefly the implications of our discussion for industrial policy. The Appendix contains extracts from an important and classic book by Yak-Yong Jung, and observations made in the 1890s by Isabella Bird Bishop relating to the late Chosun-era practices of property rights protection.

## 2.   THE PERSPECTIVE OF NEW-INSTITUTIONAL ECONOMICS: THE PROPERTY RIGHTS SYSTEM AND ECONOMIC ORGANIZATION

In this section we begin by looking into the importance of transaction costs in relation to economic institutions, particularly the property rights system. Then we present the link between property rights systems and the formation of economic organizations. Lastly, we look at the influence of property rights systems on economic development.

Under the neo-classical assumption of zero transaction costs, the issue of economic institutions is absent and any differences, especially in property rights systems, are not treated in the analyses. The new-institutional economics explicitly recognizes and introduces non-zero transaction costs, where differences in economic institutions inherently and systematically affect the size of such costs and thereby also affect resource allocation and economic performance. Moreover, an additional innovation of the new-institutional approach is not to treat economic institutions as given but as endogenously evolving. This perspective is a clear break from the traditional neoclassical approach where institutions are regarded as exogenously given and outside economic analysis.[2]

Essentially, the property rights system is an economic order that defines the inter-relationship between the various economic actors regarding the use of scarce economic resources. Such a system aims to delineate the entitlement of exclusive rights to particular economic resources, thereby resolving in advance potential disputes concerning the issue of who has the right to use and dispose of which resources.

In order to discuss the relationship between property rights systems and the structure of economic organizations in the new-institutional approach, it will be useful to start with the following remarks by North (1990, p. 67).

> Firms come into existence to take advantage of profitable opportunities, which will be defined by the existing set of constraints. With insecure property rights, poorly enforced laws, barriers to entry, and monopolistic restrictions, profit-maximizing firms will tend to have short time horizons and little fixed capital, and will tend to be small scale. The most profitable businesses may be in trade, redistributive activities, or the black market. Large firms with substantial fixed capital will exist only under the umbrella of government protection with subsidies, tariff protection, and payoff to the polity – a mixture hardly conducive to productive efficiency.

The fact that property rights are not securely protected implies that market contracts are not likely to be fully honored and observed. If a formal system of property rights protection is neither clearly established nor fully enforced, even though clearly defined, excessive transaction costs will make the formation of large firms more difficult. Forming a large business organization will inevitably require formal as well as informal economic links among various individuals and groups of individuals. Therefore, under an insecure property rights system and with high transaction costs, it is extremely difficult for large business firms to emerge in an economy out of natural economic forces.

The potentially high transaction costs resulting from an insecure property rights system, however, may induce efforts on the part of economic agents to minimize such costs by adopting types of economic organizations that will mitigate such costs, for example, through the formation of small firms, especially in the non-manufacturing trading and distribution sector. Furthermore, such small firms do not require large initial investments which need to be locked up for long periods of time as is typically the case when setting up large firms in the manufacturing sector.

Thus, the weakened enforcement of property rights tends to increase transaction costs, which, in turn, creates an environment more favorable to small firms and short-term liquid asset investment rather than to large business organizations and long-term fixed investments. These assumptions can be extended to the issue of managerial behavior. Recently, Fukuyama (1995, 1996) introduced the concept of social capital as a part of human capital in a broad sense.[3] Social capital is seen to encourage the mutual trust and cooperation between social members in forming common solidarity, and as social capital accumulates, this mutual trust becomes deeper with formal economic organizations becoming more active relative to informal organizations. According to this view, a strongly family-oriented social tradition as a particular form of social capital tends to create a social environment where members are more likely to distrust non-family members, and as such tends to discourage the formation of large economic organizations.[4] In this way, the view of new institutionalism is supported where informal constraints such as customs and traditions are seen to affect the amount of transaction costs that the society will incur and therefore will systematically influence the structure of economic organization. In sum, a country having an insecure property rights system and characterized by low levels of mutual trust among non-family members, tends to favor economic organizations relatively dominated by family-oriented management structures that are closed to outsiders, and which usually have no separation between ownership and control. This is in contrast to modern business management structures, which have both specialized managers and the separation of ownership and control. We summarize these characteristics in Table 5.1.

It is important to realize that different property rights systems affect accordingly not only the size of transaction costs but also 'the will to economize'. First, it is important that a property rights system should be designed so as to encourage individual economic agents to economize in order for that system to bring about positive contributions to economic development. Second, since economies with high transaction costs are most likely to result in poor economic performance, property rights systems should seek to minimize transaction costs in order to induce optimal allocation of resources

According to the new-institutional approach (North, 1981; Wallis and North, 1986), it turns out that the secure establishment of property rights systems has been the most crucial factor in determining long-term trends of economic development throughout economic history. North (1992), in fact, argued that centralized bureaucracies in monarchic systems tended to allow only very limited realms of private activity, including the protection of

*Table 5.1  Degree of property rights protection and economic organization*

| | Transaction cost | Type of firms | Fields in which economic activity is promoted | Firm management behavior | Economic performance level of development) |
|---|---|---|---|---|---|
| Weak system and protection of property rights | • high | • small/ medium firms<br>• self-managed firms | • marketing and distribution, which do not require fixed investment (black market transaction) | • family management<br>• unlisted (closed management)<br>• union of ownership and management | • low |
| Transparent system and protection of property rights | • low | • large firms | • industry, which needs large-scale fixed investment (manufacturing industry, etc.) | • professional management<br>• listed (open management)<br>• division between ownership and management | • high |

property rights and individual freedom, compared to decentralized feudalistic political systems. Also, according to North (1990), countries under the tradition of Spanish centralized bureaucratic monarchism exhibit *poorer* long-term economic performances relative to countries under the English tradition of decentralized feudalistic monarchism. He attributes this phenomenon to the greater uncertainty of property rights protection under the former system. In this context we may explain why feudalistic Japan, compared to Korea and China who were both under a centralized bureaucratic system, had achieved modernization earlier and with more success.[5]

## 3.   ANECDOTAL OBSERVATIONS OF THE WEAKNESS IN PROPERTY RIGHTS PROTECTION IN KOREA

### 3.1   Dilution of Property Rights Protection in the Chosun Dynasty

The private property rights system has been a prominent feature in England for a long time. The formation of modern capitalistic systems involved the establishment of various laws throughout history protecting private property rights through efforts by newly emerging bourgeois classes and citizens to resist irregular and excessive taxes levied upon them for financing wars and the extravagant lifestyles of royal families and aristocrats. The common element included in most declarations, such as the Petition of Right (1628), the Puritan Revolution (1642), the Glorious Revolution (1688), and the Bill of Rights (1689, virtually depriving kings of their absolute monarchical rights) is that they all contributed to the emergence of the private property rights system as the foremost principle of a new civil society by developing the new principle that 'kings cannot levy taxes without the Parliament's approval.'[6]

Unlike in the English tradition, rulers in the Chosun dynasty had established a centralized monarchic system from the very beginning. Consequently, there were no political processes guaranteeing the protection of private property rights. Centralized bureaucratic systems tend to have more feeble protection of individual private property relative to feudal or constitutional monarchic systems. Viewed from this perspective, it may be surmised that the protection of private property rights during the Chosun dynasty, with its centralized bureaucratic system under a monarchy, was much weaker than in most countries in Europe under feudalism.

The tax system in particular became extremely disorderly during the last century of the Chosun dynasty, and from the nineteenth century a few bureaucrats having kinship with the king seized virtual political power.[7] In fact by the mid-eighteenth century, the tax system constituted a tripartite system composed of a land tax, a military tax and a grain exchange system. Four important features of the operation of this tripartite system are as follows.

First, provinces were responsible for the collection of taxes and each were assigned a certain amount to collect. This assignment was, however, made without proper consideration for the number of taxpayers and/or the geographical characteristics of each province. Moreover, the tax system allowed provincial heads and bureaucrats to collect taxes at their own discretion and consequently residents were extorted and forced to pay high tax burdens under the arbitrary will of bureaucrats.

Second, the degree to which property rights were diluted because of the confusion in the tax system became extreme. For example, it was frequently the case that not only were additional taxes[8] and fees levied on top of regular taxes, but taxes were also levied on waste- or fallow land. Taxes on land were often raised in order to make up for the public funds that were unlawfully appropriated by public officials.

Third, the tax system was extremely unstable. The *Kyun-yuk* Act, or the 'Equal Military Burden Act', was originally intended to alleviate the burdens caused by the military tax. The Act imposed a given quantity of cotton fabric for military use for each grown male unless he volunteered for military service. However, it soon lost its original purpose and the tax was levied upon dead men, as if they were alive, as well as on children. If the assigned tax was not paid on the due date, then relatives and even neighbors of the delinquents were forced into payment. This type of extreme instability in the tax system caused people to roam around without permanently settling down and when possible, to rely on a powerful family-member for support.

The instability of the tax system can further be observed in the grain exchange mechanism. This was an institution intended to alleviate the grain shortages during the sowing season by giving out grain loans to farmers and having them repay after the harvest season. This system, however, soon degenerated into the most notorious taxing method of the tripartite system, being infected with various types of extortion that included: (a) the manipulation of the exchange rate, including arbitrary price manipulation; (b) switching the kind of grain, including forced one-to-one exchange of the same quantity of high grade for low grade grain – or of the preferred kind of grain (rice) for the ones less desired (barley or bean), and; (c) confiscation of grain without any prior loans.

Such anarchy in the tripartite tax system in the later Chosun dynasty is well described in *A Guide to Shepherding People (Mok Min Shim Suh)*, written in 1818 by Yak-Yong Jung, one of the most famous scholars who dearly wanted to reform the state at that time. The Appendix to this chapter contains abstracts from this classical work.

Isabella Bird Bishop's historical masterpiece on Korea entitled *Korea and*

*Her Neighbors* contains a vivid picture of Korea's economic and social status in the nineteenth century and includes the nature of her property rights protection as well. An understanding of the nature of the property rights system in place at the time can also be derived from the detailed and interesting pages of her book. In particular, it is interesting to contrast the farming class in Korea under the auspices of the *yang-ban* and the Koreans in Vladivostok who enjoyed a higher standard of livelihood made possible by the comparably better property right protection at the time. The Appendix at the end of this chapter contains excerpts from her book.

## 3.2    Examples of Private Property Rights Dilution in Korea's Modern Era

Turning to the modern era of private property rights dilution in Korea, we may begin with a discussion of the fall of the landlord class in the 1950s. We then discuss the brief period of the privatization of banks in the 1950s, and the confiscation of private banks by the government in the 1960s. We also look into the emergency measures for stable growth as adopted through the decree of 3 August 1972. The adverse effects on the property rights system of the structural adjustment policies of the latter half of the 1980s and the introduction of the real name financial transaction system are also discussed, as well as the general lapse of fair law enforcement.

It is a well-known and peculiar fact that the agricultural capitalists in Korea failed to transform themselves into industrial capitalists. The crucial reason for the fall of the landlord class lies in the fact that the compensation method used for land reform in the 1950s was so unfair as to discourage land ownership and as a result seriously compromised the notion of property rights. Landlords were often forced to surrender their land involuntarily on prescribed and unfair compensation terms. Furthermore, both complicated procedures and the post-Korean War disorder made it very difficult to redeem land bonds. Inflation after the war also made it common for agricultural capitalists to dispose of their bonds at prices that were 30 to 70 per cent of the face value in order to sustain themselves. As a result, contrary to the original intention of the government, which was to induce the transformation of agricultural capital into industrial capital, it was indeed very rare for agricultural capitalists successfully to establish modern firms.[9]

In the 1950s, following the liberation from Japanese rule and the Korean War, the new Korean government privatized all banks that were under Japanese ownership. However, privatization was not conducted in a fair manner as stock was allocated *not* to the highest bidder based solely on a public auction *but rather* to a lower bidder based, usually, on personal favoritism and connections. However, things changed abruptly as the military government seized power in 1961, when it confiscated the stocks of those banks held by big businesses under the official explanation of punishing 'unfair wealth accumulation'. Furthermore, an upper limit on bank stock holdings allowable to private concerns was strictly enforced and the government regained a majority stockholding in order to control bank management and thereby to finance economic development. It is also interesting to note that this incident set the precedent for many similar measures thereafter that infringe private property rights in the name of promoting economic development.

In 1972, the Korean government declared emergency measures through a presidential decree to rapidly improve economic conditions required for more profitable businesses. This included the deferment of firms' curb market liabilities, a drastic cut in interest rates for firms borrowing in the official financial market, special government lending at preferential rates, and comprehensive tax cuts for firms. Especially important among these measures were payment deferments for unofficial market borrowings,[10] which included loans from relatives, friends and neighbors as well as from professional curb market lenders. These measures infringed on the individual property rights of nearly everyone to some extent. In addition, across the board interest rate cuts on loans in official financial markets became not only a serious infringement on financial property rights but also a precedent that the Korean government repeated thereafter in the name of reviving business activity whenever firms complained about hardship from foreign competition.

The government enacted various structural adjustment policies from 1986 to 1988 in order to deal with the insolvency problem of large businesses due to over-investment during the heavy and chemical industry promotion drive of the 1970s that was adopted in order to improve Korea's industrial competitiveness. However, the criteria used for selecting troubled firms as outlined in those policies were so broadly set that there remained much room allowing for governmental discretion to play an even bigger role than transparent rules and this in turn generated far-reaching negative implications for property rights protection. Target firms were selected on the basis not of their financial solvency alone, but rather for industrial policy concerns such as upgrading industrial structures and promoting the specialization of *chaebols*. The process through which the government selected firms and forced them to undergo ownership changes, in particular, was neither transparent nor easily acceptable not only to the concerned parties but also to the general public, thereby resulting in a lot of controversies. For example, the government forced the dissolution of one of the big *chaebols*, Kukjae, but the decision was criticized thereafter as being politically oriented, that is, based not on an economic but rather political rationale.

On 12 August 1993, the Korean government introduced the real name financial transaction system[11] as a part of the reform of the income tax system and this was scheduled to be fully effective from 1997. This was done in part to prevent bribery practices in political activities. The government requires that information on all financial transactions above a certain amount be made available at all times, not only to tax authorities but also to those officials investigating sources of financial funds. This requirement, however, increases the possibility of governmental confiscation of private financial property of almost all major financial asset holders for the following reasons: (1) some major financial asset holders have been known to be connected to illegal activities such as bribery, which was widespread under past authoritarian rule; and (2) almost all financial asset holders are suspected of having violated the tax law to some extent due to its complexity and/or arbitrary application.

As a result, the real name financial transactions system runs the risk of increasing uncertainty about financial property rights. It may be desirable to minimize that risk through an open commitment on the part of the government to use the information not for political purposes but for tax purposes and for criminal investigations only. In this context, however, it is important to understand that the use of pseudo-names made bribery easier but did not cause it. As such, the real name financial transactions system is not the most effective means to eliminate bribery. Rather, bribery is the by-product of non-transparent political and/or government regulation systems that are prone to rent-seeking, and one therefore has to find a cure for bribery primarily through institutional reforms in those areas.

Law enforcement has been emphasized as an important part of economic institutions together with formal as well as informal institutional constraints (North, 1992). Moreover, even if a formal institution with an ideal economic incentive structure is legalized, that institution will be of no use if it is not fully and fairly enforced. Korea has been notorious for introducing many important economic institutions no less ideal than those in advanced countries but without due attention to the enforcement of those institutions. From the National Assembly, the nation's lawmaker, to the government's law enforce-ment authorities and administrative officials enforcing various government regulations at the lowest levels, the importance of transparent and fair legal enforcement does not seem to be well understood. Rather concern for political and administrative convenience in law enforcement has dominated concern for fairness so that even ordinary citizens have become very insensitive to the issue of fair and strict law enforcement. However, because the government can always enforce a particular law more strictly if it is convenient and beneficial to its goals, the situation tends to create a lot of uncertainties about formal economic institutions. The tax law can be regarded as a typical example.[12]

The historical experiences of property rights dilution presented in this section have led the general public into believing that society is not functioning properly or desirably under the rule of law, and in particular, that a proper property rights system is as yet not well established in Korea. It is important, however, not to lose sight of the fact that Korea's economic institutions, including her property rights system, have become strongly influenced by informal constraints rather than formal rules, which in turn has increased uncertainty about the property rights system. We shall further elaborate this point after we have looked at some of the statistical evidence on property rights systems in Korea and other countries as well.

## 4. PROPERTY RIGHTS SYSTEM AND ECONOMIC ORGANIZATIONS: SUMMARY OF EMPIRICAL EVIDENCE

In the previous sections, we discussed the nature of the property rights system in Korea through selected historical experiences. In this section, we provide empirical or statistical evidence relating to Korea's property rights system, transaction costs and industrial organization. This section is based to a large extent on quantitative work by Jwa (2001).

### 4.1  Empirical Evidence on Transaction Costs and Firm Size

There are various ways to measure the degree of property rights protection that can be found in the literature. Clague *et al.* (1996) use the *proportion of deposited money* in M2 as a proxy measure for the degree of property rights protection. Factors related to property rights protection such as political stability and the nature of the political regime are seen to affect the weight of the country's deposited money. For example, it is argued that a country characterized by political instability will have more people preferring to hold cash rather than deposited money,[13] the latter being understood as *contract-intensive money*. Similarly, we use the *cash ratio* in broadly defined money (M2) as the measure for the lack of property rights protection and the extent of transaction costs that may be saved if property rights are fully protected. That is, the higher the cash ratio, the lower the proportion of deposited money, the lower the degree of property rights protection, and the higher the transaction cost in the economy concerned.

Table 5.2 provides a summary of the cash ratios in M2 for 14 selected countries. The table also shows the share of self-employed to total employed persons (SEP) in the non-agricultural sector for the same countries, a proxy for the proportion of small firms in the country, which may be compared taking into account the level of transaction costs in the economy.

First of all, we find that the cash ratios are largely consistent with the

*Table 5.2 Cash ratio and SEP for selected countries (period averages)*

| | Cash ratio 1970–94 | SEP[a] 1970–93 |
|---|---|---|
| Australia | 8.29 | 11.60 |
| Canada | 7.61 | 6.96 |
| France | 8.48[b] | 10.60 |
| Germany | 10.18 | 8.14 |
| Italy | 9.15 | 21.68 |
| Japan | 8.36 | 13.00 |
| Korea | 13.14 | 26.87 |
| Norway | 11.07[b] | 6.71[c] |
| Portugal | 13.95 | 14.87 |
| Spain | 11.09 | 16.82 |
| Sweden | 10.70 | 5.46 |
| Taiwan | 9.30 | 21.54 |
| UK | 10.16[b] | 8.82 |
| USA | 7.02 | 7.26 |

*Notes*:  [a] SEP: Self-employed as a proportion of total employment in non-agricultural sector.
[b] Average form 1970 to 1993.
[c] Average from 1972 to 1993.

*Source*:  Jwa (2001).

perspective of new-institutional economics. For example, the cash ratio tends to be rather high in Portugal and Spain, countries characterized by North (1990) as under the Spanish tradition of centralized bureaucracy with weak property rights protection. The cash ratio is also high in Sweden, Norway and Korea. However, the cash ratio was found to be relatively low in the United States, Canada and Japan, all of which are characterized as low transaction costs countries by North (1990). It is observed that, during the 1970s to 1990s, the cash ratio in Korea was the highest among the OECD countries, second only to Portugal, and is consistent with the poor state of the private property rights system that results in high transaction costs as described above.

Second, the index of the weight of self-employed to total employed (SEP) is used to study the relationship between economic organizations and transaction costs. This follows directly from our argument in Section 2 suggesting that self-employment might be a kind of business organization that is more easily formed in an economic environment where large economic organizations are difficult to form due to insecure property rights protection and high transaction costs. Interestingly, international comparisons of the index ranked Korea among the highest, even higher than countries such as Italy and Taiwan which are well-known for being dominated by small and medium-sized firms.

We quickly test the hypothesis consistent with the view of new-institutional economics that the proportion of small firms in the economy will be positively correlated with transaction costs. Specifically, we regressed the ratio of the self-employed to total employment (SEP), which is used as a proxy for the proportion of small and medium-sized firms in the economy, on the proxy for transaction cost (the cash ratio) and per capita income.[14] We found that a greater proportion of small and medium-sized firms were exhibited in countries with higher transaction costs, and this tended to reflect the lower levels of economic development.

In sum, the cash ratio defined in a broad concept of money can be a useful proxy for transaction costs incurred due to the uncertainty of property rights protection, and Korea is seen as a relatively high transaction cost country. We have also supported through regression results the views of new-institutional economics that transaction costs have a positive impact on the proportion of small-sized firms in the economy.

## 4.2   Empirical Evidence on Private Property Rights Protection and Firm Size

Table 5.3 shows the individual property rights (IPR) index, which measures the effectiveness of government protection of individual property rights. We used the International Country Risk Guide (ICRG), where an index has been obtained from the average value of five indices, namely: the rule of law, government corruption, expropriation risk, quality of bureaucracy, and the repudiation of contracts by government.[15] As reported in Jwa (2001) and consistent with the expectations of new-institutional economics, the IPR index tended to be low in countries such as Portugal and Spain, which as mentioned above were characterized as high transaction cost countries by North. The IPR index was also low for Italy, Taiwan and Korea, all described as low-trust countries by Fukuyama (1996), but was higher for the UK, the US, Canada and Japan, all described as low transaction cost countries by North (1990) and as high-trust countries by Fukuyama (1996).[16]

Comparing the individual property rights system (IPR index) with the proportion of small and medium-sized firms (SEP index of Table 5.2), it can be observed that Korea has the highest self-employment ratio, while maintaining the lowest IPR index among the countries selected for analysis. Italy, Spain and Portugal also have relatively high self-employment ratios and low IPR indices. However, Sweden, Norway, Canada, the US and the UK, all have relatively low self-employment ratios but enjoy higher than average IPR

*Table 5.3     Inter-country comparison of individual property rights systems index*

| | Individual property rights (IPR) systems index (period average for 1982–90) |
|---|---|
| Australia | 9.33 |
| Canada | 9.80 |
| France | 9.47 |
| Italy | 8.33 |
| Japan | 9.67 |
| Korea | 6.05 |
| Norway | 9.73 |
| Portugal | 8.39 |
| Spain | 8.47 |
| Sweden | 10.00 |
| Taiwan | 8.46 |
| UK | 9.67 |
| USA | 9.63 |
| Average | 9.00 |

*Source*:   Barro and Sala-I-Martin (1995, ch. 12), which quotes the ICRG.

indices. This suggests a negative relationship between the self-employment ratio and the IPR index.

The relationship between the two variables has also been confirmed in a cross-country regression analysis, similar to that of Section 4.1.[17] Regression results seem to lend strong support to the expected negative impact the IPR would have on the weight of small and medium-sized firms in the economy. In other words, the higher the income and the more secure the protection for individual property rights, the lower the ratio of self-employed to total employed persons. Thus, we have confirmed, both directly and indirectly, the importance of property rights systems in explaining the evolution of economic organizations, and moreover our discussions lend strong support to the new-institutional economics approach.

## 5.   LACK OF PROPERTY RIGHTS PROTECTION AND BEHAVIOR OF *CHAEBOLS*

Our discussion above and the empirical evidence cited above have shown that the credibility of the Korean property rights system was damaged through the abuse and disorder in the tax system as well as through active governmental development policies. Empirical comparisons using cross-country data also suggest that the Korean economy belongs to the category of high-transaction-cost economies where the protection of property rights is very weak, and therefore the proportion of small and medium firms is relatively high. This is an interesting point because it is a common perception in Korea that large business corporations are dominant and that economic power is highly concentrated within a few *chaebol*, which unfortunately has been the basis for the implementation of various economic policies in the past.

In this section, we interpret the formation and behavior of the *chaebols* as an issue of economic organization under conditions where private property rights protection is unstable and as a result transaction costs remain very high. This argument has important implications in the search for a new paradigm of public policy toward the *chaebols*.

According to the empirical analysis briefly described in the preceding section, the proportion of large business firms in Korea is neither extraordinarily high nor low. Rather, the ratio of large firms in Korea is, in fact, low. Given these arguments and the fact that the proportion of small and medium firms in Korea is relatively high, one may raise the question of how large firms and *chaebols* were formed and developed under a lack of private property rights protection and the existence of high transaction costs. An answer to this puzzle is provided here.

## 5.1    The Process of *Chaebol* Formation

Our discussion above implies that the lack of property rights protection and high transaction costs in Korea constitute unfavorable conditions for large firms to emerge, let alone flourish. Then what explains the birth and growth of the *chaebols* in Korea given our argument that high transaction costs discourage the formation of large firms and their operation? We note that only when some external entity guarantees the protection of property rights related to massive long-term investments and when contractual arrangements for those investments are well enforced by that entity can large firms thrive.

In Chapters 2 and 4, we described in detail the process and implications of the first stage of *chaebol* formation. Essentially, the Korean government, as has been fully discussed in Chapter 2, promoted and protected large-scale heavy and chemical industries by picking out particular entrepreneurs and providing them with subsidies, entry barriers and preferential bank loans, among other measures, according to its policy for rapid economic industrialization. Through this process the government, in exchange for receiving quasi-taxes and political support, provided property rights protection with regards to large fixed investments by firms. The role of the government in this process was to provide an environment in which large firms could form and prosper. The government selectively guaranteed the protection of property rights of large firms through the exercise of the state's coercive and discretionary powers to make up for the lack of overall institutional protection and enforcement of property rights. In other words, in Korea, the government opted to use its administrative powers directly rather than adopt a more transparent method of improving formal and informal institutions.

## 5.2　Family-Centered Managerial Behavior of *Chaebols*

Although the government's strong industrialization drive has facilitated the emergence and growth of selected firms, the managerial behavior of these firms usually does not reflect the professional management style observed in organizations where property rights are institutionally well protected. Instead, the management structure of *chaebols* are family-centered and closed. At the time of the *chaebols'* formation and thereafter, the long-standing authoritarian government had pursued strong interventionist policies that included revoking the property rights of large firms at its discretion, as exemplified by various incidences discussed in Section 5.3.2. This means that the government not only promoted large firms but was also the source of uncertainty over property rights as far as the owner-managers of big corporations were concerned. Uncertain property rights protection tends to hinder the evolution of managerial behavior from traditional family-centered control to modern professional management. In fact, family-centered managerial behavior seems to be a preferred response by entrepreneurs when faced with high transaction costs so as to avoid, in particular, those costs that may be incurred if firms are managed openly and formally. Furthermore, it may also be noted that family-centered and closed management behavior provides a good environment for the existence of favoritism by the government or politician toward corporations.

## 5.3　Excessive Diversification of the *Chaebols*

As previously mentioned in Chapter 3, the far-reaching diversification into unrelated businesses has been criticized as one of the evils of the *chaebols'* behavior. We argue here that this behavior seems to have originated from, among other things, the lack of property rights protection on the part of the government and the consequent response by *chaebol* owners to protect themselves. As has been already explained, in the name of industrial rationalization, the ownership of large firms was often determined not according to market principles or through the redemption of claims by banks, but rather through the political and discretionary judgment of the government. This raised doubts about the equity and transparency of the process through which new owners were chosen. This type of intervention, of course, has greatly contributed to the attenuation of the transparency of the property rights system.

Hence it has often been the case that the government's arbitrary political decision to disregard private property rights has been blamed for causing many bankruptcies, irrespective of whether the real reason may in fact be due to poor management. General public opinion also supports such a conception. The dismantling of Kukjae in 1985 is a case in point. This induced firms to adopt the managerial strategy of increasing their size so as to reduce the likelihood of being declared bankrupt. The result of this strategy, especially under the constraint of the small Korean domestic market, could be 'unreasonably' deep diversification into various types of businesses.[18]

Viewed from this perspective, many cases of *chaebol* diversification can be interpreted as examples of this managerial strategy. For example, *chaebols'* efforts to enter the mass media industries can be viewed in the same context. Owning firms in the mass media industry appears, in this context, to be a very good investment to defend oneself against the threat of losing one's private property. The influence of the mass media on public opinion and political sentiment implies that owning businesses in the mass media can buy a significant degree of power to protect oneself from arbitrary governmental intervention into private property rights.

## 5.4   Anti-*chaebol* Sentiment and its Impact on *Chaebol* Policy

Economic policies concerning the *chaebols* cannot be formulated and implemented purely according to economic logic, especially because of the presence of what is called the 'anti-*chaebol* sentiment'. This includes, for example, government policies such as inducing *chaebols* to specialize in specific industries, reserving certain industries only for small and medium firms and prohibiting large firms from entering such industries. These policies are hardly rationalized by economic logic.

Furthermore, it is difficult to deny that the public's anti-*chaebol* leanings have been an important reason behind the public's demand for *chaebol* ownership restructuring. The government has been criticized for granting the *chaebols* permission to enter new industries or participate in the privatization of public enterprises and thereby creating the potential for increased economic concentration. It must be understood, however, that economics has never taught us that size itself can be a reason for regulating the activities of a firm.[19]

The anti-*chaebol* sentiment held by the Korean people is deeply rooted and variegated. Perhaps, looking back into the past, these feelings originate from the deep-rooted hatred of commerce and manufacturing in Confucian thought and the sympathy for absolute equality, which runs counter to the concept of wealth accumulation according to each individual's ability in the capitalistic market systems. Looking into the more recent past, the 30 years of government-led economic development raised suspicions in the general public's mind that the *chaebols* have accumulated illegitimate wealth through connections with despotic political leaders. This has been described as a prominent feature in the first stage of the decision-making process of *chaebol* formulation in Chapter 4. Distrust regarding the process of wealth accumulation contributed directly to the formation of the anti-*chaebol* sentiment.

The problem is not whether this sentiment is right or wrong. Its mere existence brings an important institutional problem. It is an informal type of institution ranking among others such as culture, traditions, common practices, customs and way of thinking. This sentiment plays the role of an informal constraint. Even if there does not exist any formally written anti-*chaebol* law, once people come to possess such a negative sentiment towards the *chaebols*, government policies are bound to be influenced by it. Therefore, the anti-*chaebol* sentiment amounts to an institution regulating the *chaebols* that is much stronger than any formally coded anti-*chaebol* law regulating their behavior. Current *chaebol* policy-making in Korea faces a very difficult dilemma of whether to take into consideration the general public's anti-*chaebol* sentiment. As a result, the content of government policy on the *chaebols* is greatly restrained by this informal constraint.

What can be expected of the organizational behavior of the *chaebols* given the strength of such anti-*chaebol* sentiment? First of all, the fact that the anti-*chaebol* sentiment works as a powerful informal institution means that any formally written law regarding private property rights may not guarantee the actual protection of property rights. From the standpoint of the *chaebols*, this means that it is difficult for them to trust the government's efforts to fairly enforce a proper property rights system. Therefore the widespread anti-*chaebol* sentiment and the political pandering to such a feeling are tantamount, for the *chaebols*, to an actual lack of property rights protection. In this situation, it is quite natural for them to seek various ways of self-protection.

In such an economic environment, large firms will bear high transaction costs and they will seek the most cost-efficient means to protect their property rights in order to survive. For example, family-centered management, certain behavioral characteristics of *chaebols* aimed at acquiring political power or establishing political connections, their 'excessive' diversification strategy, and the ownership of the mass media can all be interpreted as an aggressive effort to obtain cost-efficient property rights protection. The strategy of building strong connections between the *chaebols* and political power aims to influence the general direction of *chaebol* policy. The *chaebols'* strategy of increasing their size and range of business activities, on the other hand, aims at reducing the risk of being driven out of the market in the event of their becoming unsound. And finally, as we have argued, the strategy of entering the mass media industry is aimed at using the mass media industry as a shield against anti-*chaebol* sentiment and other hostile government policy.

However, when we reflect on the background of the emergence of the anti-*chaebol* sentiment, it seems that, contrary to the original intention, efforts by the *chaebols* to protect themselves tend to somehow strengthen such sentiments. Unfortunately, one cannot exclude the possibility that the vicious circle of stronger anti-*chaebol* feelings and stronger pursuance of self-protection measures have become entwined and will both get worse.

## 6.  REORIENTATION OF GOVERNMENT POLICIES TOWARD BIG BUSINESSES

Following the discussions in this chapter, certain questions arise regarding a new paradigm of public policies for big businesses, which can help promote a well-functioning capitalistic market economy. First of all, is it really the case that Korea's economic development was more successful because the country's policies toward businesses was conducive to the creation of large firms? It may be the case that in the absence of such a policy, Korea may have ended up with an industrial structure in which small and medium firms would have played a major role. In relation to this, one may also ponder as to whether large firms in Korea can survive in a future characterized by open and global competition. Second, given the fact that institutional protection of private property rights in Korea, especially in relation to the *chaebols*, has been greatly lacking, what should be done to remedy this situation?

Regarding the first question, it is important to recognize that the relative superiority of an industrial structure composed of large firms to an alternative industrial structure composed of small and medium firms cannot be determined unambiguously. The economic environment at the time when Korea began its large-firm promotion policy implies that small and medium firms may have had better chances of economic survival. However, given the fact that large firms had already been promoted through the government's active industrial policy, they have contributed more than small and medium firms to Korea's economic development. As has already been examined, not only do some advanced countries have higher proportions of small and medium firms than Korea, but developing countries such as Taiwan have also demonstrated high rates of economic growth as well. Hence, determining which industrial structure is superior is not a simple matter. Furthermore, if we take an evolutionary viewpoint, each country's economic structure is the mixed product of its particular economic and institutional environment and governmental policies. Therefore, to draw any general conclusion regarding the relative superiority of an industrial structure would not be easy or even desirable.

Some may think that large amounts of investment contribute to economic development because of scale economies and hence argue in favor of the superiority of large firms over small and medium ones. However, we may also question whether such large firms, created and maintained through governmental protection, can survive over long periods of time without such governmental protection or institutional reform that can remedy the insecure property rights system. We are presently witnessing the strong and irreversible trend of globalization and consequently the weakening of the governments' ability to protect and intervene in market economies. Under the influence of these trends, unless institutional reforms regarding formal and informal property rights protection are successfully achieved, it will be very difficult positively to assess the long-run sustainability of the *chaebols*. Hence, it is important to reform the property rights system in such a way as to allow even the big corporations to evolve and prosper spontaneously.

In this regard, for future growth, economic reform should be continuously and steadily aimed at strengthening the formal property rights system and enforcing it more firmly in order to better establish it and improve its transparency. It is our only hope that informal institutions such as culture, tradition, customs, conventions and public opinion will assist in that process as well even if this process takes a considerable amount of time. We have to keep in mind that whereas we may change the content of formal rules quite easily, it is far more difficult to change informal institutions accordingly. According to new-institutionalism, institutional constraints do not change easily because they, especially informal ones, show long-run path dependence due to their own economies of scale, economies of scope, network economies and complementarity. This implies that even if the government announces the end of arbitrary regulation and protection of firms in favor of the formal protection of private property rights, the general public's ingrained perception of weak private property rights protection will not easily fade away. Therefore it is important to keep in mind that changing this perception will take a lot more effort and time.

Improving institutions related to the property rights system also has other implications. If it is desirable for the *chaebols* to focus only on economic efficiency, it is crucial for them not to worry much about any arbitrary encroachments of their private property rights by an external agent, including the government. It is also important for them to believe that they will be judged only according to their market performance and that the market alone will determine their fate. All these can be achieved only through the firm establishment of private property rights protection. In particular, we should keep in mind that almost all regulations that appear arbitrary in fact represent encroachments of private property rights in one way or the other. We should, therefore, be more aggressive about trying to reduce the amount of government intervention and instead pursue more liberal policies.

Finally, it is critical that we should be able to remedy the widespread anti-*chaebol* sentiment that reinforces the current high-transaction-cost corporate environment. In order to achieve this, we must resolve not only the anti-*chaebol* sentiment itself but we must also look to the problems resulting from the prevalence of the sentiment among the public. To tackle anti-*chaebol* sentiment directly, the government should eliminate all subsidies to large manufacturing firms that were utilized as part of the industrial development policies and thereby remove the general perception that the *chaebols* are prospering due to unfair rules and special treatment from the government. Furthermore, an objective evaluation of the *chaebols'* contribution to economic development and making this publicly known will also contribute to the mitigation of the anti-*chaebol* sentiment. On the other hand, the *chaebol* could humbly accept criticism and try to improve their image by voluntarily changing any unsound behavior and, where necessary, returning some of their profits to society. However, as was previously pointed out, the elimination of such deep-seated sentiments will not be at all easy.

Addressing the problems that derive from anti-*chaebol* sentiment, the government must try to avoid being persuaded by this usually strong public sentiment, particularly when formulating and implementing public policies regarding the corporate sector. In order for this to be achieved, economic, not political, factors should be considered as the prime concern in the development of corporate policy. However, this is never an easy task. Since the government and political leaders are more likely to follow public opinion regardless of its economic justification, we cannot expect much from the government and political leaders.

Because of these factors, as mentioned above, the anti-*chaebol* sentiment and *chaebols'* self-defense measures are likely to take the form of a vicious circle. As a result, the *chaebol* problem will remain one of the thorniest issues in the Korean economy for a considerable amount of time. Nevertheless, we have clearly to recognize that the resolution of this problem is one of the most important tasks that the Korean economy has to tackle on its rocky path to becoming an advanced capitalist economy. In fact, in this book we have already looked at the sources of anti-*chaebol* sentiment, and have argued that the main reason for the continuing vicious circle, as well as the power and responsibility to break it, lies with the government. Accordingly, we explore a new paradigm for public policy toward the *chaebol*. In this context, we must also bear in mind the fact that reforming informal practices and perceptions will require much more effort and time than reforming formal institutions under governmental jurisdiction. One cannot over-emphasize not only the importance of continued reform efforts on the part of the government but also the necessity for big corporations and the general public to coordinate their efforts toward the same goal.

# APPENDIX

## A1.   Extracts from Yak-Yong Jung's *A Guide to Shepherding People (Mok Min Shim Suh)*

We provide extracts that describe the prevailing anarchy in the tripartite tax system in the later Chosun dynasty from Yak-Yong Jung's *A Guide to Shepherding People (Mok Min Shim Suh)*, written in 1818. Yak-Yong Jung is recognized as one of the most important scholars who dearly wanted to reform the state at that time. The book was meant to explain to the local administrators how to correct contradictions and malfunctions in the local administration system and to protect farmers from extortion by bureaucrats. It consists of 12 chapters and 72 sections. Section 5 of Chapter 3, in particular, is about serving the public and discusses what is required of local heads in order to prevent exaction on the part of low-ranking officials. It further explains to officials how to accomplish their duties rightfully for the state and the people of their district. The following is an excerpt from the section:

> Property derives from people and the head of a local district is to receive it. If he can monitor well those officials through whose hands taxation is executed, he may well be generous. If he cannot monitor them well enough, he cannot be too meticulous and harsh. The land tax, either in the form of coins or cotton fabrics, is the most urgent for the needs of the State. In order to collect the due amount by the due date, the more affluent need to be taxed first, and low-ranking officials need to be closely watched for embezzlement so that there is no drainage of taxes. The military tax, collected either in the form of coins or cotton fabrics, is always urged by the Central Military Base. In order not to arouse the grievance of the people in each district, it needs to be constantly verified whether the same taxes have been levied twice, and embezzlement on the part of low-ranking officials must be prevented. To each local district high officials in the central government assign tributes, including manufactured products, to be sent to the king. This form of taxation also needs to be protected from abuse. Those manufactured products already in use but polished with care to make them look new should be acceptable as tributes. New manufactured products can take as long as a year to make and giving them as tributes can seriously impoverish craftsmen. Various obscure taxes either in cash or in kind are an object of deep sorrow for the people. When asked to send specific items as tributes by higher officials in the central government, the

local administrator is advised to send only those items that can be acquired easily in the local district and to refuse those items difficult to obtain, thus alleviating the burden of the people.[20]

Other parts of the book that illustrate the shortcomings of the tax system at the time can be found in Chapter 6, 'Government Finance', and Chapter 8, 'The Army'. In Chapter 6, Jung criticizes the land tax system based on harvest reaped and instead praises another system, *Kyungmuje* of China, which is based on the area of land owned. He also strongly emphasizes that, without true reforms, neither fairness in the tax system nor sound financing of state expenditures can ever be obtained. Let us look through some important parts of Chapter 6.

Among the 54 functions of the heads of local communities who administer people in their district, administering land taxes is the most difficult responsibility. This is so because our country does not have a good system of land tax laws. ... Improving old measures is one of the major tasks ahead in administering land taxes. Investigate old ones and shed light on the hidden. They must seek stability. Yet it is important to make efforts to improve measurement methods when it is not enough to simply seek stability. ... Arable land will be deserted only when taxes are exorbitant. Decreasing the assigned grade of the land (and hence decreasing its tax base) would be the only cure. Changing the grade would lead to many legal disputes regarding the land. New documents regarding title of ownership should be issued in every case. ... Investigating lands left fallow is also another of the major tasks to accomplish in the administration of land taxes. Taxing on fallow land creates resentment from the people. It is very important to perform the investigation. That kind of land, the whole or some part of which is not on official records, increases as time goes by. Land taxes collected for the needs of either royal family palaces or local governmental offices also increase with time. All these contribute to the reduction of the base for taxable lands. How are we going to deal with it in the future?[21]

The land tax system has already been corrupted to a large extent. Accordingly, tax laws are also in disarray. Tax is already being stolen by local officials through an unfair grading process of the year's harvest. ... Consequently, there are not many tax revenues left for the State. Investigating disasters and reducing taxes by taking these disasters into account are minor techniques for the better administration of taxes. [The major technique of tax administration is to establish fundamental principles whereby improvements will be made where it is possible to do so.] However, this great principle has already become crude and irrational because of the decrepit state of the tax system. Although local administrators may do their best heartily, it would not be so pleasing. ... When the year happens to be drought-struck, they need to carefully pick the men who are responsible for going around to record the amount of rice fields that were not able to transplant rice seedlings. ... The subsequent reduction in taxes is also difficult. If the actual harvest is less than what was assumed, a proportional reduction in tax is advised. When tax adjustments are all done, any movement in or out of the district by residents needs to be promptly prohibited [in order not to allow manipulation of the tax]. However, methods for collecting rice need to be flexible for convenience's sake. Low-ranking officials may have wicked designs, such as changing the category of taxes payable to increase the amount to be collected. Such malpractice should be clearly investigated and strictly prohibited.[22]

In January, storehouses of rice collected as tax are usually opened and the rice is then transported to the local government office. District heads had better assume the responsibility for receiving the transported rice by themselves [to avoid any wicked scheme by lower officials]. Before opening the storehouses, they had better post public notices in various places around villages warning thieves and other troublemakers of harsh punishment should they disrupt the process or steal rice. Although transportation of the rice by the people may take longer than planned, letting low-ranking officials do it to speed the process would be like setting hungry tigers free in a fold of sheep. Obviously local heads should never commit such a folly.[23]

Chapter 8 of the book by Jung discusses mainly problems related to the levy of cotton fabrics instead of conscription by males. The following is an excerpt from this chapter.

Collecting cotton fabrics instead of actual military service for adult males originated from Yang Yeon.[24] The hardships from this have been so tremendous that it has become the object of deep-rooted rancor from the people. Unless we fix this law, people will all die. ... For instead of having each adult male pay a tax in grain or cotton fabrics in order to be exempted from military service, five or six people are counted as responsible to compensate for one's military service exemption. This deplorable practice contributed to the unlawful accumulation of wealth by low-ranking officials. We cannot but be alert on this matter. Military plans and records should be kept firmly locked and out of the hands of those officials, in places such as the main administration room. Only after the head of a district has earned enough authority and a reputation for benevolence, so that low-ranking officials are afraid of him and people appreciate his benevolence, can it be possible for him to correct mistakes in the records of final military service. In order to achieve this task, he needs to investigate various tax havens that are so widespread at this time. ... On the day of collecting cotton fabric he needs to receive them by himself. If he lets low-ranking officials do it for him, the costs for the people will expand very quickly and will double.[25]

An examination of these records reminds us that farmers, the largest producers, were in a situation where they could not expect to receive any protection for either their private property or basic human rights.

## A2.   Extracts from Isabella Bird Bishop's *Korea and Her Neighbours*

Isabella Bird Bishop wrote a historical masterpiece on Korea entitled *Korea and Her Neighbors* about a hundred years ago following her fourth visit to Korea and other adjacent countries between 1894 and 1897. This part of the Appendix contains some important extracts that give a flavor of the type of property rights systems that the Korean people lived under at the time.

According to her book, Korean farming villages were so completely exacted by local officials and the *yang-ban* class that Korea appeared hopeless to her eyes. Her observations of the farming area alongside the Han river at the time do not only make a good description of the problems related to farming in Korea, but also provide a good demonstration of the importance of private property rights protection.

> The villages from about 50 *li* up the Han from Seoul may all be described as 'farming villages.' ... The people are peasant farmers in the strictest sense, most of them holding their land from the *yang-bans* at their pleasure. The proprietor has the right to turn them out after harvest, but it does not seem to be very oppressively exercised. He provides the seed, and they pay him half the yield. Some men buy land and obtain the deeds. In 1894 they paid in taxes one day's plowing, so much for barley, beans, rice, and cotton, the sum varying; but a new system of collecting tax on the assessed value of the land has come into operation, which renders 'squeezing' on the part of tax collectors far more difficult.[26]

> They [the farmers] appear lazy. I then thought them to be so, but they live under a *régime* where there is no security for the gains of their labor; and for a man to be reported to be 'making money', or attaining even the luxury of a brass dinner service, would be simply to lay himself open to the rapacious attention of the nearest mandarin and his myrmidons, or to a demand for a loan from an adjacent *yang-ban*. Nevertheless, the homesteads of the Han valley have a look of substantial comfort.[27]

Furthermore, Isabella Bird Bishop correctly observes details about the life-style of the yang-bans or privileged class, and the following is a short excerpt.

> For among the curses of Korea is the existence of this privileged class of *yang-bans* or nobles, who must not work for their own living, though it is no disgrace to be supported by their relatives, and who often live on the clandestine industry of their wives in sewing and laundry work. A *yang-ban* carries nothing for himself, not even his pipe. *Yang-ban* students do not even carry their own books from their studies to the classroom. Custom insist that when a member of this class travels he shall take with him as many attendants as he can muster. He is supported on his led horse, and supreme helplessness is the conventional requirement. His servants browbeat and bully people and take their fowls and eggs without payment. ... There is no doubt that the people, i.e. the vast mass of the unprivileged, on whose shoulders rests the burden of taxation, are hard pressed by the *yang-bans*, who not only use their labor without paying for it, but make merciless exaction under the name of loans. As soon as it is rumored or known that a merchant or peasant has accumulated a certain amount of *cash*, a *yang-ban* or official seeks a loan. Practically it is a levy, for if it is refused the man is either thrown into prison on a false charge and whipped every morning until he or his relations pay the sum demanded, or he is seized and practically imprisoned on low diet in the *yang-ban's* house until the money is forthcoming. It is the best of the nobles who disguise their exactions under the name of loans, but the lender never sees principal or interest. It is a very common thing for a noble, when he buys a house or field, to dispense with paying for it, and no mandarin will enforce payment.[28]

I believe that the fishing industry, with every other, is paralyzed by the complete insecurity of the earnings of labor and by the exaction of officials, and that the Korean fisherman does not care to earn money of which he will surely be deprived on any or no pretence, and that, along with the members of the industrial classes generally, he seeks the protection of poverty.[29]

The picture so far is gloomy, but Lady Bishop adopts a brighter forecast of the Korean people as she travels to the village of *Kwan* populated by about 20 000 Korean immigrants near Vladivostok, Siberia, after having completed her tour of Korea. The Koreans in this village developed institutions of self-rule in an orderly and very modern form. Economically, they were more successful than the Russians, Chinese or any other ethnic group in both commerce and farming. They enjoyed a standard of living cozier than the other people in the region. She begins by giving a brief account of the people in this region and further explains the nature of their rights to possess land.

The total number of Korean immigrants is estimated at from 16 000 to 18 000. It must be remembered that several thousands of these were literally paupers, and that they subsisted for nearly a year on the charity of the Russian authorities, and after that were indebted to them for seed corn. They settled on the rich lands of the Siberian valley mostly as squatters, but have been unmolested for many years. Many have purchased the lands they occupy, and in other cases villages have acquired community rights to their adjacent lands. It is the intention of Government that squatting shall gradually be replaced by purchase, the purchasers receiving legal title-deeds.[30]

Moreover, she writes.

Koreans settled in Siberia prior to 1884 can claim rights as Russian subjects, and at this time those who can prove that they have settled on purchased lands for ten years can do so, as well as certain others, well reported of as being of settled lives and good conduct. Owing to the steady influx of settlers from Southern Russia, the rich lands near the railroad are required for colonization, and further immigration from Korea has been prohibited. The sending of Koreans who are either squatters or of unsettled lives to the Amur Province is under discussion.[31]

There was also a good foundation and respect for the law among Korean settlers as is seen by the following passage.

These alien settlers practically enjoy autonomy. At the head of each district is an Elder or Headman, with from one to three assistants according to its size. The police and their officers are Korean. In each district there are two or three judges with their clerks, who try minor offences. The headmen, who are responsible for order and the collection of taxes, are paid salaries, or receive various allowances. All these officers are Korean, and are elected by the people themselves from among themselves. The Government taxation is 10 roubles (about £1) on each farm per annum. The local taxation, settled by the villagers in council for their own purposes, such as roads, ditches, bridges, and schools, is limited to 3 roubles per farm per annum. Men who are not landholders pay from 1 to 2 roubles per annum.[32]

There is also praise for the Korean people living in this region. 'It would be impossible for a traveler to meet with more cordial hospitality and more cleanly and comfortable accommodation than I did in these Korean homes.'[33] More importantly, she observes positive changes that have resulted from the increased protection of property rights.

> But there is more than this. The air of the men has undergone a subtle but real change, and the women, though they nominally keep up their habit of seclusion, have lost the hangdog air that distinguishes them at home. The suspiciousness and indolent conceit, and the servility to his betters, which characterize home-bred Korean have generally given place to an independence and manliness of manner rather British than Asiatic. The alacrity of movement is a change also, and has replaced the conceived swing of the *yang-ban* and the heartless lounge of the peasant. There are many chances for making money, and there is neither mandarin nor *yang-ban* to squeeze it out of the people when made, and comforts and a certain appearance of wealth no longer attract the repacious attentions of officials, but are rather a credit to a man than a source of insecurity.[34]

> It must be borne in mind that these people, who have raised themselves into a prosperous farming class, and who get an excellent character for industry ... were mostly starving folk who fled from famine, and their prosperity and general demeanor give me the hope that their countrymen in Korea, if they ever have an honest administration and protection for their earnings, may slowly develop into *men*.[35]

## NOTES

1. Here, the distinction between old and new institutionalism lies primarily in the difference in each school's incorporation of economic theory in explaining economic institutions. While the old school confined itself to the description of either institutional changes or institutional differences among various economic systems, thereby ignoring economic theory itself, the new school explains systematically the relationship between institutions and economic behavior (and performance) with neoclassical economic analysis. In this way, new institutionalism overcomes not only the atheoretical tendency of the old institutionalism, but also the weakness of the institution-free neoclassical approach. Some authors (for example, Eggertson, 1990) have distinguished neo-institutionalism from new institutionalism depending on the distance from the neoclassical approach, with the former being closer than the latter. However, we will use the term new-institutionalism throughout this book as a broad concept inclusive of both strands of institutionalism.
2. See Chapter 1 for a brief yet concise outline of the new-institutional economics framework.
3. The concept of social capital can be viewed from a new-institutionalist point of view as a kind of informal constraint.
4. Fukuyama argues that China and Korea, where the family-oriented tradition is strong, tend toward an economic organization based on small-sized firms, but in Japan with a group-oriented tradition that tends to create strong mutual trust among social members, large economic organizations tend to dominate.

5.  In another study Clague, Keefer, Knack and Olson (1996) have also shown that democratic political regimes tend to have relatively more secure private property rights systems, whereas unstable and insecure autocracies tend to provide weak protection of private property rights. They also point out, however, that unstable democracies may have a worse property rights protection than secure and stable autocracies.
6.  Refer to Christopher Hill (1995) for more detail.
7.  For a more detailed discussion of disorder caused by the tripartite tax system of the Chosun dynasty, see Dong Whan Ko (1991, pp. 71–125).
8.  At one time there could be more than 40 different taxes.
9.  See Byung-Tak Kwon (1984 pp. 202–4).
10. The deferment measure included cutting the curb market rate from an average 3.84 to 1.35 per cent monthly and a three-year deferment with installment payments for five years thereafter.
11. This is intended to improve tax equity by introducing a comprehensive income tax system inclusive of financial income that had been treated separately thus far, and thereby to apply an equal tax system to all incomes regardless of their source.
12. Korea's tax system, consisting of tax laws and related orders and regulations, is revised so often and is so complicated that enforcement by tax authorities and the proper use by ordinary citizens of this tax system have become extremely difficult. As a result, the system tends to have been enforced to a large extent through the arbitrary judgment of authorities.
13. According to Clague *et al.* (1996), the ratio of deposited money is low relative to cash under both unstable democratic and autocratic political regimes, where the protection of property rights is weak, but the ratio of deposited money is higher relative to cash under stable democratic and long-established autocratic regimes, where property rights are expected to be firmly secured.
14. Per capita income was added to the regression to take account of the effect of economic development, and this variable applied to the regression is actually the residual of regressing per capita income on the cash ratio. See Jwa (2001) for further details and for time series regression on the Korean case.
15. Information on IPR system index is obtained from Robert J. Barro and Xavier Sala-i-Martin (1995, Chapter 12).
16. Also, it may be useful to check if the IPR index has a systematic relationship with the Cash Ratio (CR) variable, the proxy for transaction costs. According to calculations of the correlation coefficient between the Cash Ratio variable and IPR index, a significant and strong negative relationship has been found consistent with the framework of new-institutional economics. See Jwa (2001) for further details.
17. See Jwa (2001) for further details.
18. A small domestic market can be a constraint on scale expansion and may therefore provide an environment conducive to business diversification, other things being equal. Moreover, the practice of mutual guarantee among affiliate firms also provided incentives for expansion through the creation of new affiliates. See the next chapter for further elaboration on this point.
19. For a more detailed discussion on this point, see Chapter 7.
20. Yak-Yong Jung (1982[1818], p. 111).
21. *ibid.*, p. 169.
22. *ibid.*, p. 175.
23. *ibid.*, p. 187.
24. Yang Yeon was a minister of the early Chosun dynasty and advisor to King Lee (sixteenth century).
25. *ibid.*, p. 227.
26. Isabella Bird Bishop, *Korea and Her Neighbors*, St James Gazette, London, UK, and New York: January 1998, pp. 77–8. Page numbers hereafter are based on the reprints of the New York edition by Yonsei University Press, Korea, 1997[1970].
27. *ibid.*, pp. 78–9.
28. *ibid.*, pp. 101–2.
29. *ibid.*, p. 158.

30.  *ibid.*, p. 233–4.
31.  *ibid.*, p. 234.
32.  *ibid.*, p. 234.
33.  *ibid.*, p. 235.
34.  *ibid.*, pp. 235–6.
35.  *ibid.*, p. 236.

# 6. Economic institutions, diversification and performance: empirical evidence and implications for *chaebol* behavior

## 1. INTRODUCTION

As has been seen in the previous chapters, economic concentration among the *chaebol* and the issue of the optimality of their business diversification has long been a subject of debate. Hence a proper evaluation of the current structure as well as the future direction of the optimal structural adjustment of the *chaebol* have both been given the highest priority for some time now. It is often argued that the *chaebols* are 'excessively' diversified and have grown over-large, and as a result, the Korean economy is said to suffer from excessive ownership and industrial concentration. To curb the propensity of the *chaebol's* diversification to grow even larger, many initiatives such as policies to promote business specialization and ownership diffusion have been undertaken. However, most of these policies have so far taken the form of direct regulations often curbing the business activities of the *chaebols*. Apart from restrictions on entry, ownership structure, mutual assistance within the same business group and bank borrowing, the government has also instigated measures to encourage business specialization. However, these policies, in effect, have side-stepped the issue altogether as they do not attack the sources or underlying causes of the *chaebols'* diversification behavior and have generally been regarded as unsuccessful in achieving their goals. The need for reform, nevertheless, remains an important issue deserving of careful deliberation and action, particularly in the era of globalization.

In Chapter 5, we discussed the importance of property rights protection in determining the evolution pattern of the *chaebol*. By tracing some recent historical evidence, we argued that despite the weaknesses in the prevailing property rights system and the accompanying high transaction costs, the *chaebol*, under government discretionary protection, have thus far been prompted and maintained to a large extent by both institutional factors and government intervention. Furthermore, the government may be seen as playing a dual role as the major initiator and constrainer of much of the *chaebols'* economic behavior. We also argued in detail that the presence of a weak property rights system and the availability of governmental favors have in fact motivated the *chaebols* to adopt a managerial strategy of diversification so as to secure and protect their private property rights and business activities. This often led to the consolidation of the 'too big to fail' attitude.

Today, globalization can be seen to affect a full range of political as well as economic issues. Globalization is a phenomenon driven by the strategies and behavior of individuals, firms, banks and other economic groups in the pursuit of profit beyond their national boundaries. It is usually identified with market deregulation, the spread of new information technologies, the intermeshing of financial markets and innovations in industrial and production systems.[1] Globalization constitutes a critical and difficult challenge for modern firms. It has been observed that with the advent of globalization, a crisis in the existing production system has simultaneously taken place. All the increasingly interdependent, complex and dynamic production systems – the American Fordist system, the German craft system, and even the flexible and lean Japanese production system – seem to be breaking down and are now subject to reassessment. This has sparked uncertainty about how a successful, modern firm should be organized and managed.[2] In this context, globalization also poses a serious challenge to the *chaebols* because it implies a drastic change in the business environment from a closed market setting to one that is open to competition in the global arena.

In this chapter, we examine the theoretical and empirical determinants of corporate diversification behavior by introducing institutional environment variables into the analysis, which will allow us to acquire a better under-standing of the motivations behind the firm's diversification. Furthermore, this chapter will analyze how the *chaebols'* diversification behavior is likely to evolve as globalization deepens. In order to do this, we study the implications of globalization for business and industrial organizations, the future structure of the *chaebols'* diversification behavior, and the role of the government in the *chaebols'* structural adjustment process. Policy implications for the Korean economy as regards *chaebols'* diversification behavior will follow these discussions.

In the second part of this chapter, we proceed further and ask about the effects of institutional factors on national economic growth. Specifically, we emphasize the importance of institutions on a country's economic performance by using a cross-country regression. As with the regression on diversification, we run a regression with economic performance as the dependent variable on other important institutional variables such as the degree of property rights protection, legal origin, degree of shareholder rights protection, as well as other economic environmental factors such as the level of financial development, market competition, market size and market risk. Our answer to the important question as to whether institutional factors matter to economic growth as well as corporate behavior is an emphatic 'yes'.

In Section 2, we begin by introducing the theoretical background as relates to the determinants of business diversification, which include not only institutional factors but also the globalized market and technological factors. We then report findings from our cross-country regression analysis that studies the relationship between corporate diversification and institutional factors. The advent of globalization and its implications for Korea's industrial organization are discussed both theoretically and by using empirical evidence of scale and scope economies of various industrial activities conducted by Korean business groups. We conclude this part by looking into the prospects for the diversification behavior of Korean firms and discuss policy implications. The second part contains discussion and empirical evidence of the relationship between institutional factors and economic performance, as well as other important economic variables. We begin with a brief theoretical discussion and then report the empirical evidence highlighting evidence in the context of other arguments in the book. A concluding section and an Appendix that contains in detail all the regressions performed here can be found at the end of this chapter.

## 2.   ECONOMIC INSTITUTIONS, GLOBALIZATION AND DIVERSIFICATION

### 2.1   Theoretical Overview of Determinants of Business Diversification

#### 2.1.1   Property rights systems and diversification

Traditionally, studies on business diversification have focused on why firms diversify out of their main lines of business in three contexts: market power, surplus of resources and agency costs. The market power view further emphasizes three ways in which conglomerates may yield power in an anti-competitive way through diversification: cross-subsidization, mutual forbearance and reciprocal buying. The resource view based on Penrose (1959) stresses that rent-seeking firms diversify in response to excess capacity in productive factors. The agency view, which many financial economists have adhered to, is based on the premise that managers have self-interests and as a result diversification may be a business strategy that the managers choose for their own benefit rather than for the gain of the firm's shareholders.

In the neoclassical world, with transaction costs assumed away, institutions are exogenously determined without having any significant impact on the outcome of economic analysis. In other words, because neoclassical economics is institution-free and there are no explicit transaction costs in the model, differences in economic institutions are seen to have no effect on the process of resource allocation. Recently, however, as mentioned in Chapters 1 and 5, the resurgence of new-institutionalism, led by North (1990, 1992) and Eggertsson (1990), has emphasized the importance of economic institutions in determining economic behavior and performance. Accordingly, we have shown both theoretically and empirically that in the non-zero transaction costs world, institutions influence the economic behavior and performance of economic agents by affecting the size of the transaction costs they incur and therefore become a crucial factor in determining resource allocation and economic performance in the overall economy.

According to the new-institutional approach, the economic system can be described as consisting of individual economic agents, economic organizations that organize individual agents, and finally economic institutions that regulate the agents and organizations.[3] Using this method of classification, one can analyze the effects of a given type of economic institution on the economic behavior of individual agents – for example, in this chapter we look specifically into the diversification behavior of *chaebols*.

Williamson (1975, 1985) studied the determinants of diversification under the transaction costs view, which can also be classified as belonging to new-institutionalism in a broader sense. Many proponents of the transaction cost view have focused on the analysis of vertical integration.[4] Vertical integration has the effect of reducing transaction costs that arise from transaction-specific investments between contractors. Williamson has exposed a transaction cost theory of the firm based on the two assumptions of bounded rationality and opportunism in the presence of uncertainty. He developed the concept of asset specificity as the critical characteristic of transactions that determine whether a transaction within the firm is efficient or not.[5] An asset is specific to a particular kind of transaction if it cannot be used productively in other activities of the firm. After an investment has been made, transactions that require a high specific investment are more likely to be brought into the firm to guard against possible exploitative behavior on the part of the firm's opportunistic trading partners. Thus, the potentially high transaction costs stemming from specific investments tend to encourage vertical integration.

Here we should also take note of the need to discriminate between the meanings of transaction costs among new-institutionalists. To do this, let us return to the argument of new-institutionalism by North and Eggertsson on the relationship between property rights, transaction costs and diversification. As has been made evident in the previous chapter, one of the most important economic institutions in a market economy is the property rights system, which is a rule defining the relationship among economic agents concerning the use of scarce economic resources. The transparency and security of a property rights system are considered to be the main determinants of the size of transaction costs. If a formal system of property rights protection is not clearly established or is not fully enforced – even though clearly defined – excessive transaction costs will be incurred. Therefore in the real, non-zero-transaction-cost world, diversification, which is one of several economic activities of a firm, is inevitably affected by the property rights system in place. The fact that property rights are not well protected implies a low probability that all market contracts made with other agents will be fully honored and faithfully observed.[6] Put differently, the more secure property rights are, the more active market contracts are because of lower transaction costs arising from the economic institutions in place. So we hypothesize that firms in countries with stronger protection of property rights and thus lower transaction costs should have more lines of business than firms in countries with weaker protection of property rights and higher transaction costs.

This hypothesis seems to run counter to Williamson's argument. Despite the fact that they all use the term 'transaction costs', we can see that there are differences between the arguments of North and Eggertsson and that of Williamson regarding the effects of transaction costs on diversification. North argues that firms come into existence to take advantage of profitable opportunities. With weak property rights, poorly enforced laws, barriers to entry and monopolistic restrictions, profit-maximizing firms will tend to have short time horizons and little fixed capital, and will thus tend to be small scale. This argument, as fully discussed and empirically tested in Chapter 5, implies that if a formal system of property rights protection is neither clearly established nor fully enforced then transaction costs will make the formation of large firms more difficult. Furthermore, we note that small firms have little capacity to diversify into various lines of business. Thus, we conclude that in countries where property rights are not well protected, the level of corporate diversification will tend to be lower. Williamson, on the other hand, argues that if transaction costs come from transaction-specific investments between buyers and sellers, they can be reduced through diversification. Here North and Williamson differ in their view regarding the extent of transaction costs. That is, for North, transaction costs incurred because of weak property rights cannot be alleviated through diversification because they are tied into the economic system. On the contrary, if transaction costs arise from specific transactions between contractors, as is the case with Williamson, then they may be reduced through diversification.

In sum, according to new-institutionalism, in a country where property rights become more secure, resulting in lower transaction costs, the level of diversification may increase because the strength of property rights protection encourages the formation and growth of large firms that tend to have a higher capacity to diversify than smaller firms. However, if transaction costs are not a factor determining the overall economic environment in place but rather reflect some special relationship between firms with transaction-specific investments, then these firms will be inclined to increase the level of corporate diversification in order to reduce such transaction costs. That is, transaction costs that occur from technical characteristics such as asset specificity can be reduced by diversification, as Williamson argues. However, transaction costs that stem from economic institutions such as property rights cannot be reduced simply through diversification because these institutions create an environment that acts as an absolute constraint that firms cannot overcome endogenously. If transaction costs from economic institutions are high, it is plausible that medium and small-sized firms with a lower capacity to diversify than larger firms will dominate. Thus, firms in countries with higher transaction costs as a result of weak economic institutions are less diversified compared to firms in countries having lower transaction costs.

### 2.1.2   Corporate governance and diversification

Now let us consider institutional factors related to corporate governance systems. According to the agency cost theory, corporate assets may be deployed to benefit managers rather than shareholders.[7] In particular, a manager may pursue diversified expansion as a means of reducing his employment risk, thus improving his personal position. This phenomenon may prevail when the manager has more powerful control in corporate governance than shareholders and the power distribution of control between manager and shareholders may depend on the legal conditions of the corporate governance system.

On the other hand, the structure of corporate governance systems has been recognized recently as a factor determining competitiveness and consequently the economic performance of business corporations.[8] The question of which system of corporate governance is ideal is continually asked in the field of business economics. Through the perspective of agency theory, many financial economists have come to the conclusion that managers actually pursue value-reducing strategies to further their own interests at the expense of the firm's owners. Mueller (1969) argues that mergers, particularly conglomerate mergers, appear to be a convenient vehicle for doing this. Therefore, as far as profitability is concerned, this argument implies that corporate diversification may be negatively related to profitability, other things being equal.

### 2.1.3   Globalized market and technological factors

*2.1.3.1   Definition of globalization*   The term 'globalization' in the literature takes on various meanings and we need therefore to clarify our meaning of the word. First, we identify the globalization phenomenon with the integration of world economies into a single market, which in turn implies the following specific predictions for the market environment: the increase of potential market size and intensified competition for market share. In this sense, how firms will deal with the increasingly larger markets is a critical challenge that globalization presents to individual firms. But as a corollary of the extended market size, globalization can also mean intensified competition in international as well as domestic markets, so that existing monopolistic producers may face the possibility of losing their market share and economic dominance. Therefore, broadly stated, globalization gives access to greater market size in general but can also imply reduced market shares, particularly for firms that have been enjoying economic concentration backed by unfair privileges within rather limited and closed market environments.

Second, we identify the globalization phenomenon with the introduction and rapid spread of microelectronics-based information technology (IT). Improvements in information technology contribute not only to economic integration through better telecommunications but also to changes in production technologies and managerial relationships among various economic activities. Specifically, it is expected that scope economies among various economic activities will be strengthened through improved information technology, computers and automation systems.[9] In addition, it may be the case that improved microelectronics-based information technology creates new synergistic managerial relationships among formerly unrelated economic activities and reinforces existing relationships by improving the information network system, thereby making it increasingly difficult to isolate a particular economic activity from other activities. So, in this sense, the additional challenge of globalization may be how to respond to the enlarged economies of scope among various economic or industrial activities generated by the stronger technological and managerial synergy effects.

Three important implications need to be mentioned. First, globalization implies the expansion of economic activity across politically defined national and regional boundaries through the increased movement of goods, services, factors of production and economic agents via trade and investment. Preferential and discriminatory policies will become increasingly ineffective in an economic environment that is moving toward globalization. As a result, government-led economic development strategies and policy instruments will also become ineffective. It is easy to see how direct regulations to promote or protect targeted industries would eventually constitute obstacles to further economic development. Generally speaking, globalization will ensure that economic policy-making and implementation will proceed according to the principle of non-discrimination and market mechanisms.

Second, in the process of globalization, knowledge, information and technology will be the most important forces behind economic development. A few industries in the traditional sense do not constitute a sufficient basis for economic growth. Technology and industries are intermeshed with each other – no technology is industry specific:

> But the same thing has happened in the automobile industry, which increasingly has become dependent on electronics, and on the computer. It has happened to the steel industry, which increasingly has become dependent on materials science of which the original steel companies were totally ignorant – and largely still are. It has happened to the paper industry – the list could be continued indefinitely.[10]

In the twenty-first century, networking, systemization and intellectualization of economic activity will be important realities, and the cycle of technological innovation will shorten. These changes will greatly affect production systems and market structures.

Third, rapid globalization, therefore, implies the advent of an age of uncertainty. Successful economic strategies in industrial societies are not necessarily applicable to the new society of globalization and information. Additionally, rapidly increasing integration and a shorter technological innovation cycle would make the predetermination of an appropriate industrial structure for this new society not only difficult but also somewhat fruitless.

*2.1.3.2   Theory of diversification based on market and technological factors*
The market as well as technological factors will affect business diversification. Jwa (1997) develops a theory of the scope of industrial activity based on market and technological factors by integrating the theories of the multi-product firm of Stigler (1968) and Baumol, Panzar and Willig (1982, henceforth, BPW).[11]

Stigler (1968) proposed a theory of the multi-product firm based on Adam Smith's theory of specialization; that is, the division of labor is limited by the extent of the market. He suggested that the scope of activities of a multi-product firm is determined by the interaction of production technology and market size. According to Stigler, as the size of the market grows, economic activities that were initially not subject to economies of scale eventually become eligible to benefit from scale economies brought about by the increase of the market. These activities then tend to become more independent and important in their own right. Conversely, activities subject to diseconomies or weak economies of scale tend to be integrated in-house. Activities with economies of scale also become integrated if the size of the market is limited or the remaining set of activities exhibits particularly strong diseconomies of scale that dominate the concerned activity's economies of scale.

BPW (1982) developed a theory of the multi-product firm, introducing the concept of economies of scope in addition to economies of scale. According to BPW, economies of scope are a necessary and sufficient condition for the existence of multi-product firms. BPW have shown that as the degree of economies of scope among activities increases, the optimal scale of multi-activity organizations and the potential to earn supra-normal profits will also increase, encouraging an increase in multi-activity organizations. On the other hand, if activities that have not been part of a multi-activity organization experience technological innovation that creates new economies of scope with the incumbent activities of that organization, then these activities will tend to be integrated. In any case, the stronger or newly created economies of scope will imply the proliferation of multi-activity organizations.

An integration of Stigler's intuitive theory of specialization and BPW's formal multi-product firm theory into an endogenous theory of economic organization implies that equilibrium in a multi-product industry consists of firms that will either integrate various activities in-house or specialize in a single activity or subset of activities, depending on the market size and the degree of (dis)economies of scale and scope of the different activities. The resulting type of industrial organization will be determined by the interaction of the production technologies of the industry and the extent of the market.

This theory can be utilized to derive the scope of industrial activities adopted by individual firms as follows. First, as the size of the market increases, the optimal structure of an industrial organization will tend toward more specialization of activities under larger economies of scale, thereby encouraging more specialized and larger firms. Second, as technological innovation increases the degree of economies of scope, more diversified (multi-activity) firms will be encouraged. One can combine these two simple implications to derive various interesting hypotheses about the relationship between globalization and new industrial organizations.

For example, one can hypothesize about the impact of globalization on the choice between large-scale specialized versus small-scale diversified production systems. According to this theory, as the world economy becomes globalized, two opposing forces will emerge. One is the pressure for specialization due to growing market sizes, which may provide an improved environment for large-scale production systems like the Fordist system, for example. The other is the pressure for a lean and flexible, and more diversified production system (say, post-Fordist or a new system) encouraged mainly by technological innovations that create larger scope economies as well as intensified market share competition. Therefore, globalization does not guarantee the diffusion of the new system only, as has usually been assumed in the literature.[12]

Furthermore, it is interesting to bear in mind that according to Gort (1962), firms may diversify their operation in order to escape severe competition with their rivals or when they experience a loss of existing markets due to competition. On the other hand, competition may help optimize the level of diversification by driving firms to set their business organization toward their core competence, that is, to focus their limited resources toward establishing or maintaining their competitiveness relative to their rivals. Of course, even in this case, firms may continue to think that business diversification will eventually help in the competition with their rivals, in particular if the diversification, in fact, generates significant synergy effects, that is, economies of scope.

On the other hand, it can be observed that unrelated activities may induce financial economies. The best indication of financial economies arising from unrelated diversification can be found in the market and hierarchies paradigm.[13] This suggests that unrelated diversification may help overcome external capital market failures. Firms pursuing a strategy of unrelated diversification can achieve a more optimal allocation of capital and can monitor the divisions more effectively than the external capital market.[14]

## 2.2   Empirical Evidence on Diversification and Institutional Factors

The Appendix at the end of this chapter contains details of the cross-country regression analysis of firms' diversification behavior, taking into account, in particular, institutional factors, corporate governance structure, development of financial markets, overall market size, market competition and business risk. In this section, we merely report the most important findings of our analysis. We begin by looking at the data set, then move on to the regression results.

### 2.2.1   Overview of data on diversification
As of 1997, the number of industries in which firms operate is listed alphabetically by country and presented in Table 6.1, which indicates the levels of diversification for various countries, including Korea. The table shows that the level of diversification in Korea is the lowest. The figures, however, may give a misleading impression that Korean firms are the least diversified, running counter to the information in Tables 3.3 and 3.4 of Chapter 3 that show that the level of *chaebol* diversification is as high as that in other developed countries, and that the average number of affiliates of the 30 largest *chaebol* exceeds 20, while the number of sectors they diversify into also comes close to 20.

In fact, the statistics for Korea represented in Table 6.1 are not comparable to the statistics for other countries because Korea's industrial organization is dominated by the *chaebol* – conglomerates that have distinct characteristics making them different from other conglomerates in advanced countries. This takes into account only the diversification of individual firms as opposed to the *chaebol* type of diversification, and thus tends to underestimate the true degree of diversification. We need to distinguish between two types of

Table 6.1    Industry diversification of firms of various countries by mean and
             variance (1997)

|              | Mean  | Variance |
|--------------|-------|----------|
| Australia*   | 6.90  | 4.32     |
| Austria*     | 3.68  | 2.33     |
| Belgium*     | 5.65  | 3.50     |
| Bermuda      | 5.00  | 3.32     |
| Canada*      | 4.13  | 2.39     |
| China        | 2.75  | 1.98     |
| Denmark*     | 7.45  | 4.58     |
| Finland*     | 6.74  | 3.25     |
| France*      | 5.68  | 3.74     |
| Germany*     | 9.79  | 5.00     |
| Hong Kong    | 5.00  | 3.54     |
| Indonesia    | 2.45  | 1.19     |
| Ireland*     | 4.83  | 2.60     |
| Italy*       | 6.83  | 4.31     |
| Japan*       | 6.83  | 5.33     |
| Korea*       | 1.55  | 1.05     |
| Malaysia     | 10.21 | 4.13     |
| Mexico*      | 4.87  | 3.18     |
| Netherlands* | 5.53  | 4.62     |
| New Zealand* | 3.76  | 2.44     |
| Norway*      | 6.06  | 5.51     |
| Portugal*    | 2.88  | 3.16     |
| Scotland     | 4.94  | 3.32     |
| Singapore    | 8.15  | 2.98     |
| South Africa | 5.63  | 5.73     |
| Spain*       | 3.90  | 2.31     |
| Sweden*      | 6.74  | 3.11     |
| Switzerland* | 5.68  | 4.70     |
| Thailand     | 2.84  | 1.98     |
| UK*          | 7.10  | 4.73     |
| US*          | 6.88  | 4.47     |
| All          | 5.50  | 3.49     |
| OECD         | 5.61  | 3.63     |
| Non-OECD     | 5.22  | 3.13     |

Note:    * indicates an OECD country.

diversification – increasing the number of affiliates in a business group, that is, the *chaebol*, and increasing the number of business lines in a firm. The latter is often termed product line diversification, which is the subject of our investigation in this chapter (as listed in Table 6.1), while the former may be called '*chaebol* diversification', which is the popular pattern of diversification in Korea and is not easily observable in other countries.[15]

From Table 6.1 we observe that Portugal and Spain, classified as high-transaction-cost countries by North (1990), are comparatively less diversified on average. On the other hand, the levels of diversification in England, the United States and Canada, which are categorized as low-transaction-cost countries, are relatively higher than Portugal and Spain. These observations are consistent with our expectations.

At first sight, although differences between OECD and non-OECD countries are not immediately noticeable, a closer look shows that the average number of industries in which firms in OECD countries operate is somewhat higher than for non-OECD countries. This is consistent with our expectations because we expect the level of diversification to be higher for OECD countries where transaction costs, which are closely related to the stability of property rights, are lower than in non-OECD countries. However, when investigating countries individually, we observe varying levels.

### 2.2.2   Empirical results and interpretation

We used the standard ordinary least squares (OLS) regression technique to explain diversification by various constructed indices that describe the different countries' level of economic growth, property rights protection, legal environment, degree of shareholder rights, level of financial development, degree of market competition, market size, firm size, business risk and the debt–equity ratio. Our analysis further distinguishes between related and unrelated diversification, and we warn the reader to take this into consideration when interpreting the results.[16] Tables A6.1 and A6.2 in the Appendix contain a summary of the variables and the estimated coefficients from the regression analysis of diversification on the explanatory variables. What follows is a discussion of the main hypothesis and our empirical findings.

In countries where property rights are well protected, as North (1990) argues, firms tend to be large because large firms command more resources that can be used for diversification than smaller ones, and therefore the coefficient of property rights should be positive. In line with this thesis, we find that the coefficient of the property rights index is positive, which implies that the strong protection of property rights provides a good environment for firms to diversify, as reduced transaction costs in the economy allow for the easier expansion of business activities. This confirms the importance of property rights systems as an absolute business constraint that firms cannot overcome endogenously. Firms in countries with higher transaction costs arising from insecure property rights systems are expected to be less diversified than firms in countries with more secure property rights systems and hence lower transaction costs. Our empirical study does not directly distinguish between North's and Williamson's views on why a firm diversifies. Essentially, although we have directly added a property rights index, a separate measure for transaction costs due to asset specificity has not been added. Therefore one must not mistakenly assume that the type of property rights systems in place is a more important factor on the level of diversification than the internalization of transaction costs due to asset specificity.

The legal origin of the company law and the index of shareholder rights, both which measure the legal conditions affecting corporate governance, were alternately included in the regressions to test whether the corporate governance structure has any effect on firms' diversification behavior. We follow the study by Porta *et al.* (1997), where the legal system of a country is described by the origin of its legal system. Here the origin of a country's legal system is thought of as deriving from either common law or roman law. We cannot expect the signs of these variables *a priori*. Nevertheless, as regards the effect of shareholder rights and as is commonly pointed out in the literature on corporate governance, the agency cost theory suggests that corporate assets may be deployed to benefit managers rather than shareholders.[17] That is, managers may pursue diversified expansion as a means of reducing employment risk, thus improving the manager's personal position. This phenomenon may prevail when the manager has more powerful control in corporate governance than shareholders. Therefore the coefficient that measures the degree of shareholder rights, that is, anti-director rights that make specific claims against the corporation, may be negative.

Our empirical analysis shows that the legal origin of company law and the commercial code does influence the level of diversification of firms. Specifically, we find that the level of unrelated diversification in countries, such as the UK or the US, where the legal system is under the common law tradition tends to be higher than that in countries with civil law. However, with regard to the effect of shareholder rights, we find that the estimation results not only vary in sign depending on the sample of countries used, but are also statistically insignificant. Therefore we cannot say anything definite as to the effect of shareholder rights on diversification. Further research may be required to clarify the empirical effect of the corporate governance system on diversification behavior.

As regards the level of financial development, the degree of financial deepening in a country may reflect the accessibility of capital for diversification or expansion. It is reasonable to assume that the more the financial sector develops, the more opportunities to finance diversification arise. In line with Williamson's argument, however, firms may expand their lines of business to reduce transaction costs due to a weak and underdeveloped financial sector by pooling capital resources between business divisions. Thus, needless to say, we cannot predict *a priori* the direction of the financial development coefficient. The empirical results turn out to vary depending on the sample of countries used in the analysis. However, the effect of financial development on diversification tended to be positive, particularly as regards unrelated diversification. This can be understood as implying that financial deepening in a country may enhance the accessibility of capital for diversification and expansion.

Market competition may have a positive or negative effect on diversification. As already mentioned, firms may diversify their operations in order to compete with their rivals. Alternatively, firms may set their business organization to focus on their core competence in response to competition. It is important to note that market competition has the effect of mitigating inefficient diversification and therefore helps optimize the level of diversification. Nonetheless, the sign of the effect of market competition on diversification cannot be foretold *a priori*. In general, the effect of market competition on diversification was found to be negative but insignificant in most cases. However, depending on the sample of countries used, the intensity of market competition shows a significant negative effect on unrelated diversification implying that market competition drives firms away from unrelated diversification. Here it can be argued that firms tend to adopt a business strategy toward the development of their core competence the higher the degree of market competition, and hence exhibit less unrelated diversification, in order to improve competitiveness to fend off rivals in the market.

The size of the market (here measured by real GDP) should negatively affect diversification behavior since an increase of the market size will allow for the benefit of large-scale production stemming from increased division of labor. Indeed, the coefficient of market size was found to be significantly negative implying that firms are inclined to diversify when markets are of limited size. That is, as has been mentioned above, if a market is too small for the potential benefit of larger-scale production to be fully exploited, then the level of diversification will become relatively high. Adam Smith's hypothesis that the division of labor is limited by the extent of the market is therefore empirically confirmed.

Firm size and business risk variables have also been added in our analysis as these variables reflect important characteristics of the firms. According to Lemelin (1982), larger firms have a greater capacity to diversify because they command more resources than smaller firms. Therefore we expect the coefficient of the size of a firm to be positive. The risk of the firm variable is included to control for diversification influenced by a firm's motive to reduce risk. Thus, a diversification strategy to reduce risk should be reflected by a positive coefficient. Our results show that the size of firm has a positive effect on diversification as Lemelin argues, while the sign of the coefficient of risk varies depending on the sample. The relationship between business risk and diversification in our sample is unstable. Further research may be required to clarify this issue.

### 2.3    Globalization and Korea's Industrial Organization

### 2.3.1    Underlying determinants of Korean firms' diversification behavior

In this section, the underlying forces driving Korean firms' diversification behavior and its future prospects are investigated by utilizing empirical evidence of the scale and scope economies of various industrial activities that the *chaebols* are engaged in. Since the cross-country empirical analysis in the previous section did not include Korea, this section should supplement our analysis on firm's diversification behavior by discussing empirical evidence on Korean firms.

One of the most peculiar aspects of Korea's industrial policy is that it mainly concentrates on attempting to curb *chaebols'* diversification behavior without probing into the actual reasons that explain why the *chaebols* tend to be highly diversified in the first place. Korea's *chaebol* policy has been of the symptom-regulation type, by which it is meant that the regulatory framework has basically been directed at remedying the symptoms instead of attacking the roots of the problem. Obviously, before any logically and empirically sound policy prescription can be made, it is imperative to understand why the *chaebols* have become so highly diversified. However, as yet, few serious efforts have been made to explain the diversification behavior of Korean *chaebol* in a systematic way.

Our discussion in the theoretical section above implies that the following factors that form the particular business environment influencing Korean firms could explain their diversification behavior. First, market size may be a critical factor. As already mentioned, if the market for certain products subject to strong economies of scale is too small for the potential benefits of large-scale production to be fully exploited, then a relatively high degree of diversification will result. Not only has the absolute size of Korea's domestic market been limited, but also the market share of Korean firms in the international market has also remained small, despite the rapid success of Korea's export promotion strategy from the early stages of development. On the other hand, governmental support for industrial development in the form of easy policy loans continued to give major firms access to larger and larger resources. Therefore in order to make the best use of the available resources, those firms pursued diversification into various industrial activities that turned out to be individually under-scaled.

Second, the degree of economies of scope among industrial activities may be an important factor. Technological innovation during the past 30 years, including recent advancements in information technology, may be argued to have strengthened economies of scope and network economies across various industrial activities. This trend has induced Korean firms to diversify by alleviating the burden of otherwise inefficient diversification.

Third, the business environment created by government policy may also be an important factor. We observe that Korean firms are found to diversify into technologically unrelated areas. In order to explain this, it seems necessary to grasp the nature of the business environment created by the government's industrial policy during the past 30 years. As has been described in Chapter 2, a salient feature of Korea's interventionist industrial policy is the government practice of refusing to allow firms that have entered a designated business area to be declared bankrupt.[18] Here the government is seen to take every possible measure to revive these firms whenever they become inefficient or are in danger of insolvency. Under such conditions, the best choice for a business firm is to make a pre-emptive move into a business area that is subject to government entry regulation because, once allowed to enter, the firm's survival is almost surely guaranteed. The detailed examination of this type of interventionist industrial policy thus helps explain some of the aspects of diversification behavior, especially unrelated diversification.

These three factors, individually and jointly, may help explain the behavioral patterns of the *chaebols* and other Korean firms with regard to business diversification. Unless these aspects are fully understood, one cannot determine whether or not the degree of diversification is excessive, and more importantly, it will be difficult to devise an appropriate policy to alleviate the degree of diversification if it is indeed excessive.

### 2.3.2 Empirical evidence on scale and scope economies and its implications for diversification behavior

Jwa (1997) reports the results of the empirical estimation of the scale and scope economies of industrial activities conducted by Korean business groups. One can combine this empirical evidence and the theoretical implications of globalization on industrial organizations to discuss the future prospects of Korea's industrial organization. A summary of the empirical results and their implications for future prospects is presented here.[19]

Two of the most important empirical findings as regards Korea's past economic environment are as follows: first, almost all products are individually subject to constant returns to scale, but overall economies of scale turn out to be very strong. Second, it is not only product-specific economies of scope that are strong but overall economies of scope also turn out to be very strong.

The implications of these findings for Korea's industrial organization are as follows: first, a major incentive for Korean business groups to diversify can be seen to stem from the particularly strong economies of scope which are present among various business activities. Basically, strong economies of scope allow cost savings through diversification. Second, globalization may not be effective in driving industrial organizations toward greater specialization for two reasons: first, almost all industrial activities are individually subject to constant returns to scale, and so the scale of production and the degree of specialization will not be greatly affected by globalization. So, as far as the effect of market size is concerned, we do not expect any drastic changes in the economies of scale. Second, it is expected that the economies of scope among industrial activities that are already firmly established will be further strengthened by globalization through rapid innovations in information technology and microelectronics. That is, there exists the possibility that globalization will further strengthen the incentives for diversification in existing industries. Furthermore, it can also be expected that if a domestic market-oriented *chaebol* loses out to foreign exporters when competing for market share, they will tend to retreat from their existing areas of specialization and move toward more diversification. However, it is also possible that globalization may bring technological innovations that could create new economies of scale for certain industrial activities, and thus encourage the specialization of those activities as the size of the market expands more than proportionately.

### 2.4 Prospects on Diversification Behavior of Korean Firms and Policy Implications

From the empirical results, one might consider whether or not the level of diversification in Korean firms is excessive. Using the estimated coefficients we project the level of diversification for Korean firms. Table A6.3 in the Appendix contains calculation for the realized and projected levels of diversification in Korean firms and differences between them. Basically, we find that the projected level of diversification in Korean firms turns out to be much higher than the actual level. Although there are some differences in the projected level of diversification depending on model specification, in general our analysis suggests that Korean firms are less diversified than their potential level, which can also be anticipated by observing international business practices. However, this is not the whole story concerning Korean firms' diversification behavior. As has already been mentioned in the preceding section on data overview, *chaebol* diversification through the expansion of the number of affiliates exhibits a vastly different pattern.

Indeed, when firm boundaries are defined from a corporate governance point of view, we can consider *chaebol* affiliates as divisions within a firm because they are under the control of major stockholders that usually include family members. Following this concept, Table 6.2 presents the level of diversification measured by counting the number of affiliates listed on the stock market and care is taken to avoid double counting where a *chaebol* has more than one affiliate operating in the given industry. The level of diversification of the *chaebols*, as shown in Table 6.2, seems to be rather high, and is actually the highest when compared to other countries in our sample (see Table 6.1, where diversification is measured as the degree of product line diversification).

We will now investigate some factors that could explain the discrepancy in *chaebol* diversification as opposed to product line diversification. As explained earlier, in Korea, it seems to be the case that there has been a strong bias in the incentive structure toward *chaebol* diversification rather than product line diversification. One factor may stem from Korea's particular situation of property rights system, which has been characterized as relatively insecure in Chapter 5. It is reasonable to assume that large firms can survive only if property rights as well as many complicated contractual arrangements are fully honored. However, if this cannot be done through the rule of law, then arbitrary protection from some external authority may also serve the same purpose. The most obvious alternative seems to be government protection, which can override both formal and informal property rights practices. As has been fully discussed in previous chapters, the Korean government reserved for itself the power to favor an owner-manager of a corporation and to selectively provide the necessary resources for the rapid growth of that corporation. In this environment, the *chaebol* found the opportunity to expand in size even without the secure protection of property rights by the rule of law.

In this way, as has been discussed in Chapter 5, the government has not only promoted large firms but has also been the prime source of uncertainty over property rights protection as far as the owner-manager of big corporations is concerned. Once the relationship between businessmen and the government has become problematic, no guarantee of favors can realistically be expected. Therefore to avoid the actual nullification of property rights, the strategy chosen has been that of aggressive expansion in the belief that this could help reduce the probability of failure, whether by non-market factors or even by market competition. This is because the government is less likely to accept the economic impact caused by the failure of a large corporation, and will intervene to maintain its existence even though it may actually be in an

Table 6.2  Diversification in chaebol groups and the ratio of listed firms to total affiliates (1997)

| Name | Rank | Total diversification | Unrelated diversification | Listed (A) | Affiliates (B) | Ratio (A/B) (%) |
|---|---|---|---|---|---|---|
| Hyundai | 1 | 43 | 32 | 21 | 57 | 37 |
| Samsung | 2 | 41 | 27 | 13 | 80 | 16 |
| LG | 3 | 23 | 16 | 11 | 49 | 22 |
| Daewoo | 4 | 23 | 17 | 9 | 30 | 30 |
| SK | 5 | 10 | 9 | 6 | 46 | 13 |
| SsangYong | 6 | 21 | 18 | 10 | 25 | 40 |
| Hanjin | 7 | 21 | 16 | 9 | 24 | 38 |
| Kia | 8 | 8 | 8 | 4 | 28 | 14 |
| Hanwha | 9 | 21 | 16 | 7 | 31 | 23 |
| Lotte | 10 | 9 | 6 | 4 | 30 | 13 |
| Kumho | 11 | 6 | 6 | 3 | 26 | 12 |
| Halla | 12 | 8 | 8 | 4 | 18 | 22 |
| Dong Ah | 13 | 7 | 6 | 4 | 19 | 21 |
| Doo San | 14 | 19 | 14 | 8 | 25 | 32 |
| Daelim | 15 | 9 | 9 | 5 | 21 | 24 |
| Hansol | 16 | 11 | 10 | 6 | 23 | 26 |
| Hyosung | 17 | 4 | 4 | 2 | 18 | 11 |
| Dong Kuk Steel Mill | 18 | 10 | 7 | 5 | 17 | 29 |
| Jinro | 19 | 9 | 9 | 4 | 24 | 17 |
| Kolon | 20 | 6 | 4 | 4 | 24 | 17 |
| Kohap | 21 | 7 | 7 | 2 | 13 | 15 |
| Dongbu | 22 | 18 | 14 | 6 | 34 | 18 |
| Haitai | 23 | 7 | 7 | 3 | 15 | 20 |

| | | | | | |
|---|---|---|---|---|---|
| Hanil | 24 | 1 | 1 | 1 | 7 | 14 |
| Keo Pyung | 25 | 9 | 9 | 5 | 22 | 23 |
| Miwon(Daesang) | 26 | 8 | 8 | 4 | 25 | 16 |
| Shinho | 27 | 9 | 9 | 6 | 25 | 24 |
| Kang Won Ind. | 28 | 2 | 2 | 2 | 12 | 17 |
| Saehan | 29 | 4 | 3 | 2 | 11 | 18 |
| Dong Yang | 30 | 4 | 4 | 4 | 24 | 17 |
| Cheil Jedang | 31 | 5 | 2 | 1 | 8 | 13 |
| Shinsegae | 32 | 1 | 1 | 1 | 8 | 13 |
| Oriental Chemical ind. | 33 | 6 | 4 | 3 | 12 | 25 |
| Woosung | 34 | 2 | 2 | 2 | 2 | 100 |
| Byuck San | 35 | 8 | 8 | 4 | 11 | 36 |
| Shin Won | 36 | 15 | 9 | 4 | 10 | 40 |
| Tongil | 37 | 8 | 7 | 5 | 11 | 45 |
| Taihan Electric Wire | 38 | 1 | 1 | 1 | 4 | 25 |
| Tongkook | 39 | 4 | 4 | 2 | 9 | 22 |
| Chong Gu | 40 | 1 | 1 | 1 | 7 | 14 |
| Keumkang | 41 | 3 | 2 | 2 | 4 | 50 |
| Sam Yang | 42 | 1 | 1 | 1 | 7 | 14 |
| Hankook Tire Mfg. | 43 | 1 | 1 | 1 | 3 | 33 |
| Pum Yang | 44 | 1 | 1 | 1 | 7 | 14 |
| Tae Kwang ind. | 45 | 5 | 4 | 2 | 5 | 40 |
| Average | 1–20 | 15.5 | 12.1 | 7.0 | 31.8 | 22.5 |
| | 1–50 | 9.2 | 7.4 | 4.3 | 18.8 | 22.9 |

*Note:* The top 30 *chaebol* are ranked according to the Korea Fair Trade Commission and the rest according to the database from the Korea Investors Services, Inc.

insolvent state. Similarly, as has been discussed in the previous chapter, efforts
to diversify into the mass media can be considered as a strategy to reduce the
probability of any discrepancy in the property rights system. In light of the
above arguments, the 'too big to fail' strategy turns out to be rather a good
survival strategy for the *chaebols* to adopt. In this context, the fact that
industrial policy has been designed so as to prevent the failure of a firm that
has been selected to enter a priority sector must constitute an important
incentive for *chaebol* diversification through affiliate expansion.

In addition, there also exists an important practice in the financial sector
known as cross-debt guarantee that determines the nature of diversification
behavior. When making loans, all financial institutions request firms to
provide collateral in the form of tangible fixed assets, such as land and
buildings, and/or third party guarantees. This financial practice has induced
the *chaebols* to create new affiliates as a means of facilitating borrowing. The
new affiliates are practically governed by the owner-managers of a given
*chaebol*, so that they can be considered as *de facto* functional divisions of a
*chaebol*. However, from a commercial law perspective, they are not *chaebol*
divisions but *de jure* independent firms because, legally, the *chaebol* or
holding company systems were not allowed, at least until 1998.[20] That is, in
effect, financial institutions have allowed major affiliates to guarantee the debt
of other affiliates from the same *chaebol* as third parties. Even if this practice
is against what is considered sound banking practice, because those affiliates
as a group should be treated as an economically identical entity, financial
sector authorities have also tacitly allowed this practice. Consequently,
diversification by increasing the number of affiliates turns out to be a much
better strategy for business expansion than product line diversification under
the existing Korean economic environment.

Since the advent of the economic crisis of 1997, the Korean economy has
been undergoing restructuring in many fields. In particular, the structure of the
*chaebols* has been subject to some changes. Some business groups that have
felt the necessity to restructure their business organization have merged their
affiliates into one firm, thereby transforming themselves into an M-type
conglomerate.[21] The strong but non-transparent relationship among affiliates
has also been weakened through the strengthening of the corporate governance
structure, as well as the policy of prohibiting cross-debt guarantees among
affiliates and other institutional reforms.[22]

On the other hand, it has been shown by empirical evidence that a major
incentive for Korean business groups to diversify stems from particularly
strong economies of scope. However, with increased globalization, the future
path of Korea's economic transformation may become varied. Loosely
speaking, however, we expect an increase in specialization to accompany the
increases in the size of the market and degree of competition. However, one

should bear in mind our argument above that globalization may not always be effective in driving industrial organizations towards greater specialization, particularly where strong economies of scope are present.

In general, overall empirical evidence together with the future prospects for change in the economic environment seem to suggest that affiliates will grow more independent than they are now or that the number of *chaebols* that amalgamate their affiliates to form a multi-divisional firm will increase. This trend may even be expedited by various government policies intended to increase the transparency of the *chaebols'* governance structure, such as those that ban cross-debt guaranteeing among affiliates, and the recent changes in the Law that allow for the formation of the holding company system.[23]

## 3.   INSTITUTIONS AND ECONOMIC PERFORMANCE

### 3.1   Background of Study

We have repeatedly argued in this book that economic institutions are directly related to a country's economic performance as well as to corporate behavior. In what follows, after consolidating this point in this section, we shall argue that institutional reform should be at the center of *chaebol* reform. In this section, we study the relationship between economic institutions and economic growth, thereby corroborating the argument that institutions matter to national economic performance.

So, how does the institutional framework of a country affect economic growth? Of course, an answer can only be provided by the new-institutional economics. Essentially, North (1990 p. 110) asserts that a country does not grow because its 'institutional constraints define a set of payoffs to political/economic activity that do not encourage productive activity'. Thus, in effect, institutions affect both individuals and organizations as shown by Figure 1.1 in Chapter 1, and institutions matter in the economy because they are integral in determining the extent of transaction costs in the economy. For example, as seen in Chapter 5, transaction costs are higher when the protection of property rights is uncertain. So firms remain small-scale, use less-capital-intensive technology and have short-term horizons, tending to rely on personal relations to facilitate operations. Since institutions determine the rules and incentive structure as well as the amount of transaction costs and eventually the behavior of individuals as well as business organizations, it follows that all these are reflected eventually by the level of economic growth.

Ever since North's work on developing the new-institutional economics framework, there has mushroomed much empirical work to determine the extent to which institutions affect national growth. Cross-country evidence is necessary not only to determine the causes of national growth, but also is important for policy-makers who might propose the strengthening of certain institutions.

Unfortunately, defining and interpreting institutional measures for empirical study is not a straightforward matter. First, the process of integrating institutions and institutional change into economic theory has largely been absent in mainstream economic thought. The variety and extent of what constitutes institutional variables is enormous and at times overwhelming. Often, it covers institutional quality such as the enforcement of property rights and the degree of shareholder rights protection, and broader social characteristics such as the ethnic, religious and historical background. Second, there is already a large variety of data and methodology in the growth literature and this is not at all simplified by adding institutional factors. Sensitivity tests, specification and identification problems, data outliers, measurement errors, and other technical matters have at times been ignored and adding institutional variables to the traditional Solow model does not usually help.[24]

In this section, we use the data set for the regression analysis on diversification from the previous section. Since these data were carefully selected to reflect the institutions and other variables of interest for the countries included in our sample, we will be in a better position to explain the significance of the parameter estimates of the regression. In sum, we have included three important institutional variables - protection of property rights, legal origin, and an index for shareholder rights, as well as other variables of interest.

### 3.2 Empirical Evidence on Economic Growth and Institutional Factors

Following our discussion of the importance of institutional factors for a firm's business behavior, we now turn to the empirical relationship between institutional factors and the overall economic performance of a country. We highlight the empirical results which are presented in Table A6.4 of the Appendix to this chapter. Briefly, we measure the economic performance of a country by the average growth rate of real GDP for the period 1990 to 1997. The explanatory variables included in the regression are the degree of property rights protection, the legal origin of company or commercial code, the degree of protection of shareholder rights, the level of financial development, the level of market competition, the size of the market and firm characteristics such as size and the debt–equity ratio that describes a firm's leverage.[25]

The potentially high transaction costs stemming from insecure property rights protection, unless a society can design a system to compensate for costs, will be realized and built into the society and thus tend to retard economic development by impeding optimal resource allocation. It follows, therefore, that the establishment of a secure property rights system becomes a necessary prerequisite for high economic performance. Our empirical results show that the effect of the property rights system on the growth of real GDP is significantly positive as expected. That is, countries having a relatively secure property rights system tend to exhibit better economic performance.

The legal origin of company law or commercial code and the extent of shareholder rights were added to the regression to test their effects on economic performance. Results show that countries where the legal system originated from common law exhibited better economic performance than countries with a legal system that did not originate under the common law tradition. French, German and Scandinavian laws, for example, are based in part on scholar- and legislator-made civil law traditions, which date back to Roman law. Clearly, our results imply that common law is a better economic environment, conducive to stronger economic performance than the scholar- and legislator-made civil law. On the other hand, the effect of shareholder rights on economic performance, despite the varying signs depending on the sample of countries in the regression, can be said to display a significant positive effect on economic growth.

A quick look at the coefficient estimates for the other variables follows. First, it is easy to understand that the level of development of the financial sector must have a positive effect on economic performance. Needless to say, our empirical results are consistent with this expectation. Second, market competition stimulates economic activity in general, including production, marketing and R&D activities, and thus tends to increase productivity. This leads to an increase in economic performance and therefore the coefficient for market competition will most likely be positive. This is confirmed by our results. Third, real GDP is used as a proxy for market size in the regression on diversification but has been included here to capture the convergence effects in economic growth as argued by Easterly and Levine (1997). According to their study, the catch-up effect is a concave function of initial income measured by real GDP per capita. The coefficient for market size is expected to be negative if catch-up effects exist, and our empirical results are consistent with this expectation. Lastly, the size of firms in the economy turns out to have a positive effect on economic growth.

In sum, by testing whether economic institutions and other factors influence aggregate economic performance, we find that countries with secure property rights systems, a common law tradition, stronger protection for shareholder rights, higher levels of financial development and higher market competition grow faster than others. We have therefore confirmed that the institutional environment strongly influences economic growth, as well as the sustainability of economic development.

## 4.   CONCLUDING REMARKS

To sum up, the cross-country empirical analysis of this chapter has confirmed
that, in general, a secure property rights system encourages the formation of
large firms with more diversification while increased market competition
tends to discourage unrelated diversification, though the latter effect was
somewhat weak. On the other hand, both turn out to make a strong positive
contribution to economic growth. We also find that the increased size of the
market turns out to have a significant negative impact on diversification
behavior. Some aspects of the corporate governance system are also seen to be
important determinants of diversification and economic performance. The
legal system or commercial code that is based on the Roman law tradition as
opposed to those based on common law traditions tends to discourage
diversification. On the other hand, the common law tradition turns out to
contribute positively to economic development in contrast to the case of the
Roman law tradition. It seems to be the case that although strong shareholder
rights do not have any discernible effects on diversification behavior, they
have a very strong positive effect on economic growth. In general, our
empirical results support our views on economic reform presented in Chapter
8 where we stress the importance of a secure property rights system,
transparent corporate governance structure, and enhanced market competition,
including market opening, in formulating a policy to discipline *chaebol*
behavior, including its diversification strategy, while being consistent with the
goals of national economic development. We find that market competition,
which is in our view the central theme for future economic reform, is an
important element for economic growth and prosperity.

This chapter has confirmed, by providing empirical evidence in an
international setting as well as in the Korean setting, our arguments on the
importance of economic institutions and market and technological factors for
firms' diversification behavior and economic growth. It has also been learnt
that the future prospects for Korean firms' diversification behavior will
depend to a large extent on government policies to alleviate excessive affiliate
diversification. However, in this context, one has to understand that the current
diversification behavior of the *chaebols* has been influenced by the prevailing
economic environment which consists of various institutional factors, as well
as given market conditions. Therefore it has to be emphasized that if the
government wants to influence *chaebol* behavior, then it must improve the
economic environment accordingly so as to induce the *chaebols* to behave in
the desired manner. Thus, in Korea, there remains the need to reform
economic institutions, as well as to promote overall competitive pressure from
the market. These arguments will be further elaborated in the following
chapters.

# APPENDIX

## A1.   Cross-Country Regression Analysis of Diversification Behavior

This part of the appendix contains details of a cross-country empirical analysis that shows the relationship between diversification and institutional factors, corporate structure, development of financial markets, overall market size, market competition and business risk.

### A1.1   Description of the data and sample sets

For the empirical analysis we use the Standard Industrial Classification (SIC) data from the Company Analysis database supplied by PriMark. This database includes a profile indicating industries in which a firm is active by SIC code and shows data on product segment sales. We selected firms operating only in the non-financial industries and classified them according to our criteria as follows. Two data sets have been constructed in order to make appropriate deductions from the regression analysis. The first set, sample A, contains 26 countries each represented by about 20 firms, while the second set, sample B, consists of 17 countries with each country being represented by about 50 firms.[26] In selecting the countries to be included in the sample, the number of countries that could be included in the samples was determined not only by the availability of data on independent variables but also by the choice of the number of firms to represent each country. Specifically, as we increased the number of firms to represent each country, the number of countries represented in a sample falls; that is, sample B has a lower number of countries than sample A. Also, in selecting which firms should represent a country, we ranked all of a country's firms in descending order according to asset size and chose those firms that had data on product segment sales beginning from the top; that is, in descending order. However, if firms in a higher rank did not have all the required information, we looked beyond this selected group to meet the condition that all firms selected should have complete product segment data. Also, note that our regression samples do not include Korea because of the incomparability of the Korean *chaebols'* managerial diversification behavior as characterized by the extension of affiliates, this being the prevalent form of diversification in Korea, with product diversification characteristic of other countries.[27]

For data on property rights (PR), the International Country Risk Guide (ICRG) data from Barro and Sala-I-Martin (1995) was used. The index of shareholder rights (AR) and the legal origin of company law or commercial code (LO) are employed from the data listed in Porta *et al.* (1997). Where necessary, data were also obtained from the *International Statistical Yearbook*, International Financial Statistics and the International Federation of

Stock Exchanges. Table A6.1 lists the dependent and independent variables used in the cross-country regression analysis.

*Table A6.1    Variables for analysis and definition*

| Variable | | Definition | Source | Period |
|---|---|---|---|---|
| DIV  TDIV | | Number of four-digit industries in which firms operate | CA | 1997 |
| | UDIV | Number of two-digit industries in which firms operate | CA | 1997 |
| GR | | $(GDP_t-GDP_{t-1})/GDP_t$ where GDP denotes real gross domestic product | IFS | 1990–97 |
| PR | | Simple mean of five ICRG indices | Barro and Sala-I-Martin (1995) | 1980s |
| AR | | Index of shareholder rights | Porta *et al.* (1997) | – |
| LO | | Legal origin of company law | Porta *et al.* (1997) | – |
| GSR | | $(M^2 +$ the market value of stock)/ nominal GNP | IFS, FIBV | 1990–97 |
| MC | | $(N_t-N_{t-1})/N_t$ where N is the number of firms in manufacturing | ISY | 1980–97 |
| MS | | Natural log of real GDP | IFS | 1990–97 |
| SF | | Natural log of firms' assets | CA | 1997 |
| RK | | Standard deviation of each firm's profits before taxes divided by sales | CA | 1994–97 |
| DR | | Debt/equity | CA | 1994–97 |

*Note :*   CA: Company Analysis, PriMark.
        IFS: *International Financial Statistics*, IMF.
        ISY: *International Statistical Yearbook*, OECD.
        FIBV: International Federation of Stock Exchanges, www.fibv.com

## A1.2   Regression model and measurement of variables

According to the theoretical implications of the determinants of diversification, we specify a regression model as in equation (1), for the cross-country analysis at the firm level. The dependent variable is the level of diversification (DIV), and the independent variables include institutional environment variables, such as property rights (PR), corporate governance (AR) and the legal origin of company law or commercial code (LO). In addition, the level of financial development (GSR), market competition (MC), the market size of a national economy (MS), the size of firm (SF) and business risk (RK) are included in the regression as variables that may influence the level of diversification. The stochastic error term is denoted by e and the $\alpha i$'s are the parameters to be estimated.

$$DIV = \alpha_0 + \alpha_1 PR + \alpha_2 AR + \alpha_3 LO + \alpha_4 GSR + \alpha_5 MC$$
$$+ \alpha_6 MS + \alpha_7 SF + \alpha_8 RK + e \qquad (1)$$

To measure the level of diversification, the number of industries in which a given corporation operates is used. That is, we simply count the number of different industries in which a corporation operates.[28] Because diversified corporations operate in different business sectors, the number of sectors or industries in which firms operate should reveal the level of diversification. According to the Standard Industrial Classification code (SIC), industries are classified into a four-digit or two-digit code. The number of different two-digit codes tell us how many unrelated businesses a firm operates in, while the number of different four-digit codes reveals how many related as well as unrelated businesses a firm operates in. Accordingly, the number of product lines in four-digit industries and the number of product lines in two-digit industries can be classified as the degree of total diversification (TDIV) and the degree of unrelated diversification (UDIV), respectively, both of which are used as dependent variables (DIV) in equation (1).

The variable for property rights (PR) is derived using the simple mean of five indices as measured by the *International Country Risk Guide* (ICRG) – expropriation risk, risk of contract repudiation by the government, rule of law, corruption in government, and the quality of the bureaucracy in the 1980s.[29] The ICRG data on property rights have been obtained from Barro and Sala-I-Martin (1995).

The index of shareholder rights (AR) is adopted from Porta *et al.* (1997). This index was created by adding '1' when (1) the country allows shareholders to mail their proxy vote; (2) shareholders are not required to deposit their shares prior to the General Shareholders' Meeting; (3) cumulative voting is allowed; (4) an oppressed minorities mechanism is in place; (5) when the minimum percentage of share capital that entitles a shareholder to call for an Extraordinary Shareholders' Meeting is less than or equal to 10 per cent.

The legal origin of company law or commercial code (LO) also uses the data listed in Porta *et al.* If the legal system has originated from common law made by judges and subsequently incorporated into the legislature, we index this by '1'. However, if it is civil law, which originated not from common law but from Roman law, then we index this '0'. Therefore this index is a dummy variable that takes on the value of either one or zero, and shows the effect of the legal condition in company law or commercial code on diversification.

The level of financial development is generally measured using the Goldsmith ratio (GSR) and is usually expressed as the ratio of financial assets to nominal GNP. The Goldsmith ratio represents the accumulation of financial assets in a national economy. In our analysis, because we could not directly access data on financial assets, the Goldsmith ratio was constructed by the summation of M2 and the market value of stock divided by nominal GNP from 1990 to 1997.

The severity or weakness of market competition (MC) depends on the number of firms (N) that are active in a market. Using the Herfindahl index (H), we created an index reflecting the density of market competition.[30] If $s_i$ is the market share of firm $i$ in a market, then the Herfindahl index can be expressed as $H = \Sigma(s_i)^2$. Now let the change in the number of firms in a market from time $t$ to time $t–1$ be E. So $E = N_t–N_{t–1}$. We can also create another index, $ES = E \times H$, and when all firms are the same size, ES represents the market share of all entrants because H equals $1/N_t$. So E or ES represents the intensity of market competition. Note that even if the sizes of all firms are not identical, firm entry increases E and ES, and these indices reflect the intensity of competition in a market. For this analysis, we obtained the data on the number of firms from the *International Statistical Yearbook* and calculated the ES average (MC) from 1980 to the most recent year for which data were available.

As regards the market size of a national economy (MS), we measured total demand by the natural log of the real gross domestic product (GDP) averaged between 1990 and 1997.

Reflecting the characteristics of individual firms, firm size (SF) is measured by the natural log of total assets in 1997. Business risk (RK), included to control for diversification influenced by a firm's motive to reduce risk, is calculated by averaging the standard deviation of each firm's profits before taxes divided by sales in every year from 1994 to 1997. While the level of diversification is measured using 1997 data, we compute risk by using data from 1994 to 1997 to remove the causality that might run from diversification to risk.

### A1.3    Regression estimates and results

Table A6.2 shows the results for the regression analysis of diversification on the explanatory variables. Because heteroskedasticity could be important across countries, the standard error of the coefficients in all models is based on White's (1980) consistent covariance matrix.

For each sample set the regression model as described in equation (1) is first run by omitting both the Goldsmith ratio (GSR) and the level of market competition (MC) variables, results for which are shown under the 'A1' and 'B1' columns of Table A6.2. The two variables are then included as in the

Table A6.2   The effects of economic institutions on diversification

| | Total diversification | | | | | | | |
| --- | --- | --- | --- | --- | --- | --- | --- | --- |
| | Sample A | | | | Sample B | | | |
| | Model A1-1 | Model A1-2 | Model A2-1 | Model A2-2 | Model B1-1 | Model B1-2 | Model B2-1 | Model B2-2 |
| PR | 0.290*** | 0.279*** | 0.413*** | 0.404*** | 0.229*** | 0.210*** | 0.304*** | 0.221*** |
| | (3.109) | (2.913) | (3.492) | (3.293) | (3.783) | (3.579) | (3.872) | (2.761) |
| LO | | 0.242 | | 0.385 | | 0.685** | | 0.529 |
| | | (0.644) | | (0.671) | | (2.236) | | (1.226) |
| AR | -0.002 | | -0.012 | | -0.049 | | -0.253 | |
| | (-0.011) | | (-0.059) | | (-0.423) | | (-1.553) | |
| GSR | | | 0.007 | 0.003 | | | 0.029*** | 0.021** |
| | | | (0.506) | (0.214) | | | (3.361) | (2.308) |
| MC | | | -0.035 | -0.045 | | | 0.011 | -0.018 |
| | | | (-0.684) | (-0.893) | | | (0.350) | (-0.578) |
| MS | -0.857*** | -0.836*** | -1.314*** | -1.210*** | -1.123*** | -1.079*** | -1.825*** | -.564*** |
| | (-4.139) | (-3.993) | (-4.116) | (-3.550) | (-8.987) | (-8.639) | (-10.242) | (-7.552) |
| SF | 1.094*** | 1.087*** | 1.179*** | 1.132*** | 1.080*** | 1.017*** | 1.253*** | 1.136*** |
| | (6.668) | (6.648) | (5.035) | (4.785) | (12.434) | (11.194) | (11.354) | (9.231) |
| RK | 1.314 | 0.872 | 2.158 | 1.591 | 0.386 | -1.637 | 0.757 | -0.813 |
| | (0.706) | (0.449) | (0.962) | (0.680) | (0.328) | (-1.139) | (0.397) | (-0.373) |
| Constant | 12.360*** | 12.331*** | 12.190*** | 11.976*** | 13.609*** | 13.008*** | 13.579*** | 12.968*** |
| | (6.347) | (6.401) | (4.973) | (5.000) | (12.315) | (12.283) | (10.481) | (10.314) |
| Adjusted $R^2$ | 0.110 | 0.111 | 0.147 | 0.149 | 0.156 | 0.161 | 0.239 | 0.238 |
| F | 12.43*** | 12.52*** | 8.58*** | 8.66*** | 36.13*** | 37.49*** | 29.46*** | 29.31*** |
| D.F. | 456 | 456 | 300 | 300 | 945 | 945 | 626 | 626 |
| No. of countries | 26 | 26 | 17 | 17 | 21 | 21 | 14 | 14 |
| No. of firms | 462 | 462 | 308 | 308 | 951 | 951 | 634 | 634 |

Continued overleaf

147

Unrelated diversification

| | Sample A | | | | Sample B | | | |
|---|---|---|---|---|---|---|---|---|
| | Model A1-1 | Model A1-2 | Model A2-1 | Model A2-2 | Model B1-1 | Model B1-2 | Model B2-1 | Model B2-2 |
| PR | 0.063 (0.955) | 0.051 (0.775) | 0.187** (2.435) | 0.175** (2.232) | 0.055 (1.285) | 0.045 (1.151) | 0.140*** (2.790) | 0.055 (1.133) |
| LO | | 0.686*** (2.815) | | 0.933** (2.553) | | 1.064*** (5.357) | | 0.969*** (3.475) |
| AR | 0.097 (1.057) | | 0.035 (0.261) | | 0.109 (1.442) | | -0.136 (-1.242) | |
| GSR | | | 0.007 (0.873) | -0.0003 (-0.040) | | | 0.025*** (4.474) | 0.015*** (2.596) |
| MC | | | -0.033 (-0.945) | -0.054 (-1.597) | | | -0.012 (-0.557) | -0.045** (-2.180) |
| MS | -0.702*** (-5.167) | -0.639*** (-4.900) | -1.152*** (-5.540) | -0.925*** (-4.315) | -0.917*** (-10.963) | -0.839*** (-10.510) | -1.473*** (-12.733) | -1.137*** (-8.682) |
| SF | 0.707*** (6.223) | 0.691*** (6.201) | 0.778*** (4.722) | 0.678*** (4.248) | 0.716*** (12.407) | 0.642*** (11.027) | 0.860*** (11.919) | 0.711*** (9.268) |
| RK | 1.313 (1.455) | 0.395 (0.412) | 1.919* (1.758) | 0.654 (0.551) | -0.311 (-0.460) | -2.809*** (-3.290) | -0.305 (-0.301) | -2.666** (-2.176) |
| Constant | 9.157*** (6.839) | 9.142*** (7.010) | 8.948*** (5.340) | 8.503*** (5.338) | 9.954*** (12.837) | 9.466*** (13.248) | 9.992*** (11.707) | 9.382*** (11.649) |
| Adjusted $R^2$ | 0.105 | 0.116 | 0.171 | 0.188 | 0.175 | 0.203 | 0.309 | 0.324 |
| F | 11.77*** | 13.14*** | 10.06*** | 11.18*** | 41.31*** | 49.27*** | 41.42*** | 44.27*** |
| D.F. | 456 | 456 | 300 | 300 | 945 | 945 | 626 | 626 |
| No. of countries | 26 | 26 | 17 | 17 | 21 | 21 | 14 | 14 |
| No. of firms | 462 | 462 | 308 | 308 | 951 | 951 | 634 | 634 |

*Note:* t-statistics in parentheses; asterisks denote the level of significance: *** 1 per cent, ** 5 per cent.

original regression for a second run and results are presented under the 'A2' and 'B2' columns. The first regression is run, with respect to sample A, by omitting the two variables for which data were insufficient, and allows for 26 countries to be included in the regression. Including the omitted variables and re-running the regression allows for only 17 countries. Similarly, we have for sample B, 21 and 14 countries respectively. For each regression set, to avoid technical problems that may be caused by the strong collinearity between the index of shareholder rights (AR) and the legal origin of company law (LO), two separate regressions are made, each omitting the other variable.

## A2.  Diversification Projection for Korea

Table A6.3 contains calculation for the realized and projected levels of diversification for Korea derived from our estimations in the above regression.

## A3.  Institutions and Economic Performance: Regression Model and Results

Equation (2) depicts the regression equation that is constructed to analyze the effects of institutional factors on economic performance. Economic performance is measured by the average growth rate of real GDP (GR) for the period 1990 to 1997. The explanatory variables include the property rights system (PR), index of shareholder rights (AR), legal origin of company or commercial code (LO), the Goldsmith Ratio (GSR), market competition (MC), market size (MS), firm characteristics such as size (SF) and the debt–equity ratio (DR), describing a firm's leverage. The $\beta_i$'s are parameters to be estimated and $\mu$ is the error term.[31]

$$GR = \beta_0 + \beta_1 PR + \beta_2 AR + \beta_3 LO + \beta_4 GSR + \beta_5 MC$$
$$+ \beta_6 MS + \beta_7 SF + \beta_8 DR + \mu \tag{2}$$

Regression on performance is performed in a similar way to the regression on diversification, and the empirical results are presented in Table A6.4.

*Table A6.3   Diversification projections for Korea*

**Total diversification**

|  | Sample A | | | | Sample B | | | |
|---|---|---|---|---|---|---|---|---|
|  | Model A1-1 | Model A1-2 | Model A2-1 | Model A2-2 | Model B1-1 | Model B1-2 | Model B2-1 | Model B2-2 |
| Realized (A) | 1.55 | 1.55 | 1.55 | 1.55 | 1.50 | 1.50 | 1.50 | 1.50 |
| Projected (B) | 9.44 | 9.38 | 9.48 | 9.44 | 9.71 | 9.31 | 10.31 | 9.47 |
| Difference (B-A) | 7.89 | 7.83 | 7.93 | 7.89 | 8.21 | 7.81 | 8.81 | 7.97 |

**Unrelated diversification**

|  | Sample A | | | | Sample B | | | |
|---|---|---|---|---|---|---|---|---|
|  | Model A1-1 | Model A1-2 | Model A2-1 | Model A2-2 | Model B1-1 | Model B1-2 | Model B2-1 | Model B2-2 |
| Realized (A) | 1.30 | 1.30 | 1.30 | 1.30 | 1.26 | 1.26 | 1.26 | 1.26 |
| Projected (B) | 6.07 | 8.87 | 6.56 | 6.49 | 6.38 | 6.14 | 7.43 | 6.27 |
| Difference(B-A) | 4.77 | 7.57 | 5.26 | 5.19 | 5.11 | 4.88 | 6.17 | 5.00 |

Table A6.4 *Effects of economic institutions on performance*

| | The growth rate of real GDP | | | | | | | |
| --- | --- | --- | --- | --- | --- | --- | --- | --- |
| | Sample A | | | | Sample B | | | |
| | Model A1-1 | Model A1-2 | Model A2-1 | Model A2-2 | Model B1-1 | Model B1-2 | Model B2-1 | Model B2-2 |
| PR | 2.448*** | 2.583*** | 2.546*** | 2.528*** | 2.493*** | 2.623*** | 2.718*** | 2.644*** |
| | (28.602) | (25.321) | (25.690) | (27.650) | (44.224) | (37.563) | (38.263) | (42.055) |
| LO | | 3.780*** | 1.665*** | 1.615*** | | 3.747*** | | 1.767*** |
| | | (9.980) | (7.679) | (3.122) | | (15.192) | | (4.877) |
| AR | 1.123*** | | | | 1.082*** | | -0.227 | |
| | (6.636) | | | | (9.960) | | (-1.573) | |
| GSR | | | -0.020 | 0.014 | | | 0.030*** | 0.005 |
| | | | (-0.095) | (0.934) | | | (3.178) | (0.465) |
| MC | | | 0.279*** | 0.228*** | | | 0.264*** | 0.197*** |
| | | | (6.754) | (5.641) | | | (9.681) | (7.690) |
| MS | -2.251*** | -1.785*** | -3.663*** | -3.130*** | -2.167*** | -1.717*** | -3.271*** | -2.603*** |
| | (-11.138) | (-9.912) | (-11.258) | (-8.406) | (-17.641) | (-16.413) | (-15.788) | (-11.205) |
| SF | 0.281 | 0.081 | 1.665*** | 1.404*** | 0.201** | 0.042 | 1.147*** | 0.866*** |
| | (1.452) | (0.428) | (7.679) | (5.802) | (2.020) | (0.446) | (10.701) | (7.540) |
| DR | 0.0000 | -0.0000 | -0.0002 | -0.0002 | 0.0000 | 0.0000 | -0.0004** | -0.0004* |
| | (0.183) | (-0.147) | (-0.466) | (-0.459) | (0.218) | (0.143) | (-2.266) | (-2.012) |
| Constant | -17.017*** | -18.750*** | -5.730*** | -7.274*** | -17.789*** | -19.472*** | -9.625*** | -11.468*** |
| | (-8.488) | (-10.011) | (-2.719) | (3.458) | (15.522) | (-18.383) | (-8.691) | (-10.905) |
| Adjusted R² | 0.561 | 0.624 | 0.672 | 0.685 | 0.561 | 0.621 | 0.656 | 0.669 |
| F | 101.62*** | 131.29*** | 78.42*** | 83.15*** | 243.58*** | 312.14*** | 173.76*** | 184.11*** |
| D.F. | 388 | 388 | 257 | 257 | 945 | 945 | 626 | 626 |
| No. of Countries | 26 | 26 | 17 | 17 | 21 | 21 | 14 | 14 |
| No. of Firms | 394 | 394 | 265 | 265 | 951 | 951 | 634 | 634 |

*Note:* t-statistics in parentheses; asterisks denote the level of significance: *** 1 per cent, ** 5 per cent.

# NOTES

1. Recently, Oman (1993) provides a definition of the complex phenomenon of globalization along similar lines.
2. For detailed discussion, see Jwa (1999).
3. See Chapter 1, Figure 1.1, and the related discussions for further details.
4. Eggertsson argues that the theory of agency is a branch of the transaction cost view. A closer examination, however, reveals that the agency view is different from the transaction cost view in that the former focuses on agency costs from agency relationships and the latter on transaction costs from transaction-specific investments.
5. See Martin (1993, pp. 212–13).
6. See Chapter 5 for more details of this discussion.
7. Also see Mork, Shleifer and Vishnya (1988, p. 293).
8. See Jwa (1997) for an exposition of the importance of corporate governance to business performance from the perspective of new-institutional economics. Chapter 7 provides a theory of corporate governance, and a framework for corporate governance reform is laid out in Chapter 8.
9. In general, the source of scope economies is the existence of public inputs, which are similar to public goods in consumption. 'Information' is intrinsically of a public-input nature; therefore diversification across different industrial activities utilizing the same information will benefit from economies of scope. In addition, improvements in computer and automation technologies will help develop a multi-functional machinery that will become a public input to various related industrial activities, thereby creating or increasing economies of scope among those activities. All these possibilities suggest that economies of scope among economic activities will strengthen as a result of technological innovations in the information industry.
10. Drucker (1999).
11. For further details see Jwa (1997).
12. For example, see Oman (1993, 1994).
13. See C.W.L. Hill and O.E. Hoskisson (1987, p. 332).
14. Diversification to induce financial economies, illustrated by behavior such as *chaebol* cross-shareholding even in unrelated areas, has been another feature that has brought about heated discussion among the general public. This can be contrasted with the discussions in the previous chapter where diversification of the *chaebol* in the mass media was viewed as a way toward securing property rights protection.
15. Indeed, for 1997, the mean value of Korea's product line diversification among the largest 20 *chaebols* turns out to be 1.55 or 1.50, as shown in Table 6.2, compared to the level of 15.5 for *chaebol* diversification as shown in Table A6.4 in the Appendix. For these reasons, we drop Korea from the samples when performing the regression analysis, but include it in the data overview where necessary.
16. See Section A.1.2 and Table A6.1 in the Appendix for details as to the classification between related and unrelated diversification, as well as details as to how the variables were set up.
17. See Mork, Shleifer and Vishny (1988). Also, see Jensen and Meckling (1976, p. 305).
18. During the 1970s, when Korea pursued the so-called heavy and chemical industry promotion policy, the government actively intervened in selecting firms and entrepreneurs to do business in specified areas and provided the means to support them. If those selected firms were in danger of going bankrupt, the government intervened to arrange additional financial assistance or merger and acquisition procedures to rescue them. In recent years, this pattern of government intervention has been mitigated but remains effective to some extent in a weaker form. The government still has strong influence on determining those that may enter important industries such as automobiles, steel, etc. Concerning exit policy, the government has become much more permissive in letting non-competitive firms go bankrupt in recent years but is still very reluctant to see big firms in important industries fail. Therefore the perception that once a firm is allowed to enter a major industry, then it will be easy for it to survive has only somewhat weakened.
19. See Jwa (1997) for more details regarding the empirical evidence and implications.

20. See note 1 in Chapter 1.
21. M-type firm refers to multidivisional firms, which remove general office executives from partisan involvement in the functional parts and assign operating responsibilities to each business division. See Williamson (1985) for further details.
22. Further details of the corporate sector reforms in the post-crisis period can be found in Chapter 8.
23. Currently the requirements for being eligible to be a holding company are rather stringent but this is expected to be relaxed in the near future. See note 1 Chapter 1.
24. See Janine Aron (2000) for further discussions on the empirical literature that tries to link institutional factors to growth.
25. See the Appendix to this chapter for further details of the variables.
26. For certain countries where data was deficient, the actual number of firms representing the country was less than 20 and 50 for sample A and B, respectively.
27. See note 13 of Chapter 6.
28. Another possible way to measure the level of diversification is by using the entropy index; see A. Jacquemin and C.H. Berry (1979). However, our data lack information on the share of each product segment in total shipments of firms so that other complex measures for diversification could not be utilized.
29. See S. Knack and P. Keefer (1995).
30. We think that one of the most important factors affecting whether or not a firm diversifies is potential competition. However, it is almost impossible to measure the intensity of potential competition in a given market, so we measure this variable using only the number of firms existing in a market.
31. See above for details about these variables.

# 7.  Lessons from Korea's economic success and the future paradigm for corporate policy

## 1.  INTRODUCTION

Extensive government intervention has featured prominently in the Korean economy. This is true whether we are talking about the general role of the government in economic development, or whether we are addressing specific issues such as the government's policy toward the corporate sector. As has been discussed in the preceding chapters, this strategy of government-led economic management contributed to Korea's economic growth in the early phase of her economic development. Extensive government intervention has, however, often hindered the development of the market economy and the prospects of its continued success are becoming increasingly uncertain. It is paramount, therefore, that a new approach to policy formulation be put into effect to meet the challenges as Korea moves into the modern era that is characterized by the rapidly changing domestic and international economic environment.

In this chapter, we look back and evaluate the general impact of Korea's industrial policies, emphasizing issues that need to be considered when looking forward in search of an appropriate framework for sustainable economic development. The first part of this chapter discusses the various deficiencies of the government-led development strategy, and also puts into proper perspective the reasons for the 1997 financial crisis. In the second part of this chapter, we review existing literature on the debates about the roles of government and the private sector in economic management, and in doing so provide a new interpretation of Korea's development process. The last part of this chapter introduces our own unique conceptual framework based on the new-institutional economics perspective, upon which a theory of corporate governance is constructed. This theory should provide the basis for a new direction of public policy toward the private sector.

Broadly speaking, this critical chapter not only provides the reasons why Korea should break away from the past government-led economic management system, but also provides the framework needed to pave the way ahead for the introduction and consolidation of the market system. This rest of the chapter is organized as follows. Section 2 presents and evaluates past industrial policies, specifically the HCI drive, which have been adopted by the Korean government. As a recent example of the government intervention legacy, we also trace the events of the rise and fall of the Samsung Motor Company. Finally, we identify aspects of the past interventionist industrial policies that provided the ideal setting for the outbreak of the recent economic crisis. Section 3 begins by reviewing existing literature on the role of the government in economic management. We then proceed further to provide our own unique explanation of Korea's past economic growth. In Section 4, based firmly on new-institutional economics as well as the analyses carried out in this book, we construct a theory of corporate governance, which is also applied to explain the differences in corporate behavior across various countries.

## 2. A BRIEF EVALUATION OF KOREA'S INDUSTRIAL POLICIES

We begin this section by evaluating the impact of Korea's government-led industrial policies on productivity, especially in relation to the heavy and chemical industrialization (HCI) drive. In addition, as a concrete illustration of the past government-led development strategy at the micro level, we narrow down our discussion in the second part and look at the specific case of the Samsung Motor Company, as a recent example of how industrial policy has been typically applied to the corporate sector. As a general overview, we conclude this section by arguing that the legacy of past government-led industrial policies created a structural environment that encouraged moral hazard behavior, which is here identified as one of the main causes of the currency crisis of 1997.

### 2.1 The Effects of the HCI Drive on Productivity

As has been described in Chapter 2, the Korean government utilized financial institutions as an instrument for industrial policy. However, as we shall see shortly, the industrial policy put into place that aided governmental control over the financial sector did not necessarily lead to an increase in total factor productivity. Financial resources directed to selected industries, particularly the heavy and chemical industries, by government, resulted in the inefficient allocation of financial resources. Moreover, lending banks and other financial institutions, as a result of the government's direct intervention, were unable to exercise their discretionary and monitoring responsibilities in the allocation of loanable funds. The borrowing firms having easier access to scarce resources became less diligent in efficiently utilizing the available capital. Furthermore, since the government protected their investments, there was no urgent need to improve business efficiency. The lack of commercial spirit in the financial sector due to government control can therefore be seen to have led directly to the weak corporate governance structure in the business sector. This adversely affected the managers' incentive to focus on productivity and therefore led to capital over-investment and the inefficient utilization of capital. We cannot, therefore, stress enough the important role of financial markets in disciplining corporate behavior to ensure the efficient allocation and utilization of capital as well as its higher productivity.

Developing countries that seek to adopt the East Asian growth model should be interested in understanding the impact of active government intervention on economic growth. Many existing studies have analyzed the sources of economic growth in Korea in terms of the increase of factor accumulation and technological progress. In particular, Krugman (1994) had warned that the East Asian economy would reach the point of marginal growth, pointing out that the source of Asian growth lay mainly in the increase in inputs of production, implying that government-led industrial policies were ineffective[1]. He argued that the growth of the East Asian economy was due not to technological advancements but to the increase in factor accumulation, and that the East Asian economy would eventually run into diminishing returns, which would restrict rapid future growth. In order to verify this argument, we shall look at Korea's development experience in more detail.

From January 1973 to spring of 1979, the Korean government implemented the Heavy and Chemical Industry (HCI) drive to promote the development of selected key industries. One approach to evaluating Korea's industrial policy would be to measure the increase in productivity at the manufacturing level in relation not only to the whole period of economic development but also to when a particular policy was active. Table 7.1 shows that between 1967 and 1996 the growth rate of the manufacturing sector was 15.68 per cent per annum, of which only 1.59 per cent is due to growth in total factor productivity. A closer look at the same table shows that, in fact, Korean manufacturing industries experienced a steep decline in the growth rate of total factor productivity during the period of the HCI drive. Furthermore, inefficiencies in the heavy and chemical industry, which is energy-intensive in its operations, were magnified by the two oil price shocks of the 1970s. The excessive capital investment in the heavy and chemical industries also resulted in a decrease of capital investment in light industry.[2] It has also been argued that there was related deterioration in efficiency in light industries due to spillover effects.[3]

*Table 7.1    Contribution to productivity growth (1967-96) (unit %)*

| Industry | 1967-70 | 1970-75 | 1975-80 | 1980-85 | 1985-90 | 1990-96 | 1967-96 |
|---|---|---|---|---|---|---|---|
| Factors | | | | | | | |
| TFP | 3.30 | 1.56 | −3.10 | −0.26 | 0.76 | 2.43 | 1.59 |
| Capital | 5.52 | 2.19 | 4.32 | 1.95 | 3.74 | 3.82 | 3.69 |
| Labor | 1.04 | 0.78 | 0.58 | 0.20 | 0.39 | −0.16 | 0.48 |
| Intermediate goods | 13.88 | 14.67 | 11.18 | 6.15 | 9.80 | 5.47 | 9.93 |
| Output growth | 23.74 | 19.20 | 12.98 | 8.05 | 14.69 | 11.56 | 15.68 |
| Contribution of TFP as percentage of total factors | 13.89 | 8.12 | −23.93 | -3.20 | 5.16 | 21.01 | 10.11 |

*Source*:   Lee (1998).

As such, the growth in Korea's manufacturing sector exhibits an input-driven pattern, achieved mainly through the quantitative growth of factors of production. That is, the growth in the manufacturing sector has been achieved mainly through the increase in the quantity of production factors rather than by improvements of production efficiency, clearly supporting the quantitative-growth hypothesis.

Table 7.2 shows the distribution of industries whose total factor productivity growth changed between 1970 and 1996. In general, there is an increase in the number of industries whose input productivity decreased during this period. Specifically, between 1975 and 1980, the period during which the HCI drive was active, the number of industries in which the total factor productivity growth was low is seen to have dramatically increased, with almost double the number of industries showing negative total factor productivity compared to the previous five-year period. Also, the number of industries in the manufacturing sector with over 4 per cent total factor productivity more than halved during the period 1975 to 1980 compared to the previous decade and never showed any sign of recovery. The major problem industries in the manufacturing sector include the petroleum and refinery industry and the coal industry, together with the iron and steel industry and non-ferrous metal industry, all having large output shares in the manufacturing sector and where all major companies were under the HCI drive.

It is therefore evident that the efficiency of capital investment decreased during the period of Korea's HCI drive, and indeed, it can be argued that direct government intervention in the heavy and chemical industries resulted in the

*Table 7.2   Distribution of total factor productivity (TFP) at the manufacturing industrial level*

|            | 1967–70 | 1970–75 | 1975–80 | 1980–85 | 1985–90 | 1990–96 |
|------------|---------|---------|---------|---------|---------|---------|
| Below –4%  | 0       | 1       | 3       | 1       | 0       | 2       |
| –3 ~ –3.9  | 0       | 1       | 0       | 1       | 0       | 0       |
| –2 ~ –2.9  | 1       | 0       | 0       | 1       | 1       | 3       |
| –1 ~ –1.9  | 0       | 1       | 1       | 3       | 3       | 0       |
| –0.9 ~ 0   | 1       | 1       | 3       | 3       | 7       | 1       |
| 0 ~ 0.9    | 2       | 0       | 5       | 5       | 9       | 2       |
| 1 ~ 1.9    | 4       | 1       | 2       | 3       | 5       | 6       |
| 2 ~ 2.9    | 5       | 2       | 2       | 6       | 1       | 5       |
| 3 ~ 3.9    | 2       | 4       | 5       | 4       | 0       | 6       |
| Above 4%   | 13      | 17      | 7       | 1       | 2       | 3       |

*Source*:   Lee (1998).

decline of total factor productivity. We find that it is the quantitative growth of inputs rather than factor productivity that is accountable for the growth of the Korean manufacturing sector. In fact, the growth rate of total factor productivity was at its lowest during the period 1975 to 1980, when the promotion of the heavy and chemical industries was well under way. We may also note that the inefficient resource allocation caused by direct government intervention in the heavy and chemical industries in the 1970s continued to adversely affect productivity in the early 1980s. Without doubt, after 1973, the active government's intervention in the heavy and chemical industries hurt industrial productivity growth and hence economic performance.

## 2.2   The curse of the Government-led Development Strategy: The Rise and Fall of Samsung Motor Company

Various efforts have been made to transform Korea into a market economy, particularly after the mid-1980s. These attempts, however, have been somewhat feeble and sporadic, and it remains difficult for Korea to break away from the government-led development strategy. Old habits die hard and direct intervention reminiscent of the past government-led development strategy is still a persistent feature of today's economy. To see this more concretely, in this section, we discuss the case of Samsung Motor Company (SMC) and highlight how the government maintained its tight influence and control over corporate decisions from its very inception to its demise.

The Samsung group, one of the largest *chaebols* in Korea, signed a 'technology import contract' with Japan's Nissan Motor Company on 26 April 1994, which provided the signal that it was genuinely interested in participating in the automobile industry. The government had already undertaken an economic analysis of the prospects of Samsung's entry into the automobile industry, and based on the outcome of its study, on 28 April 1994, announced that it would not allow Samsung's entry into the automobile industry. The reasons for this decision were (i) duplication and over-investment in the automobile industry, (ii) exhaustive competition in the limited domestic market,[4] and (iii) delay of technological independence caused by the introduction of foreign technology.

A few months later, almost without any warning, on 30 November 1994 the government reversed its decision and allowed Samsung to enter the auto-mobile industry.[5] Subsequently, Samsung submitted a technology imports report, which the government promptly accepted, and SMC was then officially established on 28 March 1995. The production lines commenced on 12 May 1997, and SMC introduced its first model into the market on 17 February 1998.

Not only was there much controversy surrounding SMC's entry into the automobile industry, but numerous debates among economists and social reformers on SMC's competence, profitability and, in particular, the excessive amount of debt, began appearing with the deepening of the economic crisis. Although no definite reason was provided, on 7 December 1998 a 'big deal' between Daewoo Motor and SMC stipulating that Daewoo would acquire SMC was announced, and on 22 March 1999 the chief executive officers (CEOs) of both groups agreed on the principles of the 'big deal'.[6]

The controversy surrounding SMC did not end here. In fact, there were various conflicts of interests in the process of making the 'big deal'. Most important was the handling of SMC's debt of more than 4 trillion Korean won, which was estimated to be more than four times the value of its equity, and thus constituted a major headache to the government, as well as to both companies. The 'big deal' negotiations did not materialize and SMC filed for the 'Corporate Reorganization Process' on 30 June 1999, as it decided to seek court receivership for its automobile unit, backing off from its earlier plan to sell the debt-laden unit to the Daewoo group. The courts were then to decide whether the filing firm, in this case SMC, was worth reviving through reorganization, under which the creditors and the filing firm would set up a reorganization plan including debt adjustment. In this case, after the filing, the government, along with the subcontractors and the community where SMC is located, insisted on keeping SMC in production regardless of its economic viability. Furthermore, the creditors and the government asked the CEO to surrender some of his own private wealth to solve SMC's debt problem.[7]

*Table 7.3   Diary of the rise and fall of SMC*

---

**1994**

| | |
|---|---|
| 26 April | Contract of technology imports with Nissan. |
| 28 April | Government disallows Samsung's entry into the automobile industry. |
| 30 November | Government allows Samsung's entry into the automobile industry. |
| 3 December | Samsung submits its request for technology imports. |
| 7 December | Government accepts the report. |

**1995**

| | |
|---|---|
| 28 March | SMC was established. |

**1997**

| | |
|---|---|
| 12 May | The production line began. |

**1998**

| | |
|---|---|
| 17 February | SMC introduces its first model into the market. |
| 17 December | The big deal between Daewoo Motor and SMC is announced. |

**1999**

| | |
|---|---|
| 22 March | The CEOs of Daewoo Motor and SMC agree on the principles of the big deal. |
| 30 June | Collapse of the big deal. SMC files for the Corporate Reorganization Process. |
| 30 October | A part of SMC's production line was put into re-operation with new loans from creditor banks. |
| 30 December | Corporate Reorganization Process began. |

**2000**

| | |
|---|---|
| 31 March | Renault (a French motor company) starts negotiations to acquire SMC with creditor banks. |
| 27 April | Renault signs letter of intent to take over 70 per cent of SMC (Samsung group retain 20 per cent, and creditors 10 per cent). |

---

As stated above, the various events surrounding the SMC serve as a typical example of the government's interventionist industrial policy. In line with our discussion in Chapter 2, the case of SMC perfectly illustrates the cycle of Korea's industrial policies.[8] We observe how the government determines a company's entry into a market – the government determined SMC's entry into the automobile industry; the government protects the market from competitors – the Korean automobile industry was already heavily protected, and, in fact, this constituted the main motivation for SMC to enter the automobile industry as protection created rent that could be exploited; the government closely intervenes in the private sector's restructuring process, and furthermore decides whether a firm should be declared bankrupt or be acquired by another firm - as is often the case, we observe that the government goes as far as to determine which firm should acquire the other - the government determined that Daewoo Motor should acquire SMC.

The events described above also reveal the manner in which uncertainty arises as a result of intervention. First, it remains a mystery why the government reversed its decision about SMC's entry into the automobile industry? After all, there were reasons given for disallowing SMC's entry, but not for the abrupt decision reversal afterwards - the reason for the change in the government's decision remains obscure. Consequently, the qualifications required for a firm to enter the automobile industry remain unknown. Second, what caused SMC's difficulty and premature failure afterwards? Was it duplication and over-investment in the automobile industry, exhaustive competition in the limited domestic market, or management incompetence? If it was one or both of the first two, then the question of why the government's policy was reversed, from barring Samsung's entry to allowing it, remains to be answered. If the cause was management failure, it remains unclear why the government insisted on the continuation of SMC's operations, and why it intervened in the debt-handling process.

We have learnt that persistent government intervention undermines private sector autonomy and nourishes dependence on the government. At this point one has to wonder whether creditors have indeed exercised their discretion in lending money to SMC and whether they are also responsible for their lending decisions. Why did they wait for the government's decision instead of actively trying to solve the debt problem? As has been argued, governmental control of banking has made banks increasingly dependent on government guidelines or coordination.

Sometimes, government intervention creates conflicts within the system of private property rights. What allows the government to pressure the CEO of SMC into paying a corporate debt using his own private wealth? There are neither laws nor regulations in Korea about CEOs surrendering private property except in the case where shareholders give up their shares in the event of a business failure. In line with our discussion in Chapter 5, we witness here again yet another historical example of how Korea's property rights system has been subject to uncertainty

The SMC case shows the legacy of governmental arbitrary discretion in policy-making, determining the rise and fall of private firms and creating uncertainty due to inconsistent policy-making, the private sector's lack of autonomy in decision-making, and governmental infringement on private property. Should this kind of industrial policy be allowed to continue? Can the government-led development strategy guarantee Korea's future prosperity? Is there an alternative vision? These are some of the questions that we will address in the remaining part of the book. But before we proceed, to drive the final nail into the coffin, metaphorically speaking, we explain why the past interventionist strategy contained within it dangerous structural deficiencies that fueled the recent economic crisis.

## 2.3   The Legacy of Government-led Interventionist Policies as a Cause of Economic Crises

At least three major causes of the 1997 economic crisis in Korea can be identified: the widespread and deep-rooted prevalence of moral hazard behavior that provided the setting for the outbreak of the crisis, macroeconomic policy failures such as the exchange rate overvaluation during the recession period immediately preceding the financial crisis that weakened the corporate sector, and microeconomic policies that were directed to save non-viable firms resulting in the loss of government policy credibility. The inappropriate sequencing of financial liberalization measures together with inadequate prudential regulations were also responsible for providing conditions ideal for the outbreak of the financial crisis.[9]

Various structural problems generated by the government-led interventionist industrial policy need mentioning. First, these industry- and firm-targeting industrial policies greatly distorted resource allocation, frequently acting as a substitute for the price mechanism and thus resulting in over-investment in major industries, particularly in the HCIs. Preferential industrial policies have therefore exacerbated economic concentration, resulting in structural imbalances between big and small and medium firms. Second, the government's use of the financial sector as a tool to support its industrial policy undermined the financial institutions' ability to discriminate between competent and incompetent firms and projects and properly to monitor the performance of borrowing firms. These conditions eventually led to the underdevelopment of the financial sector as well as resource waste. Third, persistent government intervention destroyed private sector incentives for creative economic ventures. Government support of selected industries and firms, and government control of the financial sector, rendered the private sector dependent on governmental guidance and command, leading to widespread behavior replete with moral hazard. In addition, since the government had helped large enterprises, especially the *chaebol*, survive financial difficulties by showering them with preferential measures, the too-big-to-fail legacy emerged and moral hazard behavior ensued as well. Lastly, in a political economic sense, the government's practice of selecting and supporting strategic industries and enforcing restructuring programs generated a tendency toward rent-seeking. As such, corporations, especially larger *chaebols*, had ample incentives to lobby government officials, and this in turn raised suspicions of corruption, which nourished anti-*chaebol* sentiment.

By and large, the government's interventionist development strategy was incapable of steering Korea away from the 1997 financial crisis. The most critical problem was the fact that the government, as we have seen, frequently acted as a substitute for the proper functioning of the price mechanism, making the private sector dependent on the government – the private sector's autonomy and creativity were adversely affected. As a result, the effectiveness of the disciplinary function of market mechanisms on private economic agents declined overall, leading to the increased dominance of moral hazard behavior in the private sector. Moral hazard made the economy less sensitive to the necessity for economic restructuring and, in fact, diminished the incentives of economic agents to adapt to changes in the economic environment. The economy's lack of market discipline, incentive and ability to quickly adapt to changes in the economic environment may have rendered it insufficiently resilient to respond effectively to the onset of the 1997 economic crisis. Furthermore, in its efforts to eradicate all vestiges of past interventionist policies, including the bad loan problems of the banking sector and the excessive debt-burden of the corporate sector, the government ironically became more active in the private sector even in the midst of the crisis. As a result, economic agents may have grown even more dependent on the government during the post-crisis restructuring effort.[10] Such are the challenges that Korea faces as it tries to break away from the legacy of government-led development.

## 3.   LESSONS FROM THE PAST AND THE FUTURE PARADIGM

In the preceding section we established that the government's interventionist industrial policy did not always lead to the desired result, and may, in fact, have been a primary weakness that could not protect the economy from the recent crisis. Nevertheless, the past decades have often been regarded as a period of miraculous growth. In the first part of this section, we discuss two well-known opposing views as to the role of government in economic development, namely the neoclassical view and the revisionist view. In the second part, we present our own perspective on Korea's development process and this forms the basis of our understanding of the past as well as the future.

### 3.1 Overview of the Debate on the Role of Government in Economic Growth

There is a heated debate about whether or not the government in an underdeveloped capitalistic market economy can improve upon the market outcome of resource mobilization and resource allocation. This debate is ultimately reduced to evaluating the importance of market failure (or absence of market institutions) versus government failure (or the government's inability to assume the role of markets or to introduce appropriate market institutions).

While observing the remarkable success of economic development in East Asian countries such as Japan, Korea and Taiwan over the past 30 years or so, adherents of the neoclassical view feel that there is an important lesson to be learned from the East Asian experience.[11] In short, this lesson, as far as economic policy is concerned, is to get the basics right. They argue that the government should provide a stable macroeconomic environment and a reliable legal framework in order to create an environment where market forces can act unhindered. Minimum intervention with the lowest degree of relative price distortion is seen as a virtue. They believe that Asian economies benefited most from a strategy where the government more or less followed the lead of the market rather than trying actively to direct it.

On the other hand, a group of economists known as the revisionists[12] attribute greater significance to other aspects of East Asia's success, aspects that have gone relatively unnoticed by the neoclassicists. They observe that the government has taken a much more active role in the process of economic development than that envisaged by neoclassicists and thus argue that despite efforts to do quite the opposite, the government has actually been leading the market. Revisionists even go on to argue that during the late industrialization stage, the state should set relative prices at deliberately 'wrong' levels in order to create profitable investment opportunities.[13] Also emphasized is the existence of market failure in developing economies due to market imperfections such as the lack of relevant markets. It is thus contended that it is necessary for government to take a positive role in the treatment of these failures as markets consistently fail to guide resource allocation toward the highest growth areas in the economy. Amsden, one of the staunchest revisionists, even suggests that the central bank should support priority industries at the cost of macroeconomic stability.[14]

The World Bank (1993) answers the revisionists' argument with the reassertion of an obvious truth: 'For interventions that attempt to guide resource allocation to succeed, they must address failures in the working of markets. Otherwise, the market would perform the allocation function more efficiently.'[15]

In sum, the debate on the role of the government in economic development seems to center around the issue of market failure versus government failure. In this regard, it may be useful to remember that market failure generally reflects the failure of institutions, which is another form of government failure as suggested by the new-institutional economists (see Chapters 1 and 5). This time the failure lies in the government's inability to set up the right institutions or, in other words, the rules of the game in the economy. Therefore the existence of market failure alone cannot be considered as an automatic justification for direct government intervention. Rather, the government should try to introduce the 'right' institutions to provide an optimal environment for improved economic performance.[16] Furthermore, in most cases of apparent market failure, it should not go unnoticed that government regulation or preferential treatment usually turns out to be the major cause of those failures.

## 3.2    A New Interpretation of Korea's Economic Development: Discrimination by the Government, Not by the Market

What then has been the role of government policy in Korea's economic development? Obviously, if we can establish that high productivity resulted from industrial policy, then it is natural to credit the positive role of industrial policy with economic growth. However, even if targeted industries do not achieve a sufficient level of productivity, as was the case of Korea during the HCI drive as shown above, this does not necessarily imply overall economic retardation. The most important factor relevant to the success or failure of an economy is whether policy can allow for the effective discrimination of viable and non-viable firms through competition. Simply put, competition is nothing more than a discrimination process. Competition discriminates between viable and non-viable entities, whether these entities are individuals, firms or societies. In the spirit of the evolutionary perspective, competition is the mechanism behind the selection process whereby relatively better entities survive while the weaker entities will opt out and become extinct. This selection process is readily observable in the realm of economies. Here, competition guarantees the continued survival of efficient firms while inefficient firms will eventually exit the market due to losses incurred. Needless to say, a country with stronger and more efficient firms that survive through competition will be superior (at least economically) to those countries that continue to nurture inefficiencies in their economies.

Our argument above would imply that a country with institutions that enhance competition should exhibit continued economic development as in the case of advanced capitalist economies. Advanced capitalist economies are characterized by strong market institutions that have allowed competition to act as a discovery procedure. Although we have been critical of Korea's past policy measures so far, we cannot but acknowledge the fact that Korea experienced tremendous growth during the past decades of strong government intervention. So, an interesting question arises – how does one explain Korea's 'miracle' growth in the past three decades despite the dominance of the government-controlled system? Basically, rapid growth has been possible precisely because the government has effectively acted as the discriminating agent substituting, though imperfectly, for the market. As we have seen, the government favored the *chaebol* that were high achievers in terms of their volume of sales and exports, and these firms in turn became the driving engine of economic progress. It may be appropriate to term this process 'government-led discrimination' for which industrial policy was designed as its chief instrument.

It may be argued, given our perspective above, that as an explanation for the low productivity experienced in Korea during the period of the HCI drive, we may recall that policy emphasized a high level of sales volume and exports rather than productivity *per se*. Effective discrimination is important for economic development as mentioned above, but also critical is the criterion of discrimination implicitly or explicitly enunciated by policy. Therefore the fact that Korea's past industrial policy succeeded in generating a rapid growth in the size of firms and hence the economy, despite its meager impact on productivity is a reflection of the characteristics of the Korea-specific industrial policy as such.

We do not deny that 'government-led discrimination' in its emphasis on sales volume and exports did contribute to Korea's rapid economic development. A more critical and difficult question to which we shall shortly return is whether this strategy can continue indefinitely as a successful strategy. Although it has contributed to Korea's rapid economic growth, a system of discrimination by the government comes with its set of problems. The most critical problems are market monopolization and economic concentration in the hands of a few, moral hazard behavior, attenuation of individual property rights, excess diversification, and more generally, the anti-*chaebol* sentiment – all of which we have taken great lengths to describe in the previous chapters.

Past industrial policies have been based on the belief that the government has sufficient information about the changing economic environment and has the ability to fully anticipate the optimal industrial structure. However, the economic environment has been changing rapidly, particularly in the era of globalization, with the increasingly dynamic economy bringing along more uncertainty. It is known that market participants have more incentive to acquire relevant information about changes in the economic environment than the government. In addition, as the economy grows in size and complexity, it becomes less and less possible for the government to absorb all relevant information related to economic changes and to determine the optimal industrial structure on behalf of the private sector. In the era of globalization, it will be increasingly difficult, if not impossible, to predetermine the optimal industrial organization.[17] Therefore instead of adopting an active interventionist industrial policy that requires a tremendous volume of information but does not necessarily guarantee a correct solution, an effective response is to let the market order prevail in discovering the optimal business and industrial structure.[18] This entails allowing the private sector maximum freedom to make structural adjustments in response to the globalization of market competition. The role of the government should therefore be confined to preserving the spontaneity and endogeneity of the market order and to cultivating an enhanced economic environment for its smooth operation.

Korea's development policies should be nimble in their adaptation to the changing economic environment, both domestically and internationally. In the era of the open society, there is only one viable way forward: discrimination by the market, not the government. After all, the market is nothing else but the spontaneous institution that discriminates effectively between viable and non-viable entities through unfettered competition.[19] We assert that the revamping of the competition promotion policy to enhance the competitive environment in the Korean economy through the establishment of proper economic institutions is therefore paramount not only to improve *chaebols'* competitiveness but also to ensure Korea's continued economic development.

### 3.3 Roles of the Government Versus Private Corporations in Economic Management: A Rule of Thumb

Figure 1.1 not only provides an illustration of the new-institutional economic framework but also has profound implications on the role of the government in economic management. The behavior of an economic agent, whether an individual or corporation, is nothing more than an outcome of the best choice among strategies available to maximize the probability of its survival under a given set of constraints. The exogenous economic environment usually comprising economic institutions constitutes the most important constraint affecting business behavior. Adaptation is critical if a firm or individual is to survive in the changing environment. In fact, only those firms that win in the competition will continue to survive to face another round of challenges that require efforts to adapt on its part and the survival of yet further competition. The resulting type of corporate behavior is inevitably a part of the past and current economic environment. An important insight to be drawn from this framework is that if the government wishes to affect corporate behavior, then it can do so more efficiently by managing the economic environment surrounding corporations rather than trying to regulate corporate behavior directly. A further elaboration appears in Figure 7.1 which describes the constitution of an economic system surrounding corporations.

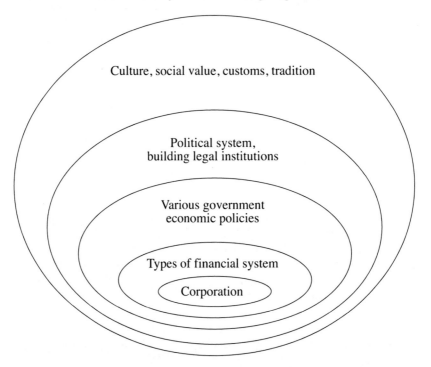

*Figure 7.1    Exogenous environment and the corporation*

Figure 7.1 shows the different levels of the exogenous variables facing a corporation. Here the corporation is dependent on the external or exogenous economic environment that ranges from the remote to the immediate, the cultural and social factors, the political system, the government's economic policies and the financial system. Culture and tradition act as the overall exogenous factor constraining all other actors in the economy from the political system to government economic policy-making, and to the type of financial system as well as the behavior of corporations. Political systems, in turn, constrain all other actors by building the legal institution (rules of the game). The government in the narrow sense affects the financial system as well as the corporate sector through economic policy. Finally, the financial system constrains corporate behavior by imposing a particular type of finance for corporations and thereby acting as a disciplinary agent on overall corporate behavior. The role of the government in a broad sense is to cultivate and enhance such an external or exogenous environment if it wishes to affect corporate behavior in a particular direction. It needs therefore to carefully distinguish between endogenous and exogenous variables in an economic system and should set policy to affect directly exogenous variables while leaving endogenous factors to be determined by individuals and corporations in their quest for their economic goals. Here it can be seen that we have placed government in a broad sense as the most extensive and critical exogenous factor in the economic system. The government must therefore resort to strengthening the country's exogenous economic institutions that include cultural and legal institutions as well as economic policy-making, and particularly the financial system, in such a way as to allow for the uninterrupted operation of the market-led discrimination mechanism in the economy. Corporate endogenous behavior should then naturally evolve within the boundaries set by the exogenous environmental factors.

Thus, as will be provided in detail in the following section, the government should establish the rules of the game in the economy, encompassing cultural and legal institutions as well as economic policy, so that the discovery function of the market order may become smooth and effective. The role of the government should be confined to defining the external economic environment and not intervening in the endogenous behavior of private agents.

## 4. A NEW THEORY OF CORPORATE GOVERNANCE: INSTITUTIONS, CORPORATE BEHAVIOR AND PUBLIC POLICY

Thus far, in this chapter, we have explained the reasons for Korea's rapid economic growth from the point of view of the role of government. In this section, we look at the issue of economic development from the point of view of the firm in the private sector. We begin with a general survey of the subject of corporate governance in the economics literature, pinpointing where current research remains weak and suggesting how it may be improved. In Section 4.2 a new theory of corporate governance is presented. In Section 4.3, an apparent contradiction between Coase and North as relates to the size of the firm is stated and resolved following insights gained by the theory in Section 4.2. Section 4.4 concludes this discussion by applying the model of corporate governance to explain the differences in corporate governance structures seen in different countries.

### 4.1 Why Corporate Governance?

The firm is a fundamental unit of economic analysis. It is commonly agreed that economic progress is impossible without the development of the firm. However, it is somewhat surprising that a well-developed 'theory of the firm' is hard to find in the literature. Existing discussions on the inner workings of the firm have usually followed the seminal article 'The Nature of the Firm' by Coase (1937). In a broad sense, we can identify at least five schools of thought: the neoclassical school, which in a strict sense cannot really claim to have a 'theory of the firm', essentially looks at the firm simply as a technical production function.[20] There is then the behavioral school (Cyert and March, 1963) and agency theory (Berle and Means, 1932; Jensen and Meckling, 1976), which although highly influential in management science provide only a narrow understanding of the issues of opportunism and asymmetric information. A broader approach is that of the evolutionary school (Hayek, 1988; Nelson and Winter, 1982), but almost nothing has been said on issues of corporate governance. Of course, there are various results based on the concept of 'transaction costs' (Coase, 1937; Commons, 1931; Williamson, 1975; Klein, Crawford and Alchian, 1978; Grossman and Hart, 1986; Hart and Moore, 1990), which seem to have converged into what is known as 'contract' theory. Although these constitute the dominant trend in the existing literature that tackles issues of why firms exist and what determines their boundaries, many important questions such as why behavioral differences in corporations exist across different countries are yet to be adequately explained. More importantly, in the context of developing countries such as Korea, where the government has had tremendous impact on the course of its economic development, there is need now to redefine the role of government and the private sector consistently with the principles of the market economy. Nevertheless, rather disappointingly, current advances in the 'theory of the firm' do not provide a useful guide to approaching public policy toward corporations.

Be that as it may, in this book, we shall argue that corporate governance is the most important feature of the firm and to understand its evolution is to understand not only those characteristics that determine firm behavior but also the role of the firm in economic development. Moreover, as we shall show, understanding the mechanisms of corporate governance is a prerequisite to developing a framework for public policy toward corporations. Accordingly, we need to develop a theory of corporate governance.

Issues of corporate governance arrive in economics with the concern of problems related to the separation of ownership and control first introduced by Adam Smith (1776) and in a more modern setting by Berle and Means (1932) and Alchian and Demsetz (1972).[21] Since managers have been found to behave in ways that may be detrimental to outside shareholders as well as to owners of the firm, the problems between ownership and management have featured prominently in the corporate governance literature. By investigating principal-agent problems Jensen and Meckling (1976) explicitly formulate the agency-cost approach to develop a theory of ownership structure of the firm, which has been hugely influential in motivating thought on corporate governance issues. Grossman and Hart (1986) and Hart and Moore (1990) have refined ownership issues and the allocation issue between managers and shareholder. The main questions commonly raised concern the degree of ownership concentration, ownership composition, the system of the board of directors, executive compensation, degree of shareholder participation in management decision-making, legal protection of shareholder rights, and transparency and disclosure requirements.

Until recently, however, the focus on corporate governance issues has been dominated by discussions surrounding shareholder value, and finding what constitutes an efficient structure that would minimize agency costs. For example, Shleifer and Vishny (1997) pose the governance question in terms of how investors may ensure that managers provide them with ample return and do not expropriate money or use capital to finance poor investments. Prowse (1998) has envisioned an efficient corporate governance system as one that depends on the right mix of competitive environment, legal protection of outside financiers, ownership structure and strength of contractual mechanisms in financial contracts. Nonetheless, with discussions revolving around issues of shareholder value, economists and legal scholars alike have been criticized for having taken too narrow an approach to corporate governance, and there is currently an effort to adopt a broader perspective. Recently, Tirole (2001) seems the most important work to break away from the 'shareholder' approach by building a framework that internalizes the welfare of 'stakeholders' when considering corporate governance.

Notwithstanding the various theoretical advancements, the recent financial crisis has given us a highly visible demonstration of the importance of a sound governance structure. Good corporate governance can be seen as having important implications that foster the performance of a firm. Therefore a proper understanding of the structure of relationships and corresponding responsibilities among shareholders, board members, managers, and other stakeholders cannot be over-emphasized. Corporate governance matters in that it has a real impact not only on the managerial efficiency of a corporation but also on the performance of the national economy. The whole issue of corporate governance becomes a matter of concern especially in the era of globalization along with the increasing role of investments by foreign financial institutions in emerging markets. Investors need to ensure that the firms in which they invest are not only managed properly but also have proper corporate governance structures – that is, corporate governance is seen to affect competitive advantage. For example, the type of corporate governance is an important factor in building market confidence and encouraging more stable, long-term domestic and international investment flows.[22] Our purpose in this section and parts of the next chapter is to address the issue of public policy toward corporations. We think that a comprehensive study of corporate governance structures is an indispensable step prior to tackling matters of corporate policy.

The subject of corporate governance is not an easy one, and at times, can be rather slippery as the sheer number of definitions demonstrates. For the purposes of our discussions in this section, we may begin by observing that corporate governance is used in both a narrow and a much wider sense. The narrow sense of the term is the traditional legal usage where corporate governance refers to the internal relations within the corporate entity that determine decision-making power and accountability. For example, the OECD (1999) guidelines on corporate governance state that:

> Corporate governance is the system by which business corporations are directed and controlled. The corporate governance structure specifies the distribution of rights and responsibilities among different participants in the corporation, such as the board, managers, shareholders and stakeholders, and spells out the rules and procedures for making decisions on corporate affairs. By doing this, it also provides the structure through which the company objectives are set, and the means of attaining those objectives and monitoring performance.

In the much wider sense, Professor Kenneth Scott (1999) of Stanford Law School has recently described corporate governance very aptly:[23]

> In its most comprehensive sense, 'corporate governance' includes every force that bears on the decision-making of the firm. That would encompass not only the control rights of stockholders, but also the contractual covenants and insolvency powers of debt holders, the commitments entered into with employees and customers and suppliers, the regulations issued by governmental agencies, and the statutes enacted by parliamentary bodies. In addition, the firm's decisions are powerfully affected by competitive conditions in the various markets in which it operates. One could go still further, to bring in the social and cultural norms of the society. All are relevant, but the analysis would become so diffuse that it risks becoming unhelpful as well as unbounded.

Our approach is in line with the broader definition as we place corporate governance issues beyond the ownership-management focus in the context of economic development. In recognizing the limitations of the traditional shareholder value approach as well as the stakeholder approach as being too narrow a view for economic analysis, we define corporate governance as those institutions that induce or force corporate management to adopt behavior that maximizes the probability of their survival. That is, we not only recognize the need to minimize agency costs, but further address explicitly institutions that enhance the role of markets and competition as these are important in shaping corporate behavior. Since the corporate governance structure is part and parcel of what constitutes a firm, the better the corporate governance structure, the better the firm's competitiveness and probability of survival.

## 4.2 A Theory of Corporate Governance: Model and System

Institutions are the main constraints on creating order and reducing uncertainty in exchange, and are responsible for defining the choice set as well as transactions and production costs, thereby affecting the profitability and feasibility of various economic activities. Furthermore, institutions provide the incentive structure of an economy pushing it toward growth, stagnation or decline. The major focus on institutions and transactions costs in economics has been on understanding institutions as efficient solutions to problems of economics organization, but this approach does not directly look into the issues of the dynamic evolutionary process of corporate governance. Our concern here is to fill this gap by providing a theory of corporate governance that will add to our understanding of the evolution of corporations, as well as the process of economic growth.

A theory of corporate governance should help explain not only the differences in corporate governance structures, but also the differences in economic performance among various countries. Accordingly, we shall begin by identifying those institutions that influence the corporate governance structure. Figure 1.1 in Chapter 1 and related discussions on the new-institutional economic perspective as well as Figure 7.1, can be reinterpreted in the context of the corporate sector as shown in Figure 7.2 with the focus on the immediate market environment surrounding corporations.

Figure 7.2 summarizes the general institutional factors affecting corporate governance, which act to monitor and check corporate behavior. These can be classified into two categories: the market disciplinary system that consists essentially of the factor and product markets, and the internal control mechanisms that constitute the firm's decision variables. The market disciplinary system acts as an important constraint on corporate behavior and consists essentially of the product market and factor markets that include the M&A, financial and CEO markets. In general, the more vibrant the market disciplinary system, the more competitive firms will become. Accordingly, increased competitive pressure provides the appropriate incentive to induce optimal behavior including good corporate behavior.

The most important market disciplinary system is the product market, which plays the role of disciplining business activity by driving out inefficient and incompetent firms through consumers' choice and selection of products. Firms cannot continue to survive in competitive markets if their products are inferior to other competitors. A country's competition promotion policy, foreign

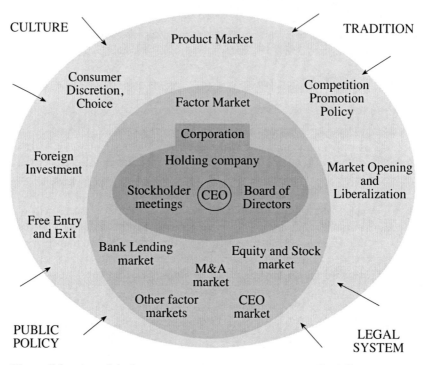

*Figure 7.2    A model of corporate governance: corporate disciplinary system*

investment climate, the degree of market opening and liberalization, as well as freedom of entry and exit, all help shape the product markets. As will be fully discussed in the next chapter, these disciplinary mechanisms, which constitute the truly exogenous factors to the firm, should be the focus of corporate policy.

Factor markets have a similar role to that of the product market in efficiently allocating scarce resources. For example, the M&A market promotes the efficiency of business management by driving out inefficient firms through the threat of hostile takeovers, and mergers and acquisitions. The CEO market, in turn, helps induce increased managerial efficiency by weeding out inefficient managers through fierce competition at the executive level. As will be discussed later, the type of financial market that emerges tends to influence the type of corporate behavior.

The market disciplinary system consists of the various markets that set the boundaries of the economic possibilities of the firm. More specifically, corporate behavior evolves depending on the balance of pressures from various external markets described above. For example, a firm's corporate behavior will differ depending on whether the firm is a monopolist or a competitive firm in the product market. Similarly, its behavior will depend on the structure of factor markets that it faces – for example, whether labor unionization exists, whether bank loans are easier to acquire than raising funds by selling stock, and so on. The degree and vitality of the M&A market also affects corporate behavior in that more efficient behavior should result if M&A markets are highly competitive and fully functional. A competitive and well-functioning CEO market is also important in guaranteeing that only the best executive managers are attracted and chosen to lead their corporations. The financial market to be discussed extensively in the next section includes the indirect (bank lending) financial market that act as a check on business management decisions through their credit screening and *ex-post* monitoring function for the smooth retrieval of loans, and, the direct (stock and equity) financial market, where shareholders influence corporate governance behavior through the exercise of their shareholders' rights.[24] In fact, a cursory glance at the findings derived in the following section reveal that the type of financial system in place, whether equity-based or bank-dominated, is an important direct link that explains the differences in corporate governance behavior as well as their structure across countries. It is important to keep in mind that the characteristics of each market are in turn influenced by institutional factors such as culture, tradition, the type of legal system, as well as the government's economic policies (also see Figure 7.1).

Internal control mechanisms, on the other hand, such as the holding company system, the structure of CEOs and the board of directors, as well as stockholder meetings, include the mechanisms within a corporation that are formed to increase business efficiency in response to various market pressures. What is important to note, as we have repeatedly emphasized in this book, is that for all intents and purposes, such business variables are basically endogenous to the firm and it is better to allow them to be determined freely without the interference of an outside mediator. Put differently, there is no reason to directly disturb or affect a firm's endogenous strategic variables, whether via government regulation or artificially created rules.

Despite the convenience of the analytical dichotomy proposed here, the distinction between the internal and market disciplinary systems is not always as clearcut in the real world. Before continuing our discussion, perhaps we can demonstrate some of the subtleties by taking a look at the role of the board of directors in a corporation. On the one hand, the board of directors can act as a signaling mechanism to consumers, potential investors, shareholders, lender and other stakeholders indicating the type of management strategy that the corporation has adopted. That is, the board of directors constitutes an essential part of the management decision variables. On the other hand, since it is composed of agents who represent various stakeholders including the shareholders as well as other interested parties, the board of directors acts as a window through which these external groups may influence the management of the corporation. As such, the board of directors acts simultaneously as part of the market disciplinary system as well as the internal control mechanism for corporate governance. It is clearly evident that the nature of the board of directors is a delicate and critical matter. Economic policy and government action, therefore, must refrain from shackling the composition and operations of the board of directors with unnecessary constraints. Rather, the management's autonomy to utilize the board of directors as an important strategic variable should be respected, as is recommended again in Chapter 8.

According to Coase (1937) markets do not operate costlessly. That is, there are costs in using the market and price systems. Coase notes that economic theory describes both the market and the firm as coordinating mechanisms but goes further and argues that the principal limitation of the market mechanism is the cost of discovering prices. Coase (1937, p. 395) writes that 'a firm will tend to expand until the costs of organizing an extra transaction within the firm become equal to the costs of organizing an extra transaction by means of an exchange on the open market or the cost of organizing in another firm'. That is, when transaction costs of market exchange are high, it may be less costly to coordinate production through an organization or firm rather than through a market. Although Coase never directly addresses corporate governance issues, the transaction costs approach suggests that it is precisely the need to reduce such costs that justifies the importance of corporate governance.

Firms exist because it is better to do things internally, by integrating markets at the margin. As will be elaborated a little later, transaction costs are implicitly reduced as a firm integrates markets. What is important to realize, however, is that only factor markets can be integrated into a firm. In economics, this is commonly known as vertical integration. Of course, the Coasian firm can arise and expand through horizontal integration, but this is besides the point here. What is important here is to recognize that factor markets and not product markets can be internalized into a firm. It is with this idea in mind that the product market and factor markets have intentionally been separated in Figure 7.2. An important implication of this distinction is that the effectiveness of the market disciplinary system should not be taken at face value. The disciplinary pressure from the factor market can be mitigated, for whatever reasons, by integrating such markets into the firm, or by finding alternatives, or even ignoring completely certain factors markets. However, such a treatment is impossible in the case of product markets – by definition, the firm cannot integrate the product market – it must sell its products in such markets. Hence, although all types of markets constitute the market disciplinary system, as previously mentioned, we find that the product market is more important than the factor market as a corporate disciplinary mechanism.

Interestingly, the terms 'corporate governance systems' and 'corporate governance structures' are often used interchangeably in the economics literature. For purposes in this book, however, when we speak of corporate governance systems, we, in fact, mean the broad external disciplinary system. Reference to corporate governance structures denotes individual components of a corporate governance system that include all forms of corporate behavior as well as the constituent agents and various organizations that are part of the internal control mechanism. Is it necessary to distinguish between 'corporate governance system' and 'corporate governance structure'? Why has no attempt been made previously to do so in the literature? Perhaps it is plausible to argue that there has been little need to distinguish between the two terms in discussions of corporate governance in advanced capitalist countries, as it is often the case that authors take the idea of markets (in terms of the distinction made earlier, here 'corporate governance system' is more appropriate than 'corporate governance structure') for granted.[25] For example, since the so-called 'arm's length' model of corporate governance that promotes the dispersed ownership of the firm through equity finance and shareholding is well established in the UK and US, discussions related to corporate governance tend to emphasize internal governance structures ('structure' rather than 'system' is the more appropriate term here) rather than directly addressing the role of markets in disciplining corporate governance behavior. It is evident that the OECD (1999) guidelines on corporate governance could not escape this trend.

In the spirit of our distinction between 'system' and 'structure', we think this distinction important and necessary, particularly in discussions of issues dealing with corporate governance in countries characterized by under-developed markets. In the example of Korea, the development of markets has been generally disturbed by strong government intervention and there is therefore the need to discuss and address the role of markets and competition in disciplining and monitoring corporate behavior as we move toward establishing a market-based economy. Hence when emphasizing 'system' over 'structure', we are basically calling for the need to establish and consolidate the market environment through appropriate institutional changes.

## 4.3 Corporate Governance Theory and Transaction Costs

To further motivate the corporate governance model developed above, it is interesting to take a closer look at an apparent theoretical contradiction between the views of North and Coase as relates to the size of the firm and transaction costs. Recall that we have already introduced North's ideas in Chapter 5. Briefly, North (1990) maintains that a country with strong property rights protection should encourage the natural growth of large firms, enhancing national economic performance. Put differently, economies with property rights systems that are not securely protected will imply a low probability that market contracts will be honored or faithfully observed, thereby adding to increased uncertainty and transaction costs which ultimately act as barriers to the formation of large firms.[26] The theory of the firm derived from Coase, which has been introduced in the previous sub-section, looks at transaction costs as arising from problems of human coordination and cooperation. Such costs are associated with information processing, costs of putting a contract together, and costs required to enforce contracts that have been put into place. According to Coase, therefore, a firm will extend its boundaries and absorb such transaction costs if it is more efficient to do so.

From the point of view of transaction costs and the theory of the firm, both Coase's and North's theories suggest contradictory implication to the size of the firm: if we accept that insecure property rights protection results in higher transaction costs, then, as we have stated above, North's theory would suggest that smaller firms prevail under such an environment, while Coase's theory will claim the opposite, suggesting that larger firms are more likely as firms tend to internalize and absorb more and more activities of higher transaction costs. Put differently, Coase's theory would claim that there tends to be smaller firms in economies with relatively lower levels of transaction costs, while at the same time, North's approach would imply that lower transaction costs due to secure property rights protection allow for the growth of larger and more diversified firms. Of course, the usual organizational costs associated with running the firm should not be ignored as they do have important implication to the size of the firm. It also remains questionable whether larger firms as implied by Coase's theory in an environment of higher transaction costs or, what amounts to the same thing, whether smaller firms arising in an economy with lower levels of transaction costs would contribute to economic development.

Although this contradiction may have to be resolved as an empirical question, it nevertheless poses an interesting theoretical inconsistency that begs reconciliation. One way is to clarify what is meant by transaction costs. The contradiction between the views of Coase and North as regards firm size and economic development can be resolved, or at least, better understood, by approaching the concept of transaction costs in a slightly different way – that is, we need to distinguish between transaction costs that can be absorbed into a firm and those that are permanently outside the domain of the firm's boundary. Certain transaction costs (for example, agency costs, costs of moral hazard, costs arising from opportunism, and so on) can be internalized or absorbed into the firm while other types of transaction costs due to the external and institutional environment (for example, the arbitrary transfer of property rights by a discriminating government, political decisions changing the law, low trust among economic actors, and so on) cannot be absorbed and remain outside the boundaries of the firm. In the world of Coase, the boundaries of a firm are determined by the extent to which the firm can internalize (internalizable) transaction costs, which is just the classical game of optimizing at the margin, while in North's perspective, the exogenous (non-internalizable) transaction costs, which are defined by the prevailing institutions are seen to limit firm size. That is, in the case of Coase, higher transaction costs is the primary incentive to increase firm size, although not all types of transaction costs can be absorbed. As we have seen under the theory of corporate governance developed earlier, only factor markets, and not the product market, can be internalized and its transaction costs avoided. Therefore, increasing firm size can be attributed to higher transaction costs in the factor market. On the other hand, the product market that the firm cannot integrate as well as other exogenous institutions makes up the broader absolute constraint on the firm. The transaction costs embodied in these exogenous factors cannot be avoided and, in the spirit of North, define the limit to firm size. This explains the general prevalence of larger firms in more developed countries characterized by lower (non-internalizable) transaction costs. A more detailed empirical study on the relationship among transaction costs, firm size and economic development under this theoretical framework should prove to be interesting.

What the new corporate governance theory developed in this book, specifically the insight that the market disciplinary system is not homogeneous (factor markets can be absorbed while product markets cannot), calls for is that we should once again revisit and question the traditional approach to corporate governance. As mentioned above, contemporary corporate governance discussions have largely aimed at addressing incentive problems between principal and agents, which often ignores the broader economic environment that includes its institutions as either fixed or unimportant. Given that a firm can internalize factor markets, its effectiveness as a corporate disciplinary mechanism is not always binding. For example, a firm can draw from its own internal accumulated capital rather than access financial markets or simply integrate existing financial firms. The product market, however, cannot be integrated into the firm and remains exogenous to the firm. Therefore, this disciplinary pressure on corporations from the product market tends to be more effective and consistent than disciplinary pressure from the factor markets. It should not be surprising therefore to find that most empirical work so far has difficulty linking traditional corporate governance theory, that emphasizes the internal governance structure as more or less reacting to factor market pressure, to firm performance.[27] This seems precisely because the traditional approach to corporate governance issues and particularly the analysis of the market disciplinary mechanism hardly recognize the intricate differences between factor and product markets explicitly stated in our theory.

Let us recapture and summarize the arguments in this section thus far. In the context of economic development, the market disciplinary system is worthier of attention when considering government policy measures than the internal control system. As argued in the previous section, the distinction between exogenous and endogenous economic variables is an important first step. That is, the market disciplinary system by definition determines the exterior environment of business management and, therefore, constitutes the exogenous variables to the firms. On the other hand, the firm's internal management is responsible for setting up internal control mechanisms – endogenous variables by definition. The most important implication is that a firm's growth may be hindered by the rigid constraints of outsiders, such as the government's direct interference in management behavior, that is, on a firm's endogenous strategic variables. More specifically, the government is duty bound to take into consideration the fact that excessively rigid and detailed regulation of the internal governance structure could become an impediment to the promotion of management efficiency by hindering the efficient transformation of firms. In this sense, it might be better to allow firms to choose internal control mechanisms suitable to their own needs. The theory of corporate governance described above has further implication for corporate policy – factor markets should be distinguished from product markets, when considering the effectiveness of the market disciplinary system. The building of an effective market disciplinary system must emphasize the product market, which directly acts as the most effective disciplinary mechanism to a private firm. The government cannot avoid overlooking this important insight in the pursuit of economic reform, as is comprehensively discussed in the following chapter. Before applying our model to corporate policy in the next chapter, it may however be useful to explain differences in corporate governance behavior as observed across various countries, which should consolidate confidence in the model developed above.

### 4.4 Culture, Finance and Corporate Behavior: The Evolution of Corporate Governance Systems

As a direct application of our theory of corporate governance developed above, by specifically looking into the differences in corporate behavior of advanced capitalist countries and that of Korea, we explain how the corporate governance system endogenously evolves under different types of financial systems. It is well known that problems with corporate behavior in Korea have been relatively well identified and usually include high debt–equity ratios, lack of transparency, low appreciation of shareholder value and so on. On the other hand, low debt–equity ratios, high management transparency, and high appreciation of shareholder value characterize the so-called global standard of corporate behavior, usually associated with the corporate governance structures of advanced capitalistic countries. However, as suggested earlier, we must appreciate the fact that not only the nature of corporate behavior and the internal governance structure but also the corporate governance system in place are essentially determined endogenously. In fact, we shall show that the type of corporate governance system is constrained by the type of financial system that evolves under a given country's cultural, historical and economic characteristics, and in addition and naturally, by the level of the nation's economic development (see Figures 7.1 and 7.2).

We first take a closer look at this intrinsic link between culture and the financial system, and then at their relationship to corporate behavior. Table 7.3 lists the essential differences between corporate governance structures in countries where equity-based finance is dominant as in Anglo-Saxon countries like the US and England and that of bank finance dominated economies like Germany, Japan, Korea and other continental European and Asian countries where the need for corporate reform continues to be a pressing issue.

As has been thoroughly discussed in Chapter 5, a high level of trust and the prevalence of the rule of law, as well as a respect for formal institutions and business contracts, characterize advanced capitalistic economies. In fact, the equity market transactions that are a dominant feature of advanced capitalist countries tend to be both impersonal and formal, requiring a high level of mutual trust between investors and corporations supported by a tradition that respects the rule of law. Since equity markets become a prominent feature of business financing in such economies, they dictate that the corporate sector cannot but maintain accountability and transparency in management and must respect shareholder value. On the other hand, the low trust countries such as Korea are heavily influenced by informal institutions and tend to be characterized by higher transaction costs. Cronyism brought about by the need to nurture personal relationships in an environment of low trust is an important factor that we may term as the 'rule of person' in contrast to the 'rule of law'. A culture of low trust where the written contract is delegated as unimportant tends to necessitate direct business contacts and personal relationships, thereby being conducive toward establishing a financial system that is relatively dominated by the bank-lending market. Since bank loans are usually made after processing background information about the borrower, it is widely observed that informal and personal relationships are a prominent feature of banking activities. It may also be noted that individual investors in equity markets in countries with low trust and a lack of the rule of law and formal relationships tend to be relatively erratic and usually have a short investment horizon. The corporate governance system that

Table 7.4   Culture, financial systems and corporate governance

| | | Equity and stock market financing (Anglo-Saxon countries) | Bank financing (continental Europe, Japan, Korea) |
|---|---|---|---|
| Endogenous financial structure | Cultural background | • High level of trust<br>• Formal Relationship | • Low level of trust<br>• Cronyism |
| Exogenous variable | National governance tradition | Rule of law | Rule of person |
| | Legal tradition | Common law | Civil law |
| Endogenous corporate behavior | Ownership structure | Widely held | Concentrated |
| | Corporate management and objectives | • High transparency<br>• Investor protection<br>• Stock-value maximisation<br>• Low debt-equity ratio<br>• Strong outside director system | • Low transparency<br>• Entrepreneur protection<br>• Expansion and conglomeration<br>• High debt-equity ratio<br>• Owner and manager discretion |

evolves under financial markets that are dominated by bank lending as the primary source of finance is usually characterized by less transparent management systems and less respect for shareholders as they are to some extent treated as being of little importance. Here banks rather than equity markets tend to play a more important role in determining corporate governance structures.[28]

Second, we may argue that the choice of the financial system is constrained by the level of capital accumulation. This critical point that links the choice of financial system and hence corporate behavior to the level of economic development begins by observing that 'catch-up' economies including Germany and Japan, particularly during the early stages of development, have usually lacked a sufficient capital base for start-ups and growth compared to more advanced capitalistic countries. In order to generate capital to finance new business start-ups and to expand existing ones, these economies tend to resort to emphasizing banking institutions, which through utilizing their deposit-taking function prove to be ideal in quickly gathering small savings into large pools of capital to be made available for bigger borrowers. Due to the nature of institutional path-dependence, the bank-dominated financial system chosen in the early catch-up stage tends to become locked in and this type of financial system continues to be emphasized in these economies. This, of course, has obvious implications for the type of corporate governance and behavior that evolves. For example, Korea and with other catch-up economies such as those in continental Europe and Japan tend to have a bank-dominated financial system that exhibits corporate behavior characterized by high debt–equity ratios as corporations have to borrow heavily, and at times excessively, from the banking market. On the other hand, advanced Anglo-Saxon countries such as England, the early mover in the Industrial Revolution, as well as the US, have been able to build well-developed equity markets supported by their early capital accumulation. We observe that in these countries the debt–equity ratio is obviously kept low, and as has already been mentioned, management transparency and respect for shareholder rights have become the norms of corporate behavior.

Our message is clear: in order to build effective reform measures for the improvement of the *chaebols'* corporate governance structures it is important that the deeper cultural and institutional parameters as well as the financial system constraint be examined and fully understood. In this context, financial sector reform aimed at promoting the equity market should be given more emphasis than before by establishing and revitalizing appropriate institutions such as measures to protect investors as well as to discipline corporations. Korea's cultural and legal institutions should also undergo reform so as to become accommodating to the growth of an equity market culture.

## 5.   CONCLUDING REMARKS

In general, this chapter has gone to great lengths to delineate the role of government and private corporations in economic development. The chapter began by evaluating Korea's past industrial policies. In particular, we found that the total factor productivity of targeted industries did not increase as expected and, in fact, showed a downturn during the period of the HCI drive. The government's active industrialization policy did not translate itself into increased productivity in many targeted industries. Nevertheless, Korea has been widely recognized as having achieved 'miracle' growth during the 30 years prior to the crisis. Various theories of the role of government in economic growth are reviewed, but none seems satisfactory in explaining the apparent contradiction of high growth rates and low productivity. We singled out the 'government-led discrimination' mechanism that effectively distinguished between viable and non-viable businesses as the key factor for successful growth. In essence, Korea's government-led discrimination mechanism was based on the criteria of increased sales volume and exports. Those firms that met the criteria set by the government were provided with tax subsidies, easy credit with preferential interest rates, and other supportive measures. It is in this sense that past industrial policy seems to have worked. Nevertheless, the nature of such policies inevitably generates side effects such as the issue of unfairness, moral hazard behavior, economic concentration, attenuation of individual property rights, excess diversification and so on.

Of course, a more urgent question follows: can we expect the government to continue its role as the ultimate economic discriminator and commander? It is clear that the status quo cannot continue. Besides, there are strong reasons to believe that continued government intervention cannot repeat the success of the past 30 years or so. Broadly speaking, not only does the sheer complexity of an expanding economy make direct government control practically impossible, but as we have argued, government-led discrimination is undesirable in its tendency to encourage moral hazard behavior on the part of private agents. Simply put, the government-led discrimination of past decades cannot be an appropriate development strategy for the future. For further economic progress, economic agents should be freed from moral hazard behavior and should be allowed to decide for themselves their future economic success. This is especially pertinent in the rapidly changing global economy of the twenty-first century.

Future development strategy should champion 'market-led discrimination', a key feature of the market economy, over 'government-led discrimination'. In this new development paradigm, we address specifically the role of government in the process of economic growth by proposing a framework based on the new-institutional economics perspective, in which the distinction between exogenous and endogenous variables is vital. Once clearly defined, the government is called upon to act on the exogenous institutional variables, while the private corporation should be allowed to freely decide upon their own endogenous decision variables.

An overview of corporate governance is discussed and a new theory based on the new institutional economics is developed. An apparent contradiction of Coase and North as related to the size of the firm is resolved following insight of the new corporate governance theory developed here, which looks at the effectiveness of the product and factor markets as disciplinary mechanisms on corporate behaviour. Specifically, we argue that institutional factors (markets in particular) influence corporate behavior by acting as a constraint on endogenous management decisions. Accordingly, the government is well advised to establish and reinforce market institutions that will enhance the competitive business environment and help strengthen market discipline on corporations, while leaving unhindered the private business decision variables internal to the firms.

We also seek to take on a broader perspective and explore the delicate link that exists between culture, financial systems and corporate governance. Utilizing the framework developed here, we establish that cultural factors, legal tradition, government policy and the type of financial system in place determine the corporate governance system. In doing so, a greater understanding of the evolution of corporate governance has been achieved and with it far-reaching implications for policy-makers interested in influencing and reforming corporate behavior have been highlighted.

What we have hinted at in this chapter is the incorporation of corporate governance issues into the literature on economic development. The bulk of the existing literature of corporate governance, as we have argued, seems to center on the discussion of shareholder value. As such, it narrowly focuses on the firm's inner structure while having little to say about its role in the process of economic development. On the other hand, we acknowledge the new-institutional economics of North (1990) as attacking directly the complicated issues in economic development, but failing to find a comprehensive application to issues of corporate governance *per se*. This is a gap that we fill by providing a new theory of corporate governance – one that goes beyond a myopic focus on shareholder value and brings the firm into the dynamic setting of the real economy and, thereby, into the realm of economic development. The essence of the firm, we argue, is reflected in its governance structure, which consists not only of the internal structure, but is also determined by constraints imposed by the exogenous institutions surrounding it. Interestingly, in this way, the 'theory of the firm' is incorporated into the broader study of economic development, with both being analyzed and studied by the application of new-institutional economics.

As a final point, we suggest that in order to improve corporate behavior wide-sweeping reforms are necessary across cultural, political, legal and financial institutions, as well as government policy. Having said this, however, the most practical path begins with the immediate task of reforming the financial system together and in line with the reform efforts in the corporate sector. Our discussions and arguments above clearly show that corporate sector reform on its own while neglecting the influence of the financial sector on corporate behavior and structure cannot be effective. In the next chapter, we set out details of corporate sector reform, specifically *chaebol* reform, in the context of the paradigm developed above.

## NOTES

1.  There is, however, another school of thought known as the revisionists led by Amsden (1989) and Wade (1990), that points to the pervasive role of the state in East Asia as prima-facie evidence of the weakness of orthodox interpretations, and holds that industrial policy has a positive effect on economic growth. In contrast, Krugman (1994) stressed that government development strategies had little significance since the East Asian economic growth could be explained simply by the quantitative growth of capital and labor. He criticized the revisionist view on the grounds that if the growth in East Asian countries is to reflect the benefits of strategic trade or industrial policies, then those benefits should be represented in the form of rapid improvements in economic efficiency. He argues, however, that in reality, there has been no sign of exceptional improvements in efficiency. Sarel (1997), approaching the problem a little differently, places high regard on the role of productivity growth in the economic growth of the East Asian countries. He compares the rates of output growth, capital accumulation, labor force participation and total factor productivity in Hong Kong, Korea, Singapore, Taiwan, Japan and the US for the period 1975–90 and finds that the growth of total factor productivity accounts for a larger part of East Asian economic growth.
2.  Yoo (1991) provides a detailed analysis of the development of the heavy and chemical industry drive during the 1970s and 1980s, and further examines the adverse effects that this had on the light industrial sector and on competitiveness in the export market. Yoo (1991) reports that capital efficiency during the 1970s was lower in the heavy and chemical industries that were favored by the HCI policy than in the light industries. Capital efficiency in the light industry was greater than in the heavy and chemical industry by 5 per cent in 1970 and this gap widened slightly to 7 per cent by 1978. However, in 1983, there was virtually no difference between the two groups in terms of capital efficiency.
3.  See Gollop (1985) for details.
4.  At the time there were three main automobile manufacturing companies in Korea, Hyundai Motor Company, Daewoo Motor and Kia Mortors. The production capacity of the first two companies constituted more than two million cars in 1997.
5.  There are various political behind-the-scenes stories and rumors regarding this event. For example, Pusan, where SMC's manufacturing unit is located, is the then President's hometown. It is said that the President decided to allow SMC's entry into the automobile industry to boost the economy of his hometown. Since these stories cannot be corroborated, it is impossible to know whether they are true.
6.  For further details about the 'big deals' see Appendix A2 of Chapter 4. The reason for SMC's participation in the big deal remains unclear. Since the government has strongly pushed the big deals, it probably intervened in the determination of SMC's exit from the automobile industry.
7.  This highly uncertain period has somehow stabilized with Renault Motors now having taken

over most of the shares and management control of SMC.

8.  See Figure 2.1.
9.  For further details of the causes of the economic crisis in Korea see Jwa (2001).
10. It is understandable that the government-led restructuring after the crisis was inevitable given the size and extent of non-viable firms in the banking and corporate sectors that needed prompt restructuring. Nevertheless, it is now time for the government-led restructuring to permit market principles to effectively guide the direction of future economic progress.
11. See World Bank (1993).
12. For example, Wade (1990), Amsden (1989).
13. 'Under such disequilibriating conditions, the state's role in late industrialization is to mediate market forces. The state in late industrialization stages has intervened to address the needs of both savers and investors, and of both exporters and importers, by creating multiple prices. Some interest rates are higher than others. Importers and exporters face different prices for foreign currency. Insofar as the state in late industrialization stages has intervened to establish multiple prices in the same market, the state cannot be said to have gotten relative prices "right", as dictated by supply and demand. In fact, the state in late industrialization stages has set relative prices deliberately "wrong" in order to create profitable investment opportunities' Amsden (1989, pp. 13–14).
14. 'Whatever the relationship between inflation and investment in theory, in practice inflation did accompany Korea's push into heavy industry under government leadership in the late 1970s. ... The pursuit of fast growth was not restrained in the interest of price stability' Amsden (1989, pp. 100).
15. See World Bank (1993).
16. See Vanberg (1991).
17. For example, the Fordist mass production system was thought of as the optimal production system throughout the first half of the twentieth century. However, changes in the market environment, such as demand diversification and technological flexibility supported by microelectronics, called for a more flexible production system. As a result, from the late 1970s to the early 1980s the German and Japanese lean-and-flexible production systems (the Just-in-Time system of Toyota Motors is a typical example) emerged and seemed to have surpassed the Fordist mass production system. But in the late 1980s and 1990s, the German and Japanese systems were in turn being challenged by new American systems such as the self-managed team or self-directed work team systems that have become even more conspicuous in recent years with the advent of the new economy.
18. Jwa (1997) presents theoretical and empirical analysis on the spontaneous evolution of industrial organizations. It is shown that, due to globalization and the progress of information technology, industrial policies based on Hayekian competition as a discovery procedure should be accepted in any event. Also, see Jwa (2001) for further detailed discussions on this issue.
19. Economic reform to establish market-led discrimination at the center of economic activity will not, however, be an easy task, not least because of the dominance and inertia of government-led discrimination practices, but also because of the many cultural differences underpinning the Korean society in contrast to that of Western countries. For example, the uniformity characteristic of the Korean culture with roots in Confucianism tends to emphasize and attach high value to the single quest of a virtuous life, that is, to aim at becoming a morally superior being. This is hardly a bad thing, perhaps, but it is somewhat difficult to justify why a morally superior being should be predefined by an elite group that purports itself to belong to such a group. Nevertheless, this monothetic thinking is a good reason why Koreans have remained a culturally homogeneous people, although certain characteristics born out of this uniformity, as opposed to pluralism, run counter to the philosophy of democracy and the workings of a market economy. In an economic sense, more importantly, uniformity in whatever form tends to look at economic diversity with remorse and suspicion, as something that disrupts social harmony and may cause social division. These reasons, as well as, at times, the general attitude toward the *chaebol* as morally incompatible have of course encouraged the growth of the anti-*chaebol* sentiment.

See Jwa (2001, Chapter 2) for the importance of Taoism, the oriental philosophy of liberalism that in contrast is supportive of diversity, and is therefore friendly to the ideas of a capitalistic market economy. We also contrast Taoism with Confucianism, the latter being responsible for the profusion of widespread government intervention. Taoism is found to be akin to Hayekian political economy.

20. The firm in neoclassical economics is simply defined by the extent of its economies of scale and scope. Like many concepts in economics, the much-discussed 'economies of scale' can be traced to Adam Smith (1776). The theory of contestable markets developed by Baumol, Panzar and Willig (1982) extends the production function approach to the firm and refines some conceptual terminology including sunk costs and the economies of scope, by introducing the concept of the 'economies of scope'.

21. Alchian and Demsetz (1972) investigate the problems of shirking and monitoring team production. Coase (1937) remains an important figure in debates on corporate governance, as the originator of the concept of 'transaction costs'.

22. The empirical link between corporate governance and business performance, however, is rather mixed. Gordon and Pound (1991) give a good account for the US. Hwang and Seo (2000) is the only real econometric study on the relationship of corporate governance and corporate performance in Korea.

23. Scott (March, 1999).

24. Shareholders' rights include: (1) vote on questions affecting the company as a whole; (2) hold a proportionate ownership in the assets of the company; (3) transfer ownership of their shares; (4) receive dividends when declared by the board of directors; (5) inspect the corporate books and records; (6) sue the corporation for wrongful acts; and (7) share in the proceeds of a corporate liquidation.

25. Strictly speaking, however, the words 'system' and 'structure' reflect the perspective or approach to addressing the issue at hand. That is, when speaking of 'corporate governance systems', it is usually the case that the writer is talking in a holistic approach (looking at the entirety of corporate governance as a single whole), most often trying to discover the broad set of factors that result in 'good' corporate behavior. On the other hand, 'corporate governance structures' adopt reductionism in that the 'system' is now reduced to its constituent parts – that is, the writer is attempting to break the problem into its elements, and from then on the subject of inquiry are the constituent elements or parts of the whole.

26. See North (1990, p. 67) and quote in Chapter 5, Section 2.

27. See Vives (2000).

# 8. Toward a new framework of *chaebol* policy

## 1. INTRODUCTION

We have come a long way in analyzing the main features and sources of *chaebol* behavior, as well as clearing up some issues regarding the nature of past and current *chaebol* policy. It is time to move forward and spell out the framework of a new paradigm for corporate policy. In this chapter we draw from results of analyses in previous chapters and, in particular, the theory of corporate governance constructed in Chapter 7, to build a framework for *chaebol* policy that is needed for Korea's sustainable development. We have suggested repeatedly that the alternative direction for Korea's *chaebol* policy should focus on the reform of the external business environment, which, as has been explained, is ultimately the main determinant of *chaebol* behavior. Broadly speaking, the government's economic policy under the new economic environment of globalization should shift from one based on government-led discrimination and direct regulation to emphasizing market-led discrimination and indirect guidance based on market principles. Only by managing the economic environment and by giving private firms the autonomy to decide on endogenous management variables will the government be able effectively to steer economic activity in the private sector in an economically efficient direction.

This chapter is structured as follows. In Section 2, the basic direction toward improving *chaebol* regulation policy, particularly in the modern era of globalization, is discussed. In Section 3, the details of what a new *chaebol* policy should look like is presented. This section follows directly from our analysis of the *chaebol* problem, as well as from our conceptual understanding of the nature of corporate governance systems as discussed in Chapter 7. In Section 4, we argue that competition promotion policy should be at the center of Korea's economic reform, and further warn about some problems that may appear. Section 5 looks at the need to transform and reform institutions to remedy the most critical defects in the property rights system in Korea, as summarized in Chapter 5. The last section concludes.

## 2.   BASIC DIRECTION OF A NEW *CHAEBOL* POLICY

First and foremost, a new framework for *chaebol* policy cannot overlook trends in the global economic environment. As already mentioned, the increased uncertainty under rapid globalization continues to weaken the already insufficient government information processing and utilizing capacity over the private sector. For example, this has made it more difficult, if not impossible, for the government to make proper and timely judgments about the optimal structure of industrial organization. Moreover, the government is incapable of resolving problems related to choices about whether specialization or diversification is a winning strategy, or whether it is optimal to have an industrial structure dominated by small and medium-sized firms or one dominated by big firms. In line with our understanding of the economic development process, it is preferable to allow individual firms to select on their own the optimal business and industrial structure most suitable to the emerging globalized business environment.

The advent of economic globalization characterized by a 'global village' economy requires a new paradigm to deal with national economic problems and this includes the *chaebol* problem. Until recently, economic problems have usually been analyzed under the given constraint of national economic boundaries. However, with the advent of globalization, economic agents will be freed from the limits imposed by national economic borders. Thus, while we had so far accepted national economic problems as partial equilibrium or disequilibrium problems under the constraint of a national economy, in the new era of globalization, we will have to approach economic issues within a wider and border-less general equilibrium context.

Most existing national economic problems result from a state of disequilibrium or partial equilibrium brought about by the limited scale of national economies. In fact, many microeconomic problems, including domestic monopoly and oligopoly problems that are the object of competition policy, can be placed in this category. The *chaebol* issue is also a prototype of this situation. For example, as partly examined in the theoretical discussion and empirical analysis of Chapter 6, unrelated over-diversification behavior of the *chaebol* can be attributed mainly to the small size of the closed domestic market.

The advent of globalization will enlarge the size and scope of markets and deepen competition both domestically and internationally, and should therefore help curb inefficient diversification. Because of these forces, the disequilibrium problem caused by limited market size can be expected to slowly disappear. Accordingly, a new *chaebol* policy in the era of globalization should be implemented by taking into account the fact that new opportunities are now quickly becoming available to achieve equilibrium in the context of global markets rather than being confined to domestic markets alone.

In line with our arguments presented in this book, we emphasize yet again that *chaebol* policy should change from the direct regulation of business behavior to the qualitative improvement of the incentive structure in the economy. More specifically, the Korean government should first reform the existing institutions under which the *chaebol* have secured an unfair competitive edge in their formation process, then should strive to dissolve the economic constraints at home and abroad that have adverse influence on *chaebol* behavior. Furthermore, all direct regulations on business operations should be removed, thereby allowing for the optimal utilization of domestic and foreign resources. That is, the government needs to promote the opening of markets and foreign direct investment as effective ways to correct the disequilibrium in the domestic economy and to induce the *chaebols* to operate more efficiently, thereby allowing for a general equilibrium under strong competitive pressure.

It is also important to establish free competition by economic deregulation and liberalization, and to protect the competitive order that ensures fair market competition. To attain this goal, the role of competition policy should be increased. Care must be observed, however, as policy created in the name of enhancing competition may itself become prone to being anti-competitive and regulation-oriented. For example, there is evidence that corporate policy introduced in the name of fair competition has at times ended up restricting *chaebol* behavior due to the anti-*chaebol* sentiment – a phenomenon that we have discussed at some length in Chapter 3. The government's antitrust and competition policies, accordingly, needs to be transformed into a competition-promotion policy in accordance with the globalization trend.

Lastly, as discussed in Chapter 5, the government should establish a well-defined property rights system at the formal as well as informal levels through the reform of economic institutions. Only then can the *chaebol* smoothly evolve as a competitive business organization operating in an efficient industrial structure without the government's active guidance, protection or direct regulation. Without such improvements in the economic institutional environment, one cannot expect policy measures to yield any lasting fruitful results.

## 3. TOWARD IMPROVING *CHAEBOL* REGULATION POLICY

### 3.1 Policy for Problems in the Process of *Chaebol* Formation

As has been established in Chapter 4, the *chaebol* problem, we argued, has its roots in the unique government-led growth strategy and industrial policy. We have seen how the Korean government directed scarce resources into the hands of a few competent entrepreneurs as a means to promote the growth of a selected few priority industries. Accordingly, financial assistance programs in the form of interest rate subsidies and preferential bank loans were established. Throughout this process, a system of cooperative relations between businessmen and the government emerged that resulted in the concentration of limited resources within these firms.

The direct cause of the *chaebol* problem, however, does not solely reside in the government's economic development strategy itself, such as, for example, the heavy and chemical industries drive that paralleled the emergence of some of the big firms. Rather, the cause of the problem lies more in the way the industry promotion policy was carried out, that is, in the government's political decisions to support particular target industries and firms through decisions often based on discretionary judgement rather than being based on fair market rules. In other words, this inclination to implement a development strategy based on government-led discrimination rather than market-led discrimination has caused the *chaebol* problem. At this point, one may argue that solving this problem is possible if, and only if, past decisions of selective assistance through political decisions are invalidated. In line with this viewpoint, some have mistakenly argued for the economic divestiture of the *chaebols* as the best available measure to solve the *chaebol* problem.

On the other hand, it has been claimed by some observers that an objective discussion on this issue is not possible unless the merits and demerits of the *chaebol* in the development of the national economy are fairly and objectively evaluated. Even if a negative evaluation of the fairness of past industrial policies continues to prevail, it seems also the case, as previously discussed, that the positive contributions of the *chaebols* to economic development cannot or should not be ignored. However, even if the issue of the merits and demerits of the *chaebols* is an important research question, it will not be easy to derive a clear-cut objective conclusion because discussions of this issue, by their very nature, involve political value judgments.

Whatever the case may be, even though we may reserve judgment on the extent of the contribution of the *chaebol* to Korea's development, the discussions on policy directions of a future industrial organization that might replace the existing *chaebol*-dominated structure will not be greatly affected. Granting that the process of *chaebol* formation might be viewed as problematic, what matters at this point is how to deal with the already existing *chaebol*-dominated economic structure. Our approach is essentially forward-looking. That is, the choice of a future industrial structure is to be determined on the basis of changes in the economic environment that will unfold in the future, and not on the basis of past merits or demerits of a certain economic structure. Therefore, by not answering the difficult question regarding the merits and demerits of the *chaebols* in the past, which will inevitably entail political value judgments, the search for the future optimal industrial and corporate organization under the newly emerging global environment will not be greatly affected. For this reason, discussions should perhaps be made more fruitful by focusing mainly on the economic validity of transforming the *chaebol*-dominated economic structure into a socially desirable one, or what some refer to as '*chaebol* divestiture'.

We must bear in mind, however, that '*chaebol* divestiture' may in fact have two different meanings.[1] The first is *chaebol* ownership divestiture, that is, the alleviation of the concentration of wealth through changes in the ownership structure of the *chaebol* using non-market government intervention. The second is the change in the production system and industrial structure from one that is dominated by big businesses to one that is 'more balanced' or dominated by small and medium-sized businesses, which in the extreme case may entail the breaking up of the *chaebol*-dominated production system and industrial structure.

As regards the first type of divestiture, the redistribution of wealth concentrated in the hands of a few persons through non-market means is seen as belonging to the realm of political decision-making, which is, in fact, reminiscent of the government-led industrial policies of the past 40 years that have resulted in the existing ownership concentration. The determination of whether transferring the wealth concentrated in person A to person B is desirable usually entails political, not economic, judgment. Consequently, the issue of *chaebol* ownership divestiture cannot be solved through economic analysis alone. Alternatively, redistribution of wealth away from the *chaebol* and eventually their dismemberment through market mechanisms together with the provision of various inducements, such as tax incentives, to disperse ownership can be regarded as accepting the legitimacy of the wealth accumulation process of the first stage *chaebol* formation process. In this respect, the transfer of ownership rights through political decision-making is in essence different from that induced by a market solution. Accordingly, if the first stage process of *chaebol* formation is deemed unfair and if one then tries to resolve the issue of wealth concentration through non-market mechanisms, the *chaebol* problem becomes an object of political value judgment and not of positive economic analysis. Granted, the political decision-making process of who will and who will not receive a certain favor from the government can also be analyzed within positive economic analysis as observed in the public choice approach to the political market. Again, the issues of whether that favor is fair or unfair and of who should or should not receive that favor belong to the realm of value judgement rather than to positive economic analysis.

As relates to the second argument regarding the dissolution of the *chaebol*-oriented production system and industrial structure, the issue can be approached from a slightly different angle. First of all, we should recognize that such a decision of divestiture is essentially a problem of economic choice. Whether a big business-dominated industrial structure will eventually be beneficial or harmful to the national economy can be regarded as an issue of pure economic judgment. In this respect, a more relevant question can be posed: which type of industrial structure will sustain Korea's economic development in the future? Second, as various forms of industrial organization are explored, the economic principle stipulating that the past, irrespective of whether it was right or not, should not have any significant impact on future decision-making must be kept in mind. In economic decision-making, only variable or avoidable costs matter. Costs that were already borne in the past and that cannot be avoided or erased at the present time are not worth considering.[2] Resource concentration in the form of production facility investments locked in the *chaebol* sectors can be viewed as some kind of sunk or historical cost for the national economy, and so these factors should not influence the search for the optimal future structure of industrial organization. Therefore at this point it is socially beneficial to explore the best alternative industrial organization by quickly dropping any lingering attachments to the already established and existing structure.

The resources that have already been invested to secure certain know-how and production facilities in the process of *chaebol* formation can be regarded as equivalent to sunk costs and therefore unavoidable, regardless of whether the *chaebols'* established production systems continue to survive or not. Accordingly, the existence of the current *chaebol* production system should not influence the choice of an optimal industrial organization in the future. On the other hand, even though the current *chaebol*-dominated industrial organization may eventually be totally discredited, the already invested sunk costs are not recoverable. Therefore whether or not we dismantle the *chaebol*-dominated industrial organization, say, even by using force, is not an economically meaningful issue with regard to the exploration for an optimal future industrial organization.

On the other hand, as discussed in previous chapters, it is our position that the government, or any other third party for that matter, should not try to impose a certain corporate structure or industrial organization on the economy. We have argued that it is almost impossible for the government to evaluate with any meaningful degree of precision the worth and optimality of alternative industrial or corporate organizations. We are faced with a compelling fact that an optimal structure can only be discovered through market competition. It therefore follows that the optimal industrial organization policy is one that, by establishing fair rules of the game, assures the survival of a corporate or industrial organization through the natural selection process of the 'survival of the fittest' based on market-led discrimination.

Here a number of conclusions can be drawn from the above discussion. First, the issue of unfairness in relation to wealth and ownership concentration, as well as how to disperse 'unfair' ownership concentration, inevitably involves political value judgment. As such (and unfortunately), the problem of ownership concentration resulting from the first stage *chaebol* formation process cannot be solved solely through positive economic analysis.[3] Second, breaking up the *chaebol*-dominated production system and industrial structure through whatever forceful means will not necessarily constitute an economically sound solution. Accordingly, we are left with hardly any choice but to go ahead with the second-best policy, that is, to alleviate the *chaebol* problem through correcting the established industrial policy framework that has induced unfair ownership concentration as well as the *chaebol*-dominated industrial organization, thus curbing further artificial aggravation.

In this case, the problem of unfairness in ownership concentration and *chaebol* domination in the country's industrial organization can be mitigated only by minimizing the influence of political decision-making and reforming the allocation process of resource utilization rights as fairly and transparently as possible, thereby raising the social legitimacy of wealth accumulation. This, in essence, means that market-led discrimination should principally be allowed to determine the pattern of ownership rather than government-led discrimination. To maintain fairness and transparency in the process of economic resource allocation and firms' acquisition of economic resources, the government should abandon interventionist industrial policy in favor of an economic management system based on the principles of non-discrimination and the market economy. For this purpose, a variety of protectionist and regulatory measures for industrial support that have been part of the government's industrial policy should be lifted as soon as possible. Moreover, entry regulations in all fields should be removed. In addition, the support system for the export-oriented manufacturing sector, which has restricted the growth of the domestic service sector, including the financial sector, should be reformed. The preferential financing practice through non-market decision-making should be abolished, thereby taking a substantial step toward financial liberalization. Then, the various ad hoc regulations on bank loans to the *chaebol*, such as the 'loan management system',[4] could be replaced by a traditional system of prudential regulation, including limits on the amount of loans to a single borrower. The collusive cronyism that exists between business and politics should be severed through the active implementation of deregulation policies and increasing policy transparency. Furthermore, to solve the problem of extreme wealth accumulation by families through the generations, clearly one of the major factors triggering the emergence of the anti-*chaebol* sentiment, a much more transparent and progressive inheritance tax system may be implemented.

Even if such policy reforms do not succeed in totally transforming the *chaebol*-dominated economic structure, they have the potential to contribute greatly to the improvement of the current economic environment, thus assisting private economic agents in making rational choices in search of an efficient corporate and industrial organization structure compatible with the rapid globalization era.

## 3.2 Policy for *Chaebol* Management Behavior: Efficiency Promotion Policy for Big Businesses

### 3.2.1 Improvement of regulations on *chaebol* management behavior

In Chapter 4 we extensively reviewed and evaluated past and present *chaebol* policy by applying the two stage decision-making process. In particular, we identified *chaebol* policy that specifically aimed at affecting second stage *chaebol* behavior. We looked at various examples of policy measures used to control *chaebol* behavior in the pre-crisis period. These include the direct regulations on diversification and business specialization, ownership concentration, the degree of separation between ownership and management, cross-debt guarantees and cross-ownership between affiliate firms, investment and sales across affiliate firms, and so on. As we have repeatedly argued in earlier chapters and especially in Chapter 4, such regulatory measures have usually aimed at intervening directly in *chaebol* behavior and as a result have distorted the smooth operation of market mechanisms.

On the other hand, we also find that nearly all of the post-crisis reform efforts turn out to focus on the second stage decision-making process or *chaebol* behavior. More importantly, there remain certain measures of the post-crisis reform that are reminiscent of the direct intervention regulations of the pre-crisis period. For example, the implementation of a uniform 200 per cent debt–equity ratio and the ban on cross-debt guarantees, as discussed in Chapter 4, are detrimental to corporate management as they directly affect endogenous decision variables that are better left to be decided upon by private corporations.[5] Even if there are reasons to resort to such measures, it is unreasonable to apply these across the board and uniformly without taking into account the inherent differences of individual corporate characteristics.

Some of the post-crisis reform efforts, however, especially those directed at improving corporate governance structures, have shown a markedly good improvement in the sense that they emphasize reforming the external economic environment rather than directly intervening in endogenous management variables. These include efforts to increase management transparency and accountability, improve the protection of shareholder rights, as well as the introduction of voting rights for institutional investors and a cumulative voting system. The introduction of the board of directors system by way of compulsory appointment of outside directors may also be added to this list, but with some reservations.[6] As explained in Chapter 7,[7] for various reasons that include social and cultural characteristics, the legal framework, type of government policy and financial system in place, and so on, it takes time for private corporations to adjust their behavior to the changing economic environment, for example, to the changes in the corporate governance system brought about by reform. While the post-crisis reform efforts have correctly focused on corporate governance structures, there are still occasions when the government has resorted to 'old-style' regulatory practices, often out of impatience to realize immediate improvements in corporate behavior and particularly in a crisis situation. Perhaps, more often than not, the misunderstanding of the intricate relationship between changes in the corporate governance system and the endogenous adaptation in corporate behavior has largely prompted 'old-style' regulation methods to creep into the reform efforts. In sum, problems with the current reform efforts usually lie more in the manner by which measures have been implemented rather than the policy prescription itself, in the sense that they occasionally try directly to push corporate behavior in a certain direction. On the other hand, at times, as we have seen above, some policy prescriptions themselves are hardly justifiable Elements of 'old style' regulation practices need to be weeded out consciously, and moreover, the 'emergency' reform measures that were set up immediately and rather abruptly in reaction to the 1997 economic crisis now need to be updated or completely revised. Later in this chapter, we show what areas are important and what needs to be done.

What is important to note is that strengthening corporate governance systems is the key to inducing proper *chaebol* behavior. Good corporate governance can be seen as having important implications that foster the performance of a firm, and therefore warrants a clear and careful understanding of the structure of relationships and corresponding responsibilities among the constituent agents of the corporate governance system, that is, shareholders, lenders, board members, managers and other stakeholders. Corporations with poor governance structures will have difficulty accessing financial markets for funds, particular in this important era of globalization, and will thus eventually lose out to competitors.

Here, we proposed that a market disciplinary system should be brought to the forefront in order to induce firms into improving their governance structure. This market disciplinary system, which would act as the external economic environment for corporations, is the responsibility of the government, as argued in Chapter 7.[8]

### 3.2.2 Strengthening of the market disciplinary system on corporate behavior

In Chapter 7, we pointed out that to a business entity the external economic environment is an exogenous variable while internal control mechanisms are strategic variables at the disposal of management that are best determined endogenously. Corporations as economic agents or organizations can be regarded as being disciplined by the prevailing institutions which set the rules of the game. This institutional environment, on the other hand, can be depicted as consisting of two ways to monitor and discipline corporations, namely through the external market disciplinary system or through internal control mechanisms. The external disciplinary system consists of exogenous factors affecting business decisions, and usually emphasizes the establishment of market institutions to enhance the corporate monitoring role of the various markets for products, capital, debt, managers and so on. Internal control mechanisms, on the other hand, constitute endogenous variables, and include mechanisms such as the holding company system or a planning and coordination office that operated as a kind of holding company, as well as the board of directors.

Current debate about corporate governance reform tends to put undue weight on internal control systems as can be seen in the OECD guidelines (OECD, 1999). For example, emphasis is placed on the proper role of the board of directors in corporate governance. This tendency seems to arise largely because such recommendations are based on the experiences of advanced economies in which the external market for corporate control in the product, capital, debt and CEO markets are well established and all operate competitively. The OECD guidelines seem to be somewhat misleading, at least from our perspective, in the sense that they fail to recognize that the system of the board of directors is in fact also an important part of the internal management system. That is, the board of directors system is often strategically utilized to meet the objectives of the corporation, and as such, the details of the internal management system should be left to be endogenously determined. Whatever the case may be, in Korea, the improvement of the role of the external disciplinary system in influencing corporate behavior is rather urgent, and will, in fact, have deep repercussions toward enhancing the efficiency of internal governance systems, including the board of director system. That is, not only is the continued development of internal control systems important, but also external control mechanisms must be established and strengthened.

In this section, we shall discuss three aspects of the external disciplinary system, some of which have traditionally experienced repeated government interference and regulation, namely the product market, the M&A market and the financial system. As a hybrid case, we shall also discuss the role of the board of directors in disciplining corporate governance behavior.

*3.2.2.1 Competition promotion in the product market* Competition in the product market is the most effective mechanism of corporate governance. The greatest incentive for firms to improve their management behavior stems from their incentive to survive cutthroat competition in the market, regardless of whether the firm is a *chaebol* or a small or medium-sized firm. Figure 7.2 shows the most important institutions that help discipline business management and its governance structure. In principle, fierce competition in the product market is one of the most effective means to induce firms toward an efficient management organization and business structure. Moreover, as we have seen, the government's ability directly to control *chaebol* behavior as well as the domestic economy is decreasing rapidly owing to globalization and the ineffectiveness of economic borders as a means of controlling the mobility of economic resources. It is therefore inevitable that the general direction of *chaebol* policy should change from direct intervention that dictated specific corporate practices to indirect management that encourages 'good' firm behavior through the promotion of competition. In the era of global competition the promotion of intense competition not only among *chaebol* affiliate firms themselves but also between different *chaebols* and competitors is the best policy to pressure them into improving the efficiency of business management.

Accordingly, the government needs to reshape the rules of market competition in accordance with global standards in order to promote competition. The Fair Trade Act as a competition promotion law currently biased toward regulations curbing economic concentration is incompatible with the globalization trend and should be redrawn.[9] Besides, the government should weaken the *chaebols'* monopoly power by raising the potential as well as the actual degree of competition among big businesses, for example, by lifting all entry regulations in domestic industries. According to survey data on entry regulations by the Department of Commerce and Industry, entry regulations still exist in more than 60 per cent of the total business sectors (205 out of 325 business sectors based on the Korean Standard Industry Classification (see Table 8.1)). Under such circumstances it cannot be expected that firms would voluntarily maximize economic efficiency with such a far-reaching entry regulation system.

Next, since the Korean economy is of limited size, policy needs to take advantage of market opening as a means of promoting competition by inviting competitive pressure from abroad. This will have the added effect of easing domestic monopoly power and ultimately achieving a general equilibrium in the industrial structure. In other words, to promote domestic competition and

*Table 8.1    Entry regulations by industry (1997)*

| Industry classification | Total no. of Industries (A) | No. of regulated industries (B) | B/A (%) |
|---|---|---|---|
| Farming, hunting and forestry | 14 | 7 | 50.0 |
| Fishery | 4 | 3 | 75.0 |
| Mining | 12 | 11 | 91.7 |
| Manufacturing | 142 | 74 | 52.1 |
| Electricity, gas and water supply | 4 | 3 | 75.0 |
| Construction | 7 | 6 | 85.7 |
| Whole/retail sale and repairs of consumer commodities | 36 | 23 | 63.9 |
| Lodging and restaurants | 4 | 4 | 100 |
| Financing and insurance | 13 | 10 | 76.9 |
| Real estates, leasing and business services | 32 | 19 | 59.4 |
| Education services | 5 | 5 | 100 |
| Health and social work | 6 | 6 | 100 |
| Other public, social and personal services | 26 | 15 | 57.7 |
| Transportation/warehouse and telecommunication | 19 | 19 | 100 |
| Household affairs services | 1 | 0 | 0 |
| Total | 325 | 205 | 63.1 |

*Note*:   Nine sectors under government monopoly are excluded.

to help drive out inefficient firms, and eventually to reshape the current industrial structure into becoming more competitive, foreign direct investment into domestic industries should be actively encouraged, and in particular, the domestic product market should be open to foreign producers.

Another point worthy of mention is that the current corporate bankruptcy system contains various pitfalls that aggravate the inefficiency in resource allocation. For example, the distinction between the corporate reorganization process and the workout program[10] remains ambiguous and the two systems are not complementary to each other. The courts are allowed to change the priority of credits, which is most likely to affect social economic efficiency through the reallocation of the creditor's expected payoffs. Furthermore, in the workout programs, there is no legal obligation for debtor firms and creditor banks to carry out the workout plan that they had agreed upon. It is therefore necessary to reform the current exit system such that firms that cannot survive the cutthroat competition will drop out of markets smoothly. The institutions relevant to the business exit system need to be simplified and rationalized because any exit barriers in the midst of increasing competition will retard industrial restructuring and cause serious distortions in resource allocation.

*3.2.2.2 Activation of the M&A market*    Although historically unimportant in the Korean economy so far, the M&A market constitutes another important component of the external disciplinary system. In modern society, it is imperative that the corporate governance system through which corporations monitor each other's management performance be strengthened by participation in the M&A market. M&A activities can be very effective at pressuring corporations into restructuring and increasing management efficiency, because a firm, undervalued due to poor management, which exhibits market value short of its potential value will be acquired or merged.

M&A activity has been restricted in Korea for a variety of reasons, such as curbing economic concentration and protecting the managerial power of the domestic owner-manager from foreign takeover. However, under the post-crisis reform program, various deregulatory measures to promote M&A activity, with the free participation of foreign capital in the stock market, have been implemented. Therefore the efforts of big businesses to promote management efficiency are expected to double.[11]

As part of the measures to revitalize the domestic M&A market, the government has strongly encouraged big deals, or more precisely business swap deals, among the large corporations.[12] The big deals, however, are controversial and run counter to the liberalization trend in that these represent government intervention, despite claims by the government that the deals stem from the *chaebols'* own initiative. As has been explained earlier, the government is in fact infringing the property rights of the companies participating in the restructuring programs.

M&A markets should be activated in line with the spirit of the market economy. Direct government control should be avoided and markets should be allowed freedom to develop according to their own needs under clear rules and procedures for merger and acquisition. Continued deregulation of M&A activities by both local and foreign firms is also important, as is increased flexibility of the labor market, as a way of improving the efficiency of M&A markets.

*3.2.2.3 Strengthening the monitoring role of the financial sector*    Following the discussions in Chapter 7, we see how the financial system plays an important role in the supervising and monitoring of corporate management behavior. Financial institutions that take on the role of creditors ceaselessly endeavor to promote the sound management of corporations through their loan-screening function in the interests of depositors and investors. In other words, corporations will make every effort to abide by good corporate behavior as they have an incentive to borrow funds, if possible, at the best possible terms (or the lowest interest rate) available by satisfying creditors. On the other hand, potential stock (equity) investors in equity markets will try to select the best corporations for their investments. At the same time, corporations will try to sell their stocks on the best possible terms (or, highest possible price) by appealing to potential investors with good corporate behavior. Thus, the resulting outcome is an improvement in corporate management efficiency.

As such, corporate behavior is directly affected by the extent to which financial markets effectively monitor corporate management. Consequently, it can hardly be desirable for the government to directly regulate corporate debt and other capital-raising behavior without due improvement in the financial market environment. That is, the government is better off trying to encourage the development of financial markets through various institutional reforms designed to strengthen their function of monitoring corporate behavior.

In Korea, however, reality differs from such ideals. Commercial banks have not played such an independent corporate-monitoring role because they were historically mobilized as a means to support the government's industrial policy under the so-called system of *kwanchi kumyung* or 'government-controlled finance' that typifies Korea's history of excessive government regulation in the financial sector. The government's heavy involvement in the activities of banks has led to the drastic weakening of many of the essential roles of banks including their loan-monitoring function. Therefore it remains a most important financial reform policy objective to upgrade the role of banks as an important institution to monitor corporate behavior.

Financial liberalization promoting the autonomous management of financial institutions and increased competition in the financial markets should help establish the credit-screening function and, more generally, the corporate-monitoring function of financial institutions. Specifically, decision-making on major corporate loans and the level of interest rate should be left to individual financial institutions, which should, at the same time, be made responsible for their lending decisions. In this way, lending institutions should become more careful so as to avoid over-borrowing and the possibility of default on the part of the private corporate sector.

On the other hand, equity markets have not functioned well enough to monitor corporate behavior effectively, not only because of government regulations, but also because of the poor institutional environment for those markets. The government should make a conscious effort to strengthen the corporate monitoring function of the equity markets by deregulating and reshaping the poorly working institutions in these markets. The securities market should also be deregulated by liberalizing the system of public stock offering and completely opening the bond and stock markets to foreign investors. Strengthening the minority shareholders' rights will also contribute to the improvement of the monitoring function of the stockmarket, which, in turn, will promote corporate management efficiency.[13] Generally, the government should aim at improving investor protection, which has historically been relegated to a minor role in the midst of Korea's past development strategy which historically emphasized entrepreneur protection.

A word of warning is perhaps needed here. The distinction between the equity markets and bank lending markets of advanced Anglo-Saxon countries and 'catch-up' economies is made in this book, particularly in Chapter 7, mainly for analytical convenience and should not mislead us into thinking that either should be emphasized over the other. What is important to note is that in the global economy the choice between a bank-dominated or equity-dominated financial system cannot and should not be made *ex ante*. It will always remain uncertain how the future course of not only the global economic scenario, but also the national economy will turn out. As things stand now, it is prudent, and perhaps therefore unavoidable, not to under-emphasize either the banking or equity markets, as they are both critical to Korea's future economic growth. In fact, this question about the future shape of not only the domestic but also international financial structures, including their role in shaping corporate governance behavior, will remain a topical research area for many years to come.[14]

*3.2.2.4   The role of the board of directors*   Despite differences in the way that the board of directors is chosen and structured across various countries, we pointed out in Chapter 7 that the role of the board of directors in corporations should be viewed as a hybrid system belonging partly to the internal as well as to the external disciplinary mechanism. Thus, when addressing the role of the board of directors in a corporation, the following implications needs to be borne in mind. Since it acts as a signaling mechanism indicating the type of management strategy that the corporation has adopted, or intends to adopt, the determination of the board of directors should be left to the discretion of the corporate management as an essential component of its management decision variables. On the other hand, since it is composed of agents who represent various interests groups including shareholders as well as stakeholders, the board of directors by acting as a window through which these external groups may directly influence corporate management, becomes an important part of the external disciplinary system.

As such, economic policy and government action must therefore refrain from putting too restrictive or overly detailed constraints on regulating the composition and operations of the board of director. Rather, the management's autonomy to utilize the board of directors as an important strategic variable should be respected, and should be free of any unfair intervention. Needless to say, we may understand that the nature of the board of directors as being simultaneously part of the internal as well as external control system for corporate governance makes this a delicate and critical matter.

In the historical context, the need for a board of directors to act as a check on professional management behavior has so far been unimportant in Korea. In fact, corporate governance in Korea has been relatively free from the principal-agent problem that occupies many of the discussions on the managerial behavior of diffused-ownership companies of advanced Western countries. Many corporations in advanced Western countries feature the separation of owner and manager, which evolved naturally during the growth of capitalism. The development of appropriate market institutions that make such a system viable was influenced by the need to accumulate large sums of capital from diffused stockholders beyond the capacity of the owner-manager. In Korea, the owner-manager usually runs most of the affairs of the company thereby avoiding the need to differentiate between managers and stockholders, as well as issues of agency costs. Recently, however, the separation of owner and manager, and the introduction of the system of board of outside directors have been prompted largely by government regulation, thereby raising issues of the effectiveness of government intervention in corporate management. That is, uncertainty surrounding the effectiveness of such government-initiated corporate reform efforts is bound to increase.[15]

### 3.2.3   Optimal diversification or specialization

The Korean government has made various attempts at inducing the *chaebol* into specializing in a few business areas to curb their so-called 'excessive' diversification behavior.[16] In line with the spirit of the market economy, instead of the current specialization guidelines, the government's policy concerning the *chaebols'* diversification behavior should be redesigned to promote competition at home and abroad while at the same time taking into consideration the new economic environment of globalization. By doing so, firms will have an incentive to pursue a strategy of discovering their own optimal diversification.

As previously pointed out, the simple dichotomized policy reasoning that specialization is right and diversification is wrong should be promptly dismissed. If, however, the government judges that the degree of *chaebol* diversification is 'excessive' compared to some optimal or desirable level and decides to intervene, it is better to resort to reforming the existing incentive structure or economic environment that constitutes the incentive for *chaebols* to diversify their business lines.

With regard to the reform of the institutional environment, the abolition of entry regulations and opening the market to foreign as well as domestic competition should make markets more competitive. As a result, the newly created competitive environment will force the *chaebols* to pursue an optimal diversification strategy centered on businesses in which they have a competitive advantage. Moreover, the government should encourage domestic firms to look further than the narrow domestic market and to freely choose a strategy between specialization and diversification, which will allow them to compete successfully in the world market.

It is also important for the government to induce firms into changing their self-protecting diversification behavior by improving the system of private property rights, which, as previously discussed, has been one of the major reasons to follow a diversification strategy. In Chapter 6, we characterized Korean firms as following a strategy of managerial diversification whereby affiliates are created and controlled, in contrast to product-line diversification where new products are simply added to a company's existing line(s) of business. As also empirically shown, it is expected that improvements in the private property rights system will induce firms to adopt 'normal' diversification behavior by discouraging managerial diversification while encouraging product-line diversification. Furthermore, letting firms voluntarily decide whether to enter or exit industries on the basis of their own economic judgment by changing the industrial policy pattern that artificially prevents big firms from going bankrupt as well as entering the designated industry will be conducive to the attainment of optimal diversification. In addition, the recent policy of prohibiting cross-debt guarantees between *chaebol* affiliates, even though their outright prohibition could severely limit the choice set available to banks and firms, will help reduce the incentives to diversify. As argued above, cross-debt guarantees are essentially part of the endogenous strategic variables of a firm.[17]

## 4.   REFORM OF COMPETITION POLICY

### 4.1   New Direction of Competition Policy

If improvements are to be made upon the alleged non-competitive behavior of the *chaebol*, then, first of all, the government should establish a competitive market economy, based on fair, free and open competition. Policy-makers also need to take into consideration the fact that the pursuit of monopoly rents, special favors and artificial protection is a common attribute of any economic agent, including big businesses.

Government-led discrimination in terms of providing special favors and protection to a selected few will no longer be effective in the global open market. The government's role in this new global era should be to coordinate the conflicting demands of complex stakeholders by establishing 'fair competition rules' and enforcing them through competition policies so that no economic agent may benefit from any unfair advantages. This also means that small and medium-sized firms should not be treated favorably compared to big firms simply because they are smaller, and at the same time big firms should not be allowed to exercise unfair market-dominant power to secure a competitive advantage over small and medium-sized firms.

The fair trade policy regarding the *chaebol*, based on the current Fair Trade Act, is biased toward the direct regulation of particular economic phenomena and market behavior, such as economic concentration and business diversification. Therefore it cannot be effective in improving market structures, and in fact, is coming under criticism for its role in unduly restraining business activity. It would be better to transform the current regime of fair trade policy based on existing antitrust laws into a competition promotion policy. For this purpose, it may be necessary to reform the existing 'Fair Trade Act' into a new 'Competition Promotion Act'.

Competition policies can generally be classified into two categories.[18] The first category focuses on competition promotion through the minimization and abolition of artificial entry barriers in the economic system. Many countries have adopted this kind of competition policy to meet the challenges of global competition. This trend is even conspicuous in the enforcement process of US antitrust laws. The primary reason why competition promotion is considered a major policy goal is because it has the desirable effect of driving inefficient firms out of the market while retaining the most efficient ones, and moreover provides for the dynamic process of discovering new potential opportunities. Only through promoting competition can economic efficiency eventually be guaranteed.

This type of competition policy requires free market entry as an important condition for competition promotion. Accordingly, competition policies, by adhering to the single goal of relaxing all unnecessary barriers to economic activity, can contribute to raising the competitiveness and economic efficiency of all economic entities. In this respect, entry barriers can be categorized into three kinds. The first kind of barriers are artificial government entry regulations, which emerge from a variety of policies such as industrial protection, protection of the weak (small/medium-sized) firms, and restraints on diversification behavior or M&A activity to alleviate economic concentration. Many studies report that such entry regulations severely restrain market competition. The second kind of barrier are natural or technological entry barriers caused by market imperfections attributable to fixed sunk costs or information asymmetry. The third kind of barrier are entry restrictions artificially erected by private monopolists or oligopolists, such as horizontal or vertical trade restrictions which have traditionally been regulated by antitrust laws. Policy of the first kind that aims at promoting competition considers the relaxation or abolition of entry barriers as the most important policy agenda above the regulation of the behavior of private monopolists or oligopolists. It is understood not only that competition pressure from potential entrants can discipline monopolistic or oligopolistic firms' anti-competitive behavior as long as free entry is guaranteed, but also that government entry regulations are themselves the most important source of entry barriers.

On the other hand, the second type of competition policy, while also having the promotion of competition as its main goal, views the curbing of monopolistic or oligopolistic market power, regardless of the existence of entry regulations, as crucial in the pursuit to promoting competition. Furthermore, adherents of this type of competition policy argue that it is desirable for the government to weaken monopoly power and in fact, that it should disperse economic power because the goal of competition policy is essentially to promote economic democratization. Germany, Japan and the EU have competition laws reflecting this view. Korea's Fair Trade Act can be included in this group as well.

In recent years, however, the policy stance emphasizing the pursuit of economic development through the growth of efficient firms, rather than one that emphasizes the pursuit of economic equity and the sacrifice of economic efficiency for the sake of protecting the economically weak, is increasingly being supported because it is expected that this is more conducive to the development of democracy. This policy stance is based on the belief that improving economic efficiency is more important than any other factor in order to survive global competition and foster the sharing of the fruits of economic growth society-wide. In line with this argument, recent trends of competition policy worldwide have begun to converge toward the first type described above, which allows maximum freedom of entry with an emphasis on competition promotion as the ultimate goal of competition policy.

Korea's competition policy needs to get in line with the globalization trend by abandoning the pursuit of mutually conflicting goals such as the simultaneous pursuit of economic efficiency on the one hand and economic equity (by regulating economic concentration in such a way as to restrict competition) on the other. Rather, competition policy needs to be reformed in line with the simple, yet important, goal of promoting competition, and thereby economic efficiency, by lifting a variety of competition-restraining regulations and also curbing the entry-restricting behavior of monopolistic firms.

## 4.2  Major Concerns in the Exercise of Competition Policy

Considering the above discussion, the lifting of entry regulations emerges as the policy measure most significant to the smooth working of competition policy. As such, artificial entry barriers erected by the government, as well as by the monopolists, should be actively and promptly eliminated. However, in the case of natural entry barriers due to inherent market imperfections, it is highly probable that these barriers could become a source of the differences in the firms' efficiency levels, and therefore simply resorting to regulations as a solution to such problems carries the potential of harming economic efficiency in general. With regard to regulatory policies prohibiting big firms in monopolistic or oligopolistic positions from engaging in anti-competitive behavior, confirming the nature of such behavior and regulating it could become very controversial owing to its close relations with the strategic behavior of firms.[19] In this respect, the following thoughts should be taken into consideration in charting the direction of competition policy, especially with regard to the *chaebol*.[20]

The uniform regulation of monopolistic firms regardless of the source of monopoly power will be highly problematic. Even though monopolistic firms are generally interpreted as firms that can directly affect market prices by adjusting the quantity supplied along the downward-sloping demand curve, two different types of monopolistic firms should be acknowledged. Specifically, it is necessary to differentiate market monopolization attributable to superiority in terms of the quality of goods and services from market monopolization due to man-made entry barriers set up by laws and regulations regardless of efficiency.[21] In this context, it is helpful to distinguish between the two when considering policies to promote competition and economic efficiency.

The former type of monopolist does not necessarily generate distortions in resource allocation and does not need to be regulated as long as it faces potential competitive pressure under free entry. This type of monopoly emerges naturally from the profit-maximizing behavior of firms that take advantage of factors affecting their business opportunities such as economies of scale, supply restraints due to high transportation costs and information asymmetry. It is common, however, to find that these factors are cited as sources of market imperfection.

In contrast, the second type of market monopolization is artificially created through various laws and regulations established by the government such as entry restrictions, advertising regulations and consumer protection measures. This type of market monopolization can also be generated by a private firm's efforts at blocking competitors, for example, by collusion among producers and competition-inhibiting mergers. It is particularly in such cases that competition policy should be more actively applied and enforced to secure fair competition.

Even though the monopolistic market structure in Korea is in part due to collusion among the *chaebol* affiliates, it has to a large extent been generated through governmental support and protection for big corporations in the name of industrial development. The most urgent measures to correct monopolistic market structures are the lifting of all existing man-made entry regulations and the active promotion of competition. Competition policies should contribute to overall efficiency by distinguishing carefully between the latter type of monopolies, which need to be the object of active correction measures, and the former, for which the need is less pronounced.

As for the exercise of competition policy on the *chaebol*, it must be noted that the concentration of market power within a few large firms does not necessarily create economic harm. The fact that a firm is big enough to yield monopoly power can be a totally different matter from the actual exercise of that power in the market. Whether a firm exerts its market power or not hinges on the possibility of increasing profits through the exercise of its power. Price increases do not always lead to profit maximization:

> Ability should not be confused with incentive. The ability to raise price is like the ability to throw my money away. (Willingness to do so is another matter.) Though a price-searcher has power to raise price by altering his output, it does not follow that he has the incentive to do so. Instead he is driven toward the wealth-maximizing price.[22]

Pricing on the part of monopolistic firms is affected to a large extent by the existence or absence of potential entrants. Even if a firm enjoys some market power, it will be significantly weakened by the existence of strong competitive pressure from potential entrants because monopoly pricing will induce new firms to enter the market. Accordingly, the amount of competitive pressure a monopolistic firm faces from potential entrants plays a pivotal role in disciplining its market behavior. For this reason, it is important to place emphasis on the correction of *chaebols'* behavior through strengthening competitive pressure as the most effective solution to the problem of economic concentration.

Hereafter, competition policy regarding the *chaebol* or for that matter big businesses should take into consideration the subtle economic behavior of such big firms. The Korean market structure will become more open and competitive with the continued relaxation and abolishment of entry regulations. As such, competition policy should also fully consider the economic implications of changes in the market environment and the incentive structure on firm behavior. Therefore, competition policy should break away from the past pattern of direct regulation. Instead, it should focus on corrective actions on the firm's fundamental structure of incentives. Such policy, by promoting competition in the market through granting maximum freedom of entry and exit, should help minimize the inclination of firms to exercise their market power.

## 5.   THE IMPROVEMENT OF ECONOMIC INSTITUTIONS

The reshaping of economic and social institutions to lower uncertainty in private property rights, which as we have suggested has been a major cause of high transaction costs, is a very important prerequisite condition for the long-term survival of big businesses in Korea. Without this, large firms will not have the institutional basis needed to secure their highly competitive edge. New-institutional economics reveals the systematic relationship between transaction costs and economic behavior, which in the context of issues addressed in this book, has also been confirmed by empirical analyses in Chapter 5 and 6. Countries subject to high transaction costs have many small-scale closed-management firms, and large firms tend not to rid themselves of parochial management behavior. Some aspects of *chaebols'* business behavior, the source of many controversies in many respects, turn out to be attributable to incentive structures emerging from the lack of a secure private property rights system and the resulting high transaction costs.

As discussed in detail in Chapter 5, eliminating the institutional and cultural tendency to violate private property rights in the name of public interest is necessary in order to lower transaction costs in Korea. As such, the argument that Korea's economic reform should focus on removing economic uncertainty regarding private property rights becomes very persuasive. To overcome the long-standing tendency to disregard private property rights in Korean society, it is important to phase out as much as possible the various restrictions on individual economic activity and property rights in the process of setting and enforcing formal institutions such as laws and regulations. In this regard, effort not only to improve the content of formal institutions but also to strictly enforce them is equally important.

Our analysis of property rights systems in Chapter 5 highlights that the society's informal institutions, such as the way of thinking, customs and traditions, may be even more important in the formation of the nation's institutional characteristics than just formal institutions on their own. As far as formal institutions are concerned, established institutions can simply be imported from a developed country, if and when necessary. However, effective institutionalization may depend on two additional factors: how strongly and transparently the government enforces them, and, consequently, the degree to which economic agents accept the rules and restrictions set by the institutions. The property rights system in Korea may be comparable to that of advanced countries in its formal content. However, the government's enforcement of property rights is too lax and discretionary, and people's thoughts and attitude toward formal property rights institutions as a rule are still not mature enough.[23]

Once adopted, laws on property rights should be strictly enforced at all times and their contents should be properly adjusted when necessary in order to minimize violations of property rights and thus keep transaction costs as low as possible. Only if formal laws are transparently adopted and fairly enforced can one expect a gradual improvement in the long-standing informal practice of ignoring property rights. As for now, questions remain and continue to be a major source of anxiety about property rights protection in Korea.

However, the process of establishing proper economic institutions, including a secure property rights system, is an evolutionary process that usually takes a long time. Even if the government imports formal institutions, their acceptance by economic agents will only come gradually through trial and error. Moreover, institutions themselves can be regarded as endogenous and tend to become mature only after a long gestation period. This occurs as the process of decision-making by the government which is responsible for the content of formal institutions becomes endogenized due to the political-economic nature of institutional reform, such as interest group politics as suggested by the public choice school.[24] Nevertheless, the importance of the government's role in this evolutionary process cannot be over-emphasized. The government plays a pivotal role not only in determining the initial settings of formal institutions, but also in determining the characteristics of informal institutions, because it can have a significant impact on economic agents' perceptions and attitudes toward informal institutions through its efforts to enforce formal institutions.

The reform of economic institutions should eventually aim at lowering the transaction costs that arise from uncertainty in the property rights system. For this reason, at the least, institutional reforms that do not reduce uncertainty and transaction costs cannot be interpreted as constituting real reforms. In cases where new institutions are introduced or even where old ones are reformed, the government needs to be very careful about the possibility that these reforms themselves may cause additional uncertainties. If the government's institutional reform of the property rights system brings about additional uncertainty, then again this cannot be termed as reform in the true sense of the word.[25]

In line with this viewpoint, one should not ignore the possibility that new reform measures introduced to correct *chaebols'* unsound management behavior may have the effect of raising uncertainty in private property rights and thus, contrary to the original intention, may result in the aggravation of 'unsound' management behavior. For this reason, the government should pay close attention to securing private property rights when it attempts to make any changes in ownership and corporate governance structures. Uncertainty is likely to escalate even further if reform measures are arbitrarily and coercively implemented by the government without any regard for private property rights.

The introduction of advanced institutions is absolutely by no means the end of institutional reform, and continuous efforts to achieve a transparent and strict enforcement of the adopted institutions are no less important than their mere introduction. As the newly adopted institutions are made effective through strict and fair governmental enforcement, positive attitudes toward the institutions on the part of economic agents will emerge and an efficient economic system will gradually evolve. Even if the introduction of new and efficient institutions is important for the success of institutional reform, no less emphasis should be put on the strict operation and enforcement of these newly adopted institutions.


## 6.   CONCLUDING REMARKS

This chapter has provided a framework for the improvement of *chaebol* policy in Korea. Various policy measures directed at the *chaebol* are here based largely on the discussions in previous chapters, and in particular, on the theory of corporate governance in Chapter 7. Having identified the essence of Korea's economic development, we have argued that market-led discrimination is the preferred mechanism to help solve the problems of the first stage decision-making process, that is, the *chaebol* formation process, problems, such as the unfair privileges and economic concentration in selected industries, that resulted from the government-led discrimination strategy. Furthermore, from the viewpoint of new-institutional economics, and by applying the theory of corporate governance of Chapter 7, we specifically discuss the roles of the product market, the M&A market, the financial sector and the board of directors in disciplining corporate behavior. This demonstrates just how and why the external business environment, which acts as a most critical and fundamental constraint on business firms, should be improved so that the various markets may effectively discipline corporate behavior. Put differently, transforming the external economic environment such that it becomes more favorable to enhancing market discipline is necessary to solving problems that arise from the second stage decision-making process, that is, *chaebol* behavior.

As a summary, Figure 8.1, which is a reinterpretation of Figure 7.2 in terms of policy contents, succinctly distinguishes, in one diagram, between the major *chaebol* policies on the one hand and institutional factors within the external economic environment on the other. In line with our theory of corporate governance, we have thus distinguished between exogenous variables and endogenous variables that influence corporate behavior.

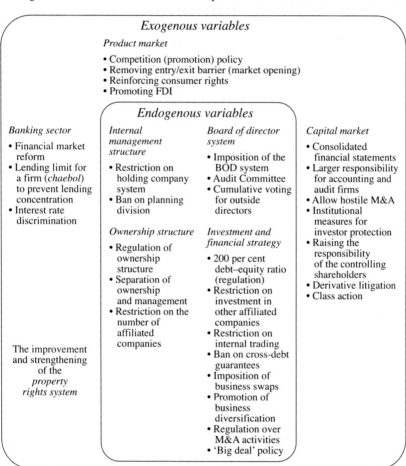

*Figure 8.1   Corporate policy map*

With reference to the corporate policy map above, it is easy to see that *chaebol* policy has often intervened in the endogenous decision variables of firms. For example, the government has tried to restrict the holding company system and has banned the planning division. Related to the above, the government has often tried to determine the ownership structure, and has encouraged the separation of ownership and management. Restrictions have been placed on the number of affiliate firms allowable, as well as on cross-investment and internal trading among affiliated firms. The government has also tried to direct business specialization as well as determine business swaps. Furthermore, we have also argued that the uniform application of a 200 per cent debt–equity ratio, the imposition of a uniform structure of a board of directors, the ban on cross-debt guarantees and restrictions on business diversification are problematic. But why did the government set up policies to control directly firms' endogenous management-decision variables? Recall that, in Chapter 7, government-led discrimination was identified as the fundamental mechanism behind Korea's past development strategy. A corollary to this fact is that this necessitates that the government intervenes directly in the management decisions of firms that it has selected in an attempt to vindicate its own policy choices by steering these firms to meet policy objectives. This is the reason why, under the government-led development strategy, with the government-led discrimination mechanism firmly in place, many endogenous decision variables have become contaminated, and often result in inefficient outcomes.

It is of fundamental importance that the roles of the government and private corporations be clearly defined. As has already been emphasized (also refer again to Figure 8.1), we suggest that the firm's management should be free from unnecessary direct intervention when deciding upon those variables endogenous to corporations, while the government should direct policy to improve the external economic environment by strengthening institutions favorable to the development of markets, by reforming competition policy, and by strengthening property rights protection. That is, first, market disciplinary systems to check corporate behavior should be strengthened. To us, this entails breaking away from the direct government intervention of the past development paradigm toward a new strategy that introduces and strengthens markets in all sectors of the economy, such as those discussed above, for example, the product market, M&A market, financial market and so on. Second, a competition promotion policy that in particular aims at relaxing all unnecessary barriers of economic activity and thereby contributes to increased competitiveness and economic efficiency should be vigorously pursued. After all, competition can be expected to drive away inefficient firms decisively, while making existing firms leaner and more efficiency-oriented, and should also stimulate the emergence of new business opportunities. Third, overall institutional improvement should be pursued, particularly as regards the protection of private property rights. Although formal institutions are becoming increasingly important, informal institutions should not be ignored either.

We should constantly bear in mind that the evolution of a country's institutions usually takes a long time and the utmost care should be observed at all times when introducing any new institutional changes. In sum, not least due to the rapid pace of globalization, or the need to adopt global standards, we have seen that as the economy advances, the government's ability to intervene effectively and directly steer its development path rapidly declines. Hence it is especially difficult, and inappropriate, for a government to design a particular industrial structure *a priori* that is supposed to be optimal for the economy. Even worse, continued government intervention in a decision-making process which is best left to be endogenously determined by the firm is a recipe for a troubled economy. Put differently, in the context of Korea's economic development, the natural evolution of her economy, including not only corporations, but also institutions – both formal and informal – should be freely encouraged. Underlying this evolutionary process, the market-led discrimination mechanism should replace the now dysfunctional government-led discrimination mechanism as the main engine that distinguishes between viable and non-viable economic agents. This is the only guarantee toward Korea's continued economic growth and prosperity.

## NOTES

1.  Here, the term '*chaebol* divestiture' has no legal meaning. The *chaebol* are not legal entities because the law officially prohibited holding companies until very recently. Therefore the term '*chaebol* divestiture' is not meaningful in legal terms. As such, this book regards the issue of *chaebol* divestiture as an issue of disaggregating a collective economic body of big businesses based on a relationship of mutual ownership.
2.  'A definite classification of costs is useful for certain purposes. It is meaningful to recognize sunk costs in cases where production planning is forgone at some point after starting production. For example, let's suppose that someone can purchase a new car for $3,000 and resale the little used car for $2,500 at most after a short period of time. Then, $500 is a loss of resale value. This amount of money is just sunk and historical. If that person buys a new car, this cost is inescapable. Even if it can be useful in estimating a cost occurred in similar cases, it can not play any role in future decision making. Because the cost is sunk, whatever choice we make in the next stage, it is already borne, unavoidable, and non-excludable. Only "escapable" or "variable" costs matter in successful decision making.' See Alchian (1977, pp. 316–17) for detailed contents.
3.  It is expected that the political solution to unfair resource concentration in the process of *chaebol* formation may take the following form. First, a national consensus on 'unfairness' must be reached, and next the national assembly must design an ad hoc law in relation to the retrieval of accumulated property and usage of the collected property. Readers following the logic of this book can easily perceive that another political problem will be brought about through this process. How much wealth is to be retrieved from which *chaebol*? How should the collected wealth be distributed and in which form and to whom? These questions cannot be objectively answered and so eventually become a problem of political value judgment. In my opinion, there is no perfect solution to the problem of the unfair formation of the *chaebol*. Nevertheless, if the government tries to divest the *chaebol* by force, the uncertainty of private property rights protection contributing to the present *chaebol* behavior will be further increased and the Korean economy will have to bear even higher transaction costs.
4.  See Table A4.1 in the Appendix to Chapter 4 for details.
5.  Also see the Appendix to Chapter 4, where we take a brief look at two aspects of corporate reforms, which have been very much reminiscent of past industrial policies, namely, the 'big

deals' that aims at improving business competitiveness by streamlining business activity, and the 'workout program' that aims at restructuring debtor firms before they become insolvent.

6. We have already seen in Chapter 7 the hybrid nature of the board of directors system, in that they are essential parts of both the internal disciplinary mechanism as well as the external disciplinary system. Also see later in this chapter for further discussions on the board of directors.

7. See Figure 7.1.

8. Research on issues of corporate governance by the international academic society has increased drastically. This tendency seems to be a result of the actual need for an efficient governance structure in the global competition era. But a matter of concern is that these studies tend to neglect the endogenous nature of corporate governance structures, which are generated and evolve differently depending on differences in the economic environments of and transaction costs incurred by each economy. Furthermore, the discussion on corporate governance structures has developed to the extent that international treaties and/or government policy force firms to adopt specific governance structures. Recently, the OECD released details about the international standard of corporate governance recommended for member countries. These may be interpreted as direct regulations on corporate behavior if the firms are forced to adopt them. The Korean government and academics' attitude favoring direct regulations on the corporate ownership/governance structure of the country reflects distrust in the *chaebols'* self-corrective behavior as well as the above-mentioned international trend. In any case, it should be kept in mind that we can hardly expect economists, management scientists and government policy-makers to be more knowledge-able than business managers as far as selecting which corporate governance structure will be beneficial to corporations.

9. For further details see the next section where we discuss in detail the direction of Korea's competition policy.

10. See the Appendix to Chapter 4 for detailed information on the workout program.

11. The laws that had obstructed the smooth working of the M&A market are as follows: Clause 10 of the Antitrust Law, prohibiting firms of the 30 largest *chaebols* from buying affiliated firms' stock beyond 25 per cent of each buying affiliated firm's pure assets; and Clause 21 of the Securities Trading Act, obliging a firm to purchase 50 per cent plus one stock of another firm if the buying firm tries to purchase more than 25 per cent of the target firm's stock. Also, even though Clause 31 of the Labor Standard Law stipulates that a firm may lay off workers in case of an emergency situation, additional Clause 1 of the same law specifying that the application of Clause 31 is postponed until March 1999 has actually limited the activation of the M&A market. But, according to the IMF agreement, the laws related to firm restructuring were recently amended to facilitate structural reforms. The obligatory stock purchasing system (Clause 21 of the Securities Trading Act) and the cross-ownership restriction system (Clause 10 of the Antitrust Law) were totally abolished. Moreover, additional Clause 1 of the Labor Standard Law was eliminated and firms can now fire employees even in cases of M&As and transfers of businesses to avoid management crises. Even though these measures are expected to promote M&As, the strict regulation of mergers on the basis of market share stipulated in the Antitrust Law is still blocking their activation. So it is deemed that merger evaluation criteria should be adjusted to revitalize M&As even between big businesses, considering the degree of potential and effective competition in addition to market share. If the opening of the product market, lifting of entry regulations and increase in foreign direct investment raise domestic competition pressure, the *chaebols* will no longer be able to enjoy monopoly rent. If so, the government need not restrain the *chaebols'* diversification behavior through direct entry regulations.

12. See Table A4.2 in the Appendix to Chapter 4.

13. Following the recommendation in the IMF agreement, the government amended the Securities Trading Act to raise corporate management efficiency and transparency on 2 February 1999 by increasing minority shareholders' rights. The required percentage of stock ownership needed for the right to file a suit against executive directors, for the right to dismiss directors and auditors, and for the right to inspect account books has decreased from

more than 3 per cent to more than 0.05 per cent, from more than 1 per cent to more than 0.5 per cent, and from more than 3 per cent to more than 1 per cent respectively.

14.  See, for example, the discussions on the universal banking system and, in particular, the roles of investment and commercial banks (the Brisbane paper on Korea's strategy for financial reform).

15.  Recall the nature and evolution of corporate behavior and its relationship to the society's culture, level of economic development, legal system, financial system and other institutional factors extensively discussed in Chapter 7. We have also explained the reason for differences between corporate governance systems in advanced capitalist countries and other 'catch-up' economies such as Korea.

16.  See, for example, the Appendix to Chapter 4, in particular Table A4.1 and the 'big deals'.

17.  See Chapter 4.

18.  See Singleton (1997) for general information and recent trends in competition policy and desirable application and direction of competition policy in the globalized world.

19.  See Singleton (1997) for a detailed discussion on a variety of problems in policy application and conceptual issues with respect to the abolition of entry barriers strategically set up by monopolistic or oligopolistic firms.

20.  The following discussion draws on Chapters 13 and 14 of Alchian and Allen (1977), as well as Demsetz (1974).

21.  Alchian and Allen (1977) call the former monopolistic firms 'market power price-searchers' and the latter 'monopoly power in restricted markets'.

22.  Alchian and Allen (1977, p. 306).

23.  The Korean Constitution states that private property rights should be exercised not to interfere with the public interest (Constitution of the Republic of Korea, Article 2 Section 23). This widely opens the possibility for private property rights to be infringed upon by public authorities. Therefore it can be said that the problem with the Korean property right system is more pronounced in the relationship between public authorities and private citizens than in relationships among private citizens.

24.  For example, Rapaczynski (1996) explains as an evolutionary process the adoption of private property rights systems in the course of introducing a market economy system in Eastern Europe after the collapse of communism.

25.  The financial real name system, which obliges people to use their real name in all financial transactions, belongs to this category. This system generates the undesirable outcome of raising uncertainty in financial property rights by failing to protect depositors' secrecy because the system is used as a general method to uncover illegal activities not only in the financial but also in the political fields. The system has even been criticized as a means of victimizing political opponents. It also infringes the property rights of the existing pseudonym depositors for the sake of implementing the financial real name system as early as possible through the imposition of extra fines on pseudonymous financial transactions. Consequently, this new system causes sharp increases in transaction costs in the financial industry and, in the end, brings about unnecessary burdens on the Korean economy.

# 9. Overview and conclusion

It has been consistently argued throughout this book that the *chaebol* is an evolutionary outgrowth of the Korea-specific economic environment that includes her unique institutional setting. In Korea, economic institutions have been critical in shaping the formation and growth of the *chaebol*. The survival of a firm, or any other economic organization for that matter, is dependent upon the decisions that it makes upon considering a set of choices subject to certain constraints. That is, a firm will survive only if its choices turn out to be in a winning set given the constraints it faces. These constraints, broadly speaking, include market variables determined by relative prices as well as policy variables as depicted in neoclassical economic theory. More importantly, they involve the institutional factors such as government policy, laws and regulations, customs, tradition and even culture. Such an institutional environment not only affects the types or sets of choices available to the firm but also determines the outcome of the firm's ultimate choices. In this sense, the genesis and evolution of Korea's economic organizations are a product of the Korea-specific economic and institutional environment, and for that matter, the *chaebol* is not an exception.

The book begins with an introductory chapter that briefly describes both the evolutionary and new-institutional economics perspectives adopted in this book. Chapter 1 also defines the *chaebol* as multi-product firms composed of smaller subsidiaries with the purpose of maximizing group benefits, and introduces what is known as the *chaebol* problem. The *chaebol* problem further evaluated in Chapter 3 is briefly introduced as consisting of aggregate concentration, market monopolization and various 'unsound' management behavior. We also mention here the policy dilemma between microeconomic and macroeconomic policies that stems from the *chaebol* problem.

In Chapter 2, we provide an overview of Korea's past government-led economic development strategy and its consequences for the formation and growth of the *chaebol*. From the early stages of Korea's industrialization, the government not only determined the market entry and exit of industries that it selected as economically and strategically important, but also actively set up policies that steered financial resources and tax support to the selected industries. Certain firms that were able to benefit from such an environment eventually grew into *chaebols* and became important players in Korea's modernization. Nevertheless, this development strategy has not been free from problems. The English proverb 'every rose has a thorn' neatly describes the growth of the *chaebol* during the past 40 years. On the one hand, the *chaebols*, nurtured by the government, were very important to Korea's rapid economic prosperity, but on the other hand, their eventual dominance in the economy became perceived as problematic both by the government and the general public.[1]

The *chaebol* has been a major subject of controversy not only domestically but also internationally, not least because of the recent financial crisis. As such, there is much confusion as to what exactly are the problems and issues concerning the *chaebol*. We critically review the traditional perception of the *chaebol* problem in Chapter 3, where we find that most of the animosity seems to spring from the fact that the *chaebol* have flourished in a privileged environment where the government allocated economic power to the *chaebol* through non-market means. Current regulation policy identifies aggregate economic concentration of the *chaebol* as their major problem, while our analysis suggests that the problem has been somewhat exaggerated and often misunderstood, thus causing government policy to become misdirected. That is, the antagonism toward the *chaebol* has not been based on solid logic. Nevertheless, it has had surprising influence on the direction of public policy. It is our contention that the real economic problems tend to derive from the monopolistic market power of the *chaebol* rather than aggregate economic concentration. In this sense, it makes better sense to shift the policy paradigm away from the existing focus on aggregate economic concentration to an emphasis on the market monopolization problem. Further problems identified in Chapter 3 relate to some aspects of *chaebol* behavior that include excessive diversification, concentration of ownership and management in the hands of a few shareholders through cross-shareholding among affiliated firms, and the practice of cross-debt guarantees.

The two stage decision-making model is a simple analytical framework that is used to reinterpret the formation and behavior of the *chaebol*. Chapter 4 identifies the first stage decision-making process as that process of *chaebol* formation in government favor during the early stages of Korea's economic development. The second stage decision-making process refers to the process by which the *chaebol* have utilized resources allocated to them during the first stage decision-making process. The latter stage is comprised of those aspects of the *chaebol* problem that can be addressed through economic analysis and these are the central issues discussed throughout the book, while the former stage tends to fall within the political decision-making process.[2] We go on to classify and evaluate past and recent *chaebol* policy within the framework presented and developed above.

In essence, the problems associated with economic concentration in the hands of a few originate mostly from the first stage decision-making process,

which is essentially of a political nature, particularly in relation to the process
through which the government promoted the growth of selected industries
through special loans and protection measures. We find that such government
decisions in the first stage can often be characterized as limiting or transferring
property rights through non-market means. The most important *chaebol* policy
that attempted to address issues related to the first stage decision-making
process was the 'Loan-Limit Management System' which basically tried to
tackle problems of lending concentration and the practice of cross-debt
guarantees. Although initially directed at a single firm, this system eventually
attempted to regulate bank loans to the *chaebol* as a group. The policy failed
to restrict loan concentration effectively as banks found it hard to distinguish
between *chaebol* affiliates, but more importantly, because the bank's capacity
to monitor loans had been eroded by the legacy of government intervention, or
the so-called *kwanchi kumyung*.

On the other hand, monopolistic *chaebol* behavior associated with market
power in their respective markets, as well as other peculiarities of their
management behavior, are seen to be the result of entrepreneurial decision-
making in the second stage. That is, it can be argued that the *chaebols*
maximize their survival probabilities through a process of monopolization and
various management strategies by taking advantage of special favors and
industry protection granted by the government. The case is made that
*chaebols*' behavior, such as their diversification into various business lines
and the practice of cross-shareholding and cross debt guarantee and so on, are
all outcomes of their survival strategy, given the Korea-specific economic as
well as institutional background. Our discussions helps delineate *chaebol*
problems into economic problems subject to positive economic analysis, that
is, the endogenous evolution of monopolistic market behavior as well as
management practices, differentiating these from political decision problems
that shift economic power to the *chaebol* through non-market means.

Regarding the *chaebol* policy that had been set up to address problems
related to the second stage decision-making process, we observe that most
of the pre-crisis and some post-crisis *chaebol* policies have been largely
'symptom-regulating' rather than addressing fundamental causes. Examples
of this tendency in the post-crisis period, for example, include amongst others,
the uniform application of the 200 per cent debt–equity ratio and the outright
ban on cross-debt guarantees. These measures are reminiscent of the 'old-
style' symptom regulation policies. The news is not entirely disappointing, as
there has been some policy improvement in the right direction. The more
recent post-crisis reform efforts, particularly those involving corporate
governance issues which tend to address institutional causes affecting *chaebol*
behavior, are an example. Nevertheless, despite such recent improvements in
the approach to policy formulation, the old habits of directly trying to

influence endogenous management decisions die hard, and so a conscious effort must be made to avoid such practices.

Having identified and clarified the misconception regarding the *chaebol* problem, in Chapter 5 we look in detail at the theory and empirical evidence of the effects of institutional factors on the evolution of the *chaebol*. Specifically, we present important evidence from the Chosun dynasty to recent times of the events that have led to the weakened protection of property rights in Korea. We apply the analytical methods of the new-institutional economics to better our understanding of the evolution of Korea's institutional environment. A simple empirical test using data from 13 countries reveals a positive relationship between transaction costs arising from insecure property rights systems and the smallness of firms in the economy. North, for example, argued that organizations tend to grow where property rights are well protected and, as such, any large investment becomes less risky as market contracts are more likely to be honored and observed. So what explains the formation of large *chaebols* in Korea despite the high transaction costs resulting from past insecure property rights systems? The answer, precisely, is the government's protection as opposed to institutional protection by the rule of law. We argue that, despite weaknesses in the prevailing property rights system and the accompanying high transaction costs, the *chaebol* have evolved under government discretionary protection and their behavior has thus far been prompted and maintained, to a large extent, by institutional factors and government intervention. Furthermore, the government is perceived as playing a dual role: the major initiator and the principal constraint on much of the *chaebol*'s economic behavior. This is what we have described as 'government-led discrimination' in Chapter 7.

In Chapter 6 we narrow our focus to business diversification of the firms. Empirical tests were carried out using a multivariate regression model containing institutional and market factors of over 25 countries to investigate the factors affecting the business diversification behavior of firms. In doing so, we confirm the positive relationship of property rights systems and product diversification, and hence, the size of the firm. The *chaebols*, it turns out, have adopted a different strategy of business diversification, through the establishment and control of affiliate companies, as opposed to the strategy of in-house diversification that focuses on product line diversification. We have termed the *chaebol*'s unique brand of diversification as 'managerial diversification behavior'. A major motivation for this behavior seems to lie in the practice of cross-debt guarantees among affiliate firms, which the *chaebols* have utilized as a means to receive finance from the banks. More specifically, this type of diversification has been encouraged by government negligence in enforcing the prudential banking regulations of lending limits on a single borrower. Banks have tolerated cross-debt guarantees among *chaebol* affiliates, which even though they are all legally independent entities, essentially belong to a single economic identity, that is, the *chaebol*. In this way, the *chaebols* succeeded in increasing their relative size *vis-à-vis* the banks and quickly took advantage of the 'too-big-to-fail' business strategy. Hence we have argued that diversification and growth of the *chaebol* are the results of Korea-specific institutional factors, of which government protection has been a prominent feature. It remains of interest to see how the *chaebol's* diversification behavior as well as the shape of its business organization will evolve in the future given the recently imposed ban on the practice of cross-debt guarantees.

In the latter part of Chapter 6, we established the importance of institutional factors such as the property rights system, the origin of the legal system and the degree of shareholder rights, as well as economic environment factors such as the level of financial development, market size and degree of competitive pressure, to a country's economic performance. In fact, we find empirical evidence to support our view that not only various institutional factors but also competitive market pressure are important factors that encourage economic growth. This is supportive of the framework of *chaebol* policy developed in the latter part of the book, where we champion competition promotion and institutional reform as important ingredients of *chaebol* policy.

Chapter 7, in a sense, contains the main methodological contribution of this book to the already extensive literature on economic development and to the theory of corporate governance. We study the impact of Korea's past industrialization policy on productivity and ask how Korea's 'miraculous' growth can be explained despite the lackluster impact of industrial policy on productivity. To make things more concrete, we look at the case of the Samsung Motor Company, which serves as a nice example showing how the government intervened, and continues to intervene, in the decision making process of private corporations. History reveals that Korea lacked the appropriate institutions necessary for the development of a market economy, and, in fact, the government played the leading role in the country's modernization. It is essential to note that it was the discrimination function, on this occasion taken up by the government, which was somewhat successful in selecting viable from non-viable entities, thereby contributing to Korea's rapid economic growth. This we have called 'government-led' discrimination. Closer inspection of the issues and problems has led us to suggest, however, that in the era of rapid globalization, the past strategy of 'government-led discrimination' will be neither an effective nor a desirable strategy for sustained growth in the future. Rather, 'market-led discrimination' – the introduction of market competition as a discovery procedure – is the more viable development strategy in the modern era.

We have also reviewed some of the recent literature on the roles of government and the private sector in economic development. In our attempt to go further to develop a general approach to *chaebol* policy, we suggest that a careful distinction between factors endogenous and exogenous to corporate behavior is an important step toward constructing effective public policy. We argue that the government can no longer play the role of an omnipotent determinant of the *chaebol's* future in the era of fierce global competition. Accordingly, we suggest that the government's role should focus on shaping exogenous economic factors to promote competition. Private corporations, on the other hand, should be allowed to decide freely upon their endogenous management-decision variables without outside interference. In fact, under this new framework, only business organizations, the *chaebol* included, that become efficient will survive and, in turn, serve the country's economic prosperity.

A new corporate governance theory is developed that helps not only to solve an apparent contradiciton between Coase and North as relates to the size of the firm, but also, puts corporate governance as an important issue in the context of economic development. Our model neatly shows how the external economic environment influences the evolution of corporate behavior. Furthermore, we show how the product market is more effective than the factor market as part of the market disciplinary system affecting corporate behavior. The external environment includes the country's institutions such as the type of financial system in place, the type of government policies and the legal setting, as well as the broader and more informal institutions such as culture, customs and traditions.

We demonstrate the high applicability of the corporate governance model developed here more specifically by showing how it can be used to explain the difference between corporate governance systems across different countries. Corporate governance behavior can be explained by the differences in the type of financial system in place – whether it is dominated by equity markets or by bank lending markets – which is in turn influenced by the country's cultural, legal and policy traditions. By doing so, we have incorporated the study of corporate governance, which hitherto has been confined to management science, into mainstream economics. We have also hinted that our approach and understanding of the firm may, hopefully, lead us to better understand why different countries have had different development experiences.

In Chapter 8, we suggest more concretely what *chaebol* policy in the future should look like. Following our analysis in Chapter 7, we suggest that in order to guide *chaebol* behavior effectively, corporate policy should be rid of the 'old-style' government intervention by placing market competition, backed by appropriate institutions, at the heart of all reform efforts. In other words, the Korean government should first focus on institutional reform and critically review policies under which the *chaebol* have secured an unfair competitive edge in their formation process. Next, it should strive to increase competition among the *chaebols* by dissolving those economic constraints and protection at home and abroad that have encouraged any of the *chaebols*' non-competitive and inefficient behavior. It should also move decisively to remove all existing direct regulations on business operations. In the same vein, we further emphasize the importance of the external disciplinary mechanisms in shaping corporate governance systems in that this affects the managerial efficiency of corporations. That is, we argue for institutional reforms needed to strengthen the corporate monitoring role of the product market, the financial as well as the M&A markets. We have also discussed the role of the board of directors in a corporation and shown how care must be observed when approaching this issue in general. Furthermore, the role of competition policy should be increased so as to protect the competitive order, thus ensuring fair competition and the establishment of market-led discrimination mechanisms to allow for the optimal allocation and utilization of economic resources. Last, but not least, the government should establish a well-defined property rights system at both the formal and informal levels, through reforming and enforcing the private property rights system. In the end, it cannot be over-emphasized that policies to promote competition as well as to strengthen institutions across all sectors of the economy are indispensable if Korea is to continue its path to being an advanced country in the twenty-first century.

From our discussions in identifying *chaebol* problems in Chapters 3 and 4, we highlighted the various criticisms of the legitimacy of the existence and growth of the *chaebol*, which may in fact be unwarranted from the point of view of positive economics, unwarranted because the *chaebol*, as a rational economic agent, makes decisions that it believes will prolong its survival and existence. It can only make decisions from a set of feasible choices, which are conditioned by the external economic and institutional environment. We have argued that 'government-led discrimination', through direct intervention and regulation, has determined the type of industrial organization in Korea, and is partly responsible for the *chaebol* problem. The purpose of this book, however, is not to criticize what the government has done, but rather to gather insights and learn in advance what is important if Korea is to achieve continued sustainable development in the modern era. We claim that criticisms of past government policy and *chaebol* behavior by hanging on to the past are unnecessary, in the sense that the future of the *chaebol* cannot be determined by looking at what has happened in the past alone. Despite the fact that there may be lessons to learn from past mistakes and successes, to borrow another English phrase, we prefer to 'let bygones be bygones' as we take the bold step of looking into the future. The analytic framework of the two stage decision-making model distinguishes between the problems with *chaebol* formation and those of *chaebol* behavior. From our discussions and analysis we find that the divestiture of the *chaebol* may not be a prudent choice even if its legitimacy has been questioned, but rather it is more important to induce the *chaebol* to behave in a competitive manner.

The main message of the book as relates to the direction of future reform is that control of the external economic environment such as its laws and regulations, its financial system, government policy, customs and tradition and so on, is the key toward influencing the future decisions and behavior of the *chaebol*. However, competition left on its own is ambiguous, and perhaps even anarchic. Institutions that support fair and free competition are necessary for its proper and efficient functioning. There is therefore an essential role and responsibility for government to ensure that the proper institutions are created and allowed to mature. In this sense, the rule of law is critical not only for the proper formation of institutional factors such as the property rights system, corporate governance and commercial law, but also for the smooth evolution of organizations themselves. Nothing remains the same and surely the *chaebol* will evolve out of the current form into a new organization within the already changing business environment, and if they continue to survive and perform well, the *chaebol* should be vindicated. That is, with the proper institutional setting firmly in place, if the *chaebol* proves to be a winner in the competition process, then we would expect that there should be no reason to question its existence and economic behavior. Otherwise, of course, the *chaebol* will either cease to exist or will take on an entirely different form.

## NOTES

1. In response, the government set up the Regulation on Monopoly and Fair Trade Act in the 1980s to specifically address *chaebol* issues that were thought to be problematic such as economic concentration and business diversification.
2. As elaborated in Chapter 4, the 'political decision-making' denotes an action that influences the distribution of income by transferring property rights from one group (of any number of individuals) to another through non-market processes.

# References

Alchian, Armen A. and Harold Demsetz (1972), 'Production, Information Costs and Economic Organization', *American Economic Review*, **62**(5), 777–95.

Alchian, Armen A. (1950), 'Uncertainty, Evolution and Economic Theory', *Journal of Political Economy*, **58**(3), 211–21.

Alchian, Armen A. (1977), 'Cost', in Armen A. Alchian (ed.), *Economic Forces at Work*, Indianapolis: Liberty Press, pp. 301–33.

Alchian, Armen A. and William R. Allen (1977), *Exchange and Production: Competition Coordination, and Control*, 2nd edn, Belmont, CA: Wadsworth Publishing Company, Inc.

Amsden, Alice H. (1989), *Asia's Next Giant*, Oxford: Oxford University Press.

Aron, Janine (2000), 'Growth and Institutions: A Review of the Evidence', *The World Bank Research Observer*, **15**(1), 99–135.

Arrow, Kenneth J. (1963), 'Uncertainty and the Welfare of Economics of Medical Care', *American Economic Review*, **53**, 941–73.

Bain, Joe S. (1959), *Pricing, Distribution and Employment: Economics of an Enterprise System*, New York: Henry Holt.

Bain, Joe S. and D.P. Qualls (1987), *Industrial Organization: A Treatise*, Greenwich, Conn.: JAI Press.

Barro, Robert J. and Xavier Sala-I-Martin (1995), *Economic Growth*, Boston, MA: McGraw-Hill International Editions.

Baumol, William J., John C. Panzar and Robert D. Willig (1982), *Contestable Markets and The Theory of Industry Structure*, New York: Harcourt Brace Jovanovich, Inc.

Berle, Adolph A. and Gardiner C. Means (1932), *The Modern Corporation and Private Property*, New York: Macmillan.

Bishop, Isabella Bird (1970[1898]), *Korea and Her Neighbors*, Seoul: Yonsei University Press.

Cho, Dong Sung (1991), 'A Study on Korean *Chaebol*', *Maeil Economic Daily* (in Korean).

Chung, Byong Hyou and Young Shik Yang (1993), *An Economic Analysis of Korean Chaebol*, Seoul: Korea Development Institute (in Korean).

Clague, Christopher, Philip Keefer, Stephen Knack and Mancur Olson (1996), 'Property and Contract Rights in Autocracies and Democracies', *Journal of Economic Growth*, **1**(1), 243–76.

Coase, Ronald H. (1992), 'The Institutional Structure of Production', *American Economic Review*, 713–19.

Coase, Ronald H. (1984), 'The New Institutional Economics', *Journal of Institutional and Theoretical Economics*, **140**, 229–32.

Coase, Ronald H. (1960), 'The Problem of Social Cost', *Journal of Law and Economics*, **3**, 1–44.

Coase, Ronald H. (1937), 'The Nature of the Firm', *Economica*, **4**, 386–405.

Commons, John R. (1931), 'Institutional Economics', *American Economic Journal*, **21**, 648-57.

Cyert, Richard and James March (1963), *A Behavioral Theory of the Firm*, Englewood Cliffs, NJ: Prentice-Hall.

Davis, Lance E. and Douglass C. North (1971), *Institutional Change and American Economic Growth*, Cambridge: Cambridge University Press.

Dawkins, Richard (1976), *The Selfish Gene*, Oxford: Oxford University Press.

Deaton, Angus and John Muellbauer (1980), *Economics and Consumer Behaviour*, Cambridge: Cambridge University Press.

Demsetz, Harold (1983), 'The Structure of Ownership and the Theory of the Firm', *The Journal of Law and Economics*, **26**(2), 375-93.

Demsetz, Harold (1974), 'Two Systems of Belief about Monopoly', in Harvey J. Goldschmidt, H. Micheal Mann and J. Fred Weston (eds), *Industrial Concentration: The New Learning*, Boston, Columbia University Center for Economics Studies: Little Brown and Company, pp. 164-83.

Drobak, John N. and John V.C. Nye (1997), *The Frontiers of the New Institutional Economics*, San Diego: Harcourt Brace Jovanovich.

Drucker, Peter (1999), *Management Challenges for the 21st Century*, New York: HarperCollins Publishers, Inc.

Easterly, William and Ross Levine (1997), 'Africa's Growth Tragedy: Policies and Ethnic Divisions', *Quarterly Journal of Economics*, **112**(4), 1203-50.

Eggertsson, Thráinn (1990), *Economic Behavior and Institutions*, Cambridge: Cambridge University Press.

Friedman, Milton (1953), 'The Methodology of Positive Economics', in Milton Friedman (ed.), *Essays in Positive Economics*, Chicago, Ill.: University of Chicago Press, pp. 3-43.

Fukuyama, Francis (1996), *Social Capital and Future of Asia*, Seoul: Samsung Economic Research Institution Seminar Paper.

Fukuyama, Francis (1995), 'Social Capital and the Global Economy', *Foreign Affairs*, **74**(5), 89-103.

Furubotn, Eirik and Rudolf Richter (1997), *Institutions and Economic Theory: The Contribution of the New Institutional Economics*, Ann Arbor: University of Michigan Press.

Gallop, Frank (1985), 'Analysis of Productivity Slowdown: Evidence for a Sector-Biased and Sector-Neutral Industrial Strategy', in W. Baumol and K. McLennan (eds), *Productivity Growth and US Competitiveness*, New York: Oxford University Press.

Gordon, Lilli and John Pound (1991), 'Governance Matters: An Empirical Study of the Relationship between Corporate Governance and Corporate Performance', John F. Kennedy School of Government, June, mimeograph.

Gort, Michael (1962), *Diversification and Integration in American Industry*, US National Bureau of Economic Research, General Series no. 77, Princeton NJ: Princeton University Press.

Grossman, Sanford and Oliver Hart (1986), 'The Costs and Benefits of Ownership: A Theory of Vertical and Lateral Integration', *Journal of Political Economy*, **94**, 671-719.

Hart, Oliver D. and John Moore (1990), 'Property Rights and the Nature of the Firm', *Journal of Political Economy*, **98**, 1119-58.

Hayek, Friedrich von (1988), *The Fatal Conceit: The Errors of Socialism*, London: Routledge.

Hayek, Friedrich von (1968), 'Competition as a Discovery Procedure', in Nishiyama Chiaki and Kurt R. Leube (eds) (1984), *The Essence of Hayek*, Stanford, CA: Hoover Institution Press, pp. 254–65.

Hayek, Friedrich von (1945), 'The Use of Knowledge', *American Economic Review*, **35**(4), 519–30.

Hayek, Friedrich von (1937), 'Economics and Knowledge', in idem (1948), *Individualism and Economic Order*, London: Routledge and Kegan Paul, pp. 33–56.

Hill, Christopher (1955), *The English Revolution 1640: An Essay*, London: Lawrence & Wishart Ltd.

Hill, C.W.L and O.E Hoskisson (1987), 'Strategy and Structure in the Multiproduct Firm', *Academy of Management Review*, **12**(2), 331–41.

Hirshleifer, Jack (1977), 'Economics from a Biological Viewpoint', *Journal of Law and Economics*, **20**(1), 1–52.

Hodgson, Geoffrey M. (1993), *Economics and Evolution: Bringing Life Back into Economics*, Cambridge: Polity Press.

Holmstrom, Bengt (1979), 'Moral Hazard and Observability', *Bell Journal of Economics*, **10**, 74–91.

Huang, Inhak and Jung-Hwan Seo (2000), 'Corporate Governance and Chaebol Reform in Korea', *Seoul Journal of Economics*, **13**(3), 361–89.

Hwang, Inhak (2000), 'Aggregate Concentration, Market Concentration and Diversification: The Korean Case', *Korean Journal of Industrial Organization*, **8**(1), 49–74 (in Korean).

Hwang, Inhak (1999), 'The Ownership and Control of Chaebols', in S. Lee, S.H. Jwa, K.S. Jung and K.T. Kim (eds), *Present and Future of Corporate Governance Structure in Korea*, Seoul: Korea Institute for Management Development, pp. 459–500.

Hwang, Inhak (1998), *Market Structure and Economic Efficiency*, Seoul: Korea Economic Research Institute (in Korean).

Jacquemin, A. and C.H. Berry (1979), 'Entropy Measure of Diversification and Corporate Growth', *Journal of Industrial Organization*, **137**(4), 359–69.

Jensen, Michael C. and William H. Meckling (1976), 'Theory of the Firm: Managerial Behavior, Agency Costs and Ownership Structure', *Journal of Financial Economics*, **3**(4), 305–60.

Jones, Leroy, P. and Sekong Il (1980, *Government, Business and Enterpreneurship in Economic Development: The Korean Case*, Cambridge, MA: Harvard University Press.

Jwa, Sung-Hee (2001), *A New Paradigm for Korea's Economic Development: From Government Control to Market Economy*, London: Palgrave.

Jwa (2000), 'A New Institutional Economics Perspective of Corporate Governance Reform in East Asia', *Seoul Journal of Economics*, **13**(3), 215–23.

Jwa, Sung-Hee (1997), 'Globalization and Industrial Organization: Implications for Structural Adjustment Policies', in Takatoshi Ito and Anne O. Krueger (eds), *Regionalism vs. Multilateral Trade Arrangement*, NBER-East Asia Seminar on Economics, vol. 6. Chicago: University of Chicago Press, pp. 313–43.

Jung, Yak-Yong (1818), *A Guide to Shepherding People*, trans. Taejun Noh (1982), Seoul: Hong Shin Publishing Company (in Korean).

Klein, Benjamin, Robert G. Crawford and Armen A. Alchian (1978), 'Vertical Integration, Appropriable Rents, and the Competitive Contracting Process', *Journal of Law and Economics*, **21**, 297–326.

Knack, S. and P. Keefer (1995), 'Institutions and Economic Performance: Cross-

Country Tests Using Alternative Institutional Measures', *Economics and Politics*, **7**(3), 207–27.

Ko, Dong Whan (1991), 'The Change and Nature of 19th Century Tax Administration', in *1984 Agrarian Policy Research*, Seoul: Historical Criticism Publishing

Korea Fair Trade Committee (1996), *Fair Trade Annual Report*, Seoul: Korea Fair Trade Commission (in Korean).

Krugman, Paul (1994), 'The Myth of Asia's Miracle', *Foreign Affairs*, **73**(6), 64–78.

Kwack, Tae Won (1984), *Industrial Restructuring Experience Policies in the 1970s*, presented at the workshop on Industrial Restructuring Experience and Policies in the Asian NICs, Honolulu: East-West Center.

Kwon, Byung-Tak (1984), 'The Process of Economic Contribution of Farmland Contract', *Agricultural Policy Research*, **11**(1), 191–207.

Lee, Byoung Ki (1998), *Factors of Korean Economic Growth and Roles of Industrial Policies*, Seoul: Korea Economic Research Institute (in Korean).

Lee, Jae-hyung (1996), 'Characteristics of Conglomerates: Costs, Competitiveness, Diversification, Ownership Structure', *KDI Policy Research* (Fall), Seoul: Korea Development Institute (in Korean).

Lee, Jae-hyung and Kyu-Ok Lee (1990), 'Industrial Conglomerates and Concentration of Economic Power', Seoul: Korea Development Institute (in Korean).

Lee, Sung Soon (1988), *Government-led Industrial Organization Policies: Accomplishment and Problems*, Seoul: Federation of Korean Industries (in Korean).

Lemelin, A. (1982), 'Relatedness in the Patterns of Interindustry Diversification', *Review of Economics and Statistics*, **64**(4), 646–57.

Macneil, Ian R. (1978), 'Contracts: Adjustments of Long-Term Economic Relations under Classical, Neoclassical, and Relational Contract Law', *Northern University Law Review*, **72**, 854–906.

Marshall, Alfred (1920), *Principles of Economics*, 8th edn, London: Macmillan Press.

Martin, Stephen (1993), *Advanced Industrial Organization*, Cambridge: Blackwell Press.

Mork, R., Andrei Shleifer and Robert W. Vishney (1988), 'Market Ownership and Market Valuation: An Empirical Analysis', *Journal of Financial Economics*, **20**, 293–315.

Mueller, Dennis C. (1969), 'A Theory of Conglomerate Mergers', *Quarterly Journal of Economics*, **83**(4), 643–59.

Nelson, Richard A. and Sidney G. Winter (1982), *An Evolutionary Theory of Economic Change*, Cambridge, MA: Harvard University Press, Belknap Press.

North, Douglass (1981), *Structure and Change in Economic History*, New York: Norton.

North, Douglass C. (1992), *Transaction Costs, Institutions, and Economic Performance*, San Francisco, CA: An International Center for Economic Growth Publication.

North, Douglass C. (1990), *Institutions, Institutional Change and Economic Performance*, Cambridge, MA: Cambridge University Press.

OECD (1999), *Principles of Corporate Governance*, Paris: Organization for Economic Cooperation and Development.

Oman, Charles (1993), *Globalization and Regionalization: The Challenge for Developing Countries*, Paris: OECD Development Center.

Pejovich, Svetozar (1995), *Economic Analysis of Institutions and Systems*, Dordrecht: Kluwer.

Penrose, Edith T. (1959), *The Theory of the Growth of the Firm*, New York: John Wiley and Sons Inc.

Porta, Rafael L., Florencio Lopez-de-Silanes, Andrei Schleifer and Robert W. Vishny (1997), 'Legal Determinants of External Finance', *Journal of Finance*, **52**(3), 1131–50.

Rapaczynski, Andrzej (1996), 'The Roles of the State and Market in Establishing Property Rights', *Journal of Economic Perspectives*, **10**(2), 87–107.

Sarel, Michael (1997), *Growth in East Asia: What We Can and What We Cannot Infer*, IMF Economic Issue 1, Washington DC: International Monetary Fund.

Scherer, Fred M. (1980), *Industrial Market Structure and Performance*, Chicago: Rand McNally College Publishing Company.

Scherer, Fred M. and D. Ravenscroft (1984), 'Growth by Diversification: Entrepreneurial Behavior in Large-scale United State Enterprises', *Zeitschrift für Nationalökonomie*, Supplement 4.

Scherer, Fred M. and David Ross (1990), *Industrial Market Structure and Economic Performance*, 3rd edn, Boston: Houghton Mifflin.

Scott, Kenneth (1999), 'Institutions of Corporate Governance', *Journal of Institutional and Theoretical Economics (JITE) (Zeitschrift für die Gesamte Staatswissenschaft) (Germany)* **155**(1), 3–21.

Shleifer, Andrei and Robert W. Vishny (1997), 'A Survey of Corporate Governance', *Journal of Finance*, **52**(2), 737–83.

Simon, Herbert A. (1961 [1947]), *Administrative Behavior*, 2nd edn, New York: Macmillan.

Singleton, Ross C. (1997), 'Competition Policy for Developing Countries: A Long-Run, Entry-Based Approach', *Contemporary Economic Policy*, 15.

Smith, Adam (1976), *The Wealth of Nations*, Edwin Cannan (ed.), Chicago: The University of Chicago Press.

So, Byung-hee (1994), 'The Effect of Industrial Policy and Rent-Seeking on Chaebol Growth', *Korea Policy Study Report*, 3.

Stigler, George J. (1968), 'The Division of Labor is Limited by the Extent of the Market', in George J. Stigler (ed.), *The Organization of Industry*, Homewood, Ill.: Irwin, pp. 129–41.

Tirole, Jean (2001), 'Corporate Governance', *Econometrica*, **69**(1), 1–35.

Vanberg, V. (1991), 'Spontaneous Market Order and Social Rules: A Critical Examination of F.A. Hayek's Theory of Cultural Evolution', in John Cunningham Wood and Ronald N. Wool (eds), *Friedrich A. Hayek: A Critical Assessment*, vol. IV, London: Routledge, pp. 177–201.

Vives, Xavier (2000), *Corporate Governance: Theoretical and Empirical Perspectives*, Cambridge: Cambridge University Press.

Wade, Robert (1990), *Governing the Market: Economic Theory and the Role of Government in East Asia Industrialization*, Princeton: Princeton University Press.

Wallis, John Joseph and Douglass C. North (1986), 'Measuring the Transaction Sector in the American Economy, 1870–1970', in Stanley I. Engerman and Robert Gallman (eds), *Income and Wealth: Long-Term Factors in American Economic Growth*, Chicago: University of Chicago Press.

Werin, Lars and Hans Wijkander (1992), *Contract Economics*, Cambridge, MA: Blackwell.

White, Herbert (1980), 'A Heteroscedasticity-consistent Convariance Matrix Estimator and a Direct Test for Heteroscedasticity', *Econometrica*, **48**(1), 817–38.

World Bank (1993), *The East Asian Miracle: Economic Growth and Public Policy*, New York: Oxford University Press.

Williamson, Oliver E. (2001), 'Why Law, Economics, and Organization?', mimeograph, UC Berkeley.

Williamson, Oliver E. (1985), *The Economic Institutions of Capitalism*, New York: Free Press.

Williamson, Oliver E. (1975), *Markets and Hierarchies: Analysis and Antitrust Implications*, New York: Free Press.

Williamson, Oliver E. (1971), 'The Vertical Implication of Production: Market Failure Considerations', *American Economic Review*, **73**, 519–40.

Yang, Won Keun (1992), *Analysis of the Efficiency of Large Business Groups*, Research Report no. 250, Seoul: Korea Institute for Industrial Economics and Trade (in Korean).

Yoo, Jungho (1991), 'Effects of Heavy and Chemical Industrialization Policy in 1970's on Capital Efficiency and Export Competitiveness', *Research on Korea Development*, **13**(1), Seoul: Korea Development Institute.

Yoo, Jungho (1989), 'The Government in Korean Economic Development', KDI Working paper no. 8904, Seoul: Korea Development Institute.

Yoo, Seoung Min (1995), 'Chaebol in Korea: Misconceptions, Realities, and Policies', KDI Working Paper no. 9507, Seoul: Korea Development Institute.

Yoo, Seoung Min (1992), 'The Ownership Structure of Korea's Big Business Conglomerates and Its Policy Implications', *Korea Development Review*, **14**(1), Seoul: Korea Development Institute (in Korean).

Yoshihara, Hideki (1981), 'Research on Japan's General Trading Firms: An Overview', *Japanese Economic Studies*, **1**(3), 61–86.

# Index

evolutionary mechanism 6–7

theory of the firm 176; *see* Coase, transaction costs
Northian versus Coasian views 177–179
Tirole, Jean 171
'too-big-to-fail' legacy 27, 138, 162
total factor productivity (TFP) 157–158
transaction costs 8, 122; *see* Coase, diversification, property rights,
international comparison and empirical evidence 99–101
internalizable versus non-internalizable 178
relation to theory of firm 176
trust 92, 101, 182
two-stage decision making process 62–64; *see* first-stage policies and problems, second-stage policies and problems

uniform regulation 34, 73–74, 97, 208

vertical integration 121

Williamson, Oliver 121–123
workout program 70, 83–84, 86, 200
World Bank 164
Willig, Robert 125–126

*yang-ban* class 113, 115

# Name index

Alchia, Armen 7, 89, 170, 188, 215, 217
Allen, William 217
Amsden, Alice 186, 187
Aron, Janine 153
Arrow, Kenneth 8

Bain, Joe 38, 61
Barro, Robert 116, 143, 145
Baumol, William 125–126, 188
Berle, Adolph 170
Berry C.H 153
Bishop, Isabella Bird 96, 112–115

Cho, Dong Sung 12
Chung, Byoung Hyou 12
Clague, Christopher 99, 116
Coase, Ronald 8, 15, 89, 170, 176–179, 188
Commons, John 170
Crawford, Robert 170
Cyert, Richard 170

Darwin, Charles 6
Davis, Lance 8
Dawkins, Richard 7
Deaton, Angus 87
Demsetz, Harold 8, 15, 61, 89, 170, 188, 217
Drobak, John 15
Drucker, Peter 152

Easterly, William 141
Eggertsson, Thrainn 8, 15, 89, 121-122

Friedman, Milton 7
Fukuyama, Francis 92, 101, 115
Furubotn, Eirik 15

Gollop, Frank 186
Gordon, Lilli 118
Gort, Michael 126
Grossman, Sanford 170, 171

Hart, Oliver 170, 171
Hayek, Friedrich von 7, 8, 15, 170
Hill, Christopher 116
Hill, CWL 152
Hirshleifer, Jack 7
Hodgson, Geoffrey 7
Holmstrom, Bengt 8
Hoskisson O.E 152
Hwang, In-hak 12, 30, 61, 188

Jacquemin A 153
Jensen, Michael 152, 170, 171
Jones, Leroy 12
Jung, Yak-Yong 95, 110-112
Jwa, Sung-Hee 12, 87, 99, 116, 125, 133, 152, 186, 187

Keefer, Philip 99, 116, 153
Klein, Benjamin 170
Knack, Stephen 99, 116, 153
Ko, Dong Whan 116
Krugman, Paul 156, 186
Kwack, Tae Won 26
Kwon, Byung-Tak 116

Lee, Byoung Ki 25, 26
Lee, Jae-hyung 12, 46
Lee, Kyu-Ok 12
Lee, Sung Soon 30
Lemelin, Andre 131–132
Levine, Ross 141
Lopez-de-Silanes, Florencio 130, 143, 145

Macneil, Ian 8
March, James 170
Marshall, Alfred 6
Martin, Stephen 152
Means, Gardiner 170
Meckling, William 152, 170, 171
Moore, John 170, 171
Mork R. 152